to Sophie —

the boy
behind the
curtain

TIM WINTON

the boy
behind the
curtain

HAMISH HAMILTON
an imprint of
PENGUIN BOOKS

HAMISH HAMILTON

Penguin Books is part of the Penguin Random House group of companies
whose addresses can be found at global.penguinrandomhouse.com.

Penguin
Random House
Australia

First published by Penguin Random House Australia Pty Ltd, 2016

1 3 5 7 9 10 8 6 4 2

Text copyright © Tim Winton, 2016

Cover design by Alex Ross & John Canty © Penguin Random House Australia Pty Ltd
Text design by John Canty © Penguin Random House Australia Pty Ltd
Typeset in Adobe Garamond Pro by Samantha Jayaweera, Penguin Random House Australia Pty Ltd
Colour separation by Splitting Image Colour Studio, Clayton, Victoria
Printed and bound in Australia by Griffin Press, an accredited ISO AS/NZS
14001 Environmental Management Systems printer.

National Library of Australia
Cataloguing-in-Publication data:

Winton, Tim – author.
The boy behind the curtain/Tim Winton.
9781926428765 (hardback)
Winton, Tim. Australian essays – 21st century. Authors, Australian – Biography.

A823.3

penguin.com.au

FOR MUM AND DAD

Nothing's said till it's dreamed out in words
and nothing's true that figures in words only.

LES MURRAY
'Poetry and Religion'

Contents

The Boy Behind
the Curtain

When I was a kid I liked to stand at the window with a rifle and aim it at people. I hid behind the terylene curtain in my parents' bedroom with the .22 and whenever anyone approached I drew a bead on them. I held them in the weapon's sight until they passed by. They had no idea I was lurking there – thirteen years old, armed and watchful – and that was the best part of it.

The family rifle was a single-shot .22 Lithgow. When the old man first acquired it, in a swap for a fishing rod, it was already a rather homely looking pea shooter, but after he gave its battered stock a generous coat of mission brown, he rendered it genuinely ugly. Even so, I couldn't get enough of that thing. I loved to be out with him on brisk evenings hunting rabbits or whistling up a fox. Some

Sunday afternoons I was given five or six bullets and entrusted to roam at liberty in the lonelier paddocks of local farms. This was a big deal, a privilege earnt from months of training and supervision during which the dogma of firearms safety was drilled into me. I knew about the folly of climbing through fences with a weapon. Likewise the dangers of ricochet near water. I understood trajectory, the effects of wind, and the perils of firing into vegetation that could obscure livestock or an unsuspecting hiker. I observed the sanctity of the safety-catch. I never walked with the rifle cocked. Nor would I travel even the shortest distance in a vehicle with a round in the breech. And once the shooting was over I knew how to render the weapon safe, to clear the breech and check twice in a manner both ritualistic and pedantic.

Often enough on these solo excursions I came back without having fired a shot. True, the rabbits were skittish and the foxes wily. But there were moments when, having got the drop on something, I just couldn't bring myself to pull the trigger. Not that I was squeamish. I'd killed snakes, birds and roos with hardly a thought. And it didn't have to be a creature in my sight. Sometimes I couldn't even let loose at a rusty tin. Because I was stricken by the very idea of the rifle, its eerie potential and authority, cowed by the sinister power of the thing, and burdened by the weight of responsibility that came with it.

The Lithgow was no blunderbuss – it made a noise like a damp Christmas cracker – and it lacked the slick glamour of the Winchester repeater Chuck Connors made famous in the TV show *The Rifleman*, or the Tommy gun Vic Morrow toted so nonchalantly in *Combat!* All the same, our family gun was a killer; I'd destroyed enough things and creatures with it to know that. Some Sundays it was enough to cradle death in your hands and just hold fire. I was appalled by its atavistic potency, yet I was entirely in its thrall.

At our place during the seventies, in the days before mandatory gun safes, the Lithgow lived at the back of my parents' wardrobe, behind a thicket of jackets and ties and police tunics. The bolt – the rifle's firing mechanism – was kept separately in the drawer on my father's side of the bed, next to the envelopes for the church collection. Lying snug against it were packs of antacids as big and orange as shotgun cartridges. In the cut-glass jars on the dressing table, salted in with the old man's uniform buttons and old coins, were a few tarnished rounds of ammunition – .22 shorts and longs, the odd hollow-point, perhaps a .38. None of this was a secret. My parents understood that I knew it was all there. But I was not allowed to touch any of it. Handling the rifle indoors without adult supervision was forbidden; this was a fundamental rule. Of course there were worse sins, like pointing a gun at another person – that was completely unthinkable, the action of a dangerous fool or a 'crim', in the family parlance. I saw the sense in these regulations and mores and accepted them without reservation. I would have been disgusted by someone who flouted them.

And yet, at thirteen, whenever I had the house to myself, I went straight to the wardrobe and drew the rifle out. I handled it soberly, with appropriate awe, a respect laced with fear, but then I carried it to the window and aimed it at innocent passers-by. This didn't happen only a time or two – I did it for months. I stood behind the filmy curtain, alert and alone, looking down the barrel of a gun. At strangers.

We hadn't been in town long that year. The house was a modest fibro affair in a working-class suburb of Albany, but from its position on the ridge where Campbell Road crested the hill it commanded quite a view, and without even knowing why, I was compulsively converting that vista into a field of fire, reducing our new home to a pillbox. Below me lay the slumping rooftops and rainswept trees of a peaceful southern port and from my eyrie I was keeping a vigil, the purpose of which eluded me. I was a placid kid in a loving, supportive family in a home where there was neither machismo nor violence. And there I was, acting like a sniper.

None of the townsfolk labouring uphill to pass by had wronged me – I didn't know any of them, I was a total newbie – so I had no intention of harming or frightening them. But to view something through a gun sight is to see it jump or fall or explode in your mind's eye. You know perfectly well that if you pull that trigger your target will be transformed in an instant, perhaps forever. I convinced myself that without its firing bolt the rifle wasn't even a weapon. Moreover, it was only a *lethal* weapon if I slipped a bullet into the breech. And of course I was hardly about to do that, was I? But all this was sophistry and self-justification. Because some dark part of me knew I had the means of destruction close at hand. The makings were all about me in the room. And therein lay the queasy buzz.

Furtive as I was, I saw nothing sinister in this new habit. It didn't strike me as creepy or nefarious. No one knew they had a gun pointed at them, so I wasn't causing any fear. I did feel guilty about abusing my parents' trust, but I told myself there wasn't anything bad in what I was up to, and certainly nothing dangerous.

When I think of that kid at the window, the boy I once was, I get a lingering chill. Back then I had only the murkiest notion of how much trouble I was courting. Not for a moment did I imagine being one of those unsuspecting pedestrians or drivers, how it might feel to look up and see a gunman training a weapon on me. I'd never had a firearm aimed my way. At thirteen I didn't yet know what that felt like. I was careful to remain unseen, but all it would have taken was for the barrel to snag on the curtain, for a neighbour to glance up, for someone to catch my silhouette, and things could have unravelled very quickly indeed. Appearing to 'go armed so as to cause fear' is a serious offence in most Australian jurisdictions. All over the world adults and minors brandishing replicas or toys have been mistakenly shot dead by officers of the law, and even before the so-called Age of Terror and the mass panics it has spawned, it was no small thing to be seen menacing strangers with an actual firearm. To be caught doing it in a country town where your dad's a cop – well, an event like that can be life-defining.

So what, you might ask, did I think I was doing all those months? It's an uncomfortable question, and even now I struggle to answer it. I was a rational, intelligent and obedient child. But for a season, in the matter of the family gun, I just couldn't help myself.

It was such a charged and sneaky compulsion. I waited for any opportunity; anticipation was part of the thrill. An empty house brought a febrile mood that was almost erotic. Having checked to see I was truly alone I'd stalk into the front room, reach into the cupboard, lay the rifle on the bed and survey the street and the valley below. And only when I took up my sentry post with the weapon in my arms did the jangly feeling begin to recede. Soon enough a stranger would come by, on the way to the Spencer Park shops or heading up to the rec centre in the lee of the school. It didn't matter if they were an adult or a child, a man or a woman, I'd draw a bead on them and everything around me and within me would slow down. Once they were contained by the rifle's simple open sight a person seemed smaller, easier to apprehend. The narrow focus calmed me. The visual imposition of the basic notch and tongue defused something. Not that I could have expressed it in those terms then. I'm not even sure they're the right words now.

Looking back I recognize this period as a time when I felt besieged. Suddenly confronted by a fresh town and another house, with the strange new high school hulking ominously out there on the opposing ridge, and puberty doing weird things to my body and mind, I didn't just treat the rifle as a source of talismanic power – it was a stilling point, a centring locus, like a religious icon. After all, there's no shape or image in modern culture to match that of the gun. Nothing else has its universal authority or saving promise. In our time the image of the cross has lost its potency, the national flag is debased and divisive. No, the gun is the supreme image. Only the dollar sign can rival it for the visceral response it produces, the power it radiates.

As it turned out, nothing happened. Nothing bad, that is. Thankfully, I didn't shoot anyone, and neither was I sprung. After a few months I just stopped playing with the rifle and to this day I don't know why. There was no revelation and no intervention. My mood changed, which is to say I grew out of the infatuation. Besides, with three siblings, a father who worked shifts and a stay-at-home mother to contend with, I found it increasingly rare to get the house to myself. For a while I wondered if my parents had twigged, but it turns out they had no idea what I'd been up to. When I asked them about it decades later they were mortified, and understandably so.

Somehow I stopped needing the rifle. By the time summer came around I was more resigned to my new life, less threatened by the alien worlds of the town and the school. In fact I began to enjoy them. I made friends, went surfing, fell in love, discovered ways of rendering myself amusing and within six months went from being a fearful, meek little fellow to a bit of a mouthy pest in class. Much of it, no doubt, was mere performance, faking it until I was making it, but it was better than cowering. I hadn't even consciously recognized how miserable I'd been, but come Christmas I was a different boy, as if, out of rank desperation, I'd recast myself entirely. I rediscovered words, learnt to project myself with new and better ones, to defend myself with jokes and stories. As a little boy I was always a reader, and adults often remarked upon how articulate I was, but for a period there in 1973 I lost the means of expression. I felt I'd been consigned to exile but I lacked a language that matched my apprehensions and anxieties. Without words I was dangerously powerless. The gun served as a default dialect, a jerry-built lingo that may have been less sophisticated than a laundry list, but it came with ready-made scripts that had been swilling about in the back of my mind since infancy. These were storylines as familiar as the object itself. But the lexicon of the gun is narrow and inhuman. Despite its allure it was insufficient to my needs. Once I found that life in Albany, Western Australia was not quite as threatening as I thought, I left the secret gunplay behind and forgot I ever did such things.

For another boy, a kid in tougher circumstances than mine, the outcome might not have been so happy. The gun's slinky power has a special appeal to the young, the weak, the confused and the powerless. To those overlooked or spurned, access to a firearm is the spark of agency. With a gun in your hands, everything is possible. In a moment you imagine the respect it demands. You see yourself suddenly getting some attention, or exacting revenge. There's nothing like those sleek contours, that baleful heft to make you feel larger, greater, wiser. Perhaps, deep down, everyone wants to feel dangerous. Being rich can do that for you. So can being very smart. For the rest who are neither, the gun is a short-cut. And whatever our circumstances, we're all steeped in its romance. We've marinated in this cult all out lives; it's inescapable. Even in a country where there is no fetishized right to bear arms, gunplay is a staple of entertainment. Researchers estimate that by the age of eighteen the average American child is likely to have been exposed to as many as twenty-six thousand gun murders on TV, and there's no reason to assume Australian children's exposure differs much. In TV, movies and video games, the underlying showbiz message is that the world is a dangerous place and the only tool that will make a difference in it is a firearm. The gun ends the discussion, solves the dispute, and, of course, brings the episode to its 'natural end'.

This is a potent trope against which our children are largely undefended. All-pervasive as it was in my childhood, it's even more raw and brutish now. I'm not suggesting entertainment is uniquely responsible for gun violence, but in a country like ours, where gun ownership is uncommon, most young people's knowledge of firearms is drawn from the festival of screentime killings. And as the internet has made plain, humans are suckers for a script. In recent years terror organizations have prospered by broadcasting real executions and assassinations, showing young men and women all across the world that they're 'getting things done', just as the gunslinging idols of every generation have, from Randolph Scott to Idris Elba, from *Dirty Harry* to *Harry Brown*. Jihadis don't upload these outrages solely for their own masturbatory gratification; the fact is, these video clips work as propaganda, as recruiting tools, they hit home. For those who claim to believe that God is Greatest, the AK-47 ends the discussion. In their minds, it would seem, even the most sacred words utterable are insufficient to the needs of the faithful.

A youth who is confused, depressed, or fearful will be tempted to resort to whatever means he has to make himself felt, if not understood, even if his problems, like those of my puberty, are minor and ephemeral, and a truly angry kid is liable to do something extreme and impulsive. In countries where firearms are commonplace in the home, this often extends to more than self-harm. Mass shootings have become a fixture of American news. The carnage in schools and public places is so unremarkable that ritual 'outpourings of grief' border on the perfunctory. Gun murder is so normal in the US it's banal. And the gun itself is sacrosanct. The right to bear it outstrips a citizen's right to be protected from it, and even a tearful president is impotent in the face of this cult. In 2016 Barack Obama declared that modest gun restrictions were 'the price of living in a civilized society' but it seemed few were listening. By all accounts, God is Great in America, too, but in truth the nation has always lived as if the gun is greater. In God they trust, but armed they must proceed.

Most Australians have never owned a firearm. Few will ever handle or discharge one, and I think this is something to be glad of. In moments of turmoil the mere presence of a gun alters the atmosphere. In a domestic dispute, a roadside altercation or a bout of depression, the thing most likely to push the scene out of shape beyond saving is a firearm. It so often gets the wrong job done.

I can't say I ever really outgrew my fascination with guns. In high school I only joined the cadets so I could shoot big-calibre weapons and blow stuff up. I was a fair shot with a 7.62 SLR and could not resist the thought of Audie Murphy as I sprayed bullets from a rattling F1 submachine-gun. I continued to hunt occasionally with my father until I was in my twenties. And then I stopped shooting altogether. I spent some years in the inner city where there was no legitimate use for a firearm. Here guns were alien. They had no place in ordinary life and I didn't miss them. If anything, I developed an aversion. Living abroad for a couple of years and having a weapon jerked my way once or twice by paramilitary police only intensified it. Whenever I visited relatives in the bush I was uncomfortable with weapons being displayed or passed around. Not because the presence of a Ruger or a Winchester was strange, but perhaps because it wasn't yet strange enough. Secretly I liked the feel of a rifle in my hands again, but if a farmer asked me to come out and help shoot a few foxes I declined.

Apart from kitchen knives, my children never saw any kind of killing tool in the home. When they were little my wife and I refused to buy them toy weapons of any sort. Not that they escaped the romance of the gun, for despite our best efforts to monitor their screen time, firearms were everywhere they looked. If they picked up sticks at play and made guns of them, then that was their right, we weren't about to tell them what they could and could not imagine, but we had no intention of collaborating with the purveyors of the cult. Our kids were strangers to violence, but perhaps, like children everywhere, they play at war to ward it off.

My kids were still small in the autumn of 1996 when a disturbed young man with a very low IQ murdered thirty-five people at Port Arthur in Tasmania. Twenty-three others were injured that day. It was a rare and traumatic event in the recent life of this nation. It prompted a review of national gun laws and many Australians were surprised to see how stridently the locally emergent gun lobby resisted all talk of reform, which mainly focused on restricting access to semiautomatic weapons. So violent was their discourse that while addressing a hostile pro-gun rally in Sale that winter the prime minister, John Howard, resorted to wearing a Kevlar vest. These were scenes once unimaginable in modern Australia. I was never a fan of John Howard. I despised his retrograde social policies and was dismayed by his nostalgia for the unchallenged whiteness and patriarchy of the 1950s, but at a pivotal moment in our history he literally stuck his neck out and did something vital and brave. By following through on gun reform he made this country a little safer. Fronting angry rednecks from the dais that day, he looked pale and stiff, like a man unwell, but that sick look was the face of courage. That was the spectacle of a man exceeding himself.

In the days immediately after the slaughter in Tasmania a woman bailed me up at the gate of my kids' primary school. She'd taken offence at something in one of my books and thought I could do with a little consciousness-raising. As she rehearsed her many opinions about men in general and me in particular, her three-year-old son waved a plastic machine-gun at me. The little fellow's eyes were like slits and beneath them were shadows dark as bruises. His toy gun was the colour of bubblegum but for some reason it reminded me of rendered flesh. Making all the sounds of televised murder, the kid 'shot' me about twenty times. Deprived of a response, he began to shove the barrel into my hip again and again, wheezing and squinting, stamping his feet, raging. I kept expecting his mother to make some token effort at curbing his assault, but she hadn't taken a breath since she collared me. So it was a war on two fronts. He was only an infant, but the kid's aggression was startling and demoralizing. Perhaps, I told myself, he's just picked up on her mood and is trying to please her, but if that explained things his efforts were in vain because she appeared not to notice. In fact she paid this little man in the making no mind at all. It seemed she had bigger fish to grill. Maybe it was the proximity of the massacre and the images of that dead-eyed murderer in Tasmania, or perhaps I'm just thin-skinned, but this encounter with the Rumpelstiltskins rattled me. By the time my daughter skipped up to rescue me from the righteously jabbing hippie finger and the porn-pink Tommy gun, I was shaking.

The only time my kids heard a firearm discharged they were more scandalized than awed. When my brother-in-law set up a skeet trap in his home paddock they were wild with excitement, but when they heard what a shotgun really sounded like their enthusiasm waned. They stuck their fingers in their ears and retreated, pale and big-eyed, to the nominal shelter of the clothes hoist. After I'd watched their uncle for fifteen minutes and resisted all his entreaties for me to have a go, I relented. I don't know what shocked the children more, seeing me fire a gun or realizing I was good at it. For half an hour, with a curious and rising exultation, I blasted away, blowing clay discs to dust, and nothing died, no one was in danger. I was out in the open, a threat to nobody. Everyone, including my own kids, could see it. And not even the mood of umbrage and inner-city disapproval radiating from the rear seat on the long drive home could make me regret it.

These days I'm back living in the bush. And the awkward fact is I could really do with a rifle. The local success of the government's fox-eradication program has meant the whole peninsula we live on is overrun with rabbits and feral cats. The bunnies ravage the vegetation and the cats are killing everything from birds and small marsupials to baby turtles. Now and then a friend comes out with his .22 and we shoot as humanely as we can with low-velocity ammo and telescopic sights, but even the subsonic report makes the dog anxious, and my wife, despite acknowledging the need, hates having a gun in the house. So I'll never buy one. Because however much I still like to let off a round or two, I'd prefer not to have a weapon at home. There are no longer any small kids to fret over, little chance one of my own will stand at the window and point the thing at passing roadtrains, but even secured in a safe somewhere discreet, a firearm would be a dark presence I can do without under my own roof. Too much sinister potential. Too much unearnt power.

Some of my friends and neighbours have no such qualms, though there are times when I wish they did. A few have veritable arsenals at home and one or two are genuine enthusiasts. Not in any rabid gun-nut way, they're more like trainspotters or collectors. But I worry about them, sometimes, worry *for* them. The sanest and safest people go through low patches, awful things happen out of the blue. Not many people have access to such ultimate and instantaneous temptation. Whether a gun owner acknowledges this or not, that's what a proximate gun presents, and no one is immune.

A child is a strange creature, and a boy perhaps strangest of them all. He befuddles his parents and confounds his friends; most of the time he's a mystery to himself. As a kid there are times when you brim with things that need saying but lack the words or suspect there's no one willing to listen. It doesn't matter if you're wrong about this apprehension you're hostage to; you're stuck, you feel you're cornered. I guess that was my experience. Lurking there behind my parents' curtain I put a gun between myself and the world. I reduced my neighbours to objects, made targets of them. Anything could have happened, none of it good. And just in time, it would seem, before anything irreparable could come of this impulse, I found words. God knows I was a happier, safer boy once I did.

A Space Odyssey
at Eight

On a winter's day in 1969 our teacher wheeled a television into the classroom. The Grade Fours, she said, were about to witness a moment of history, though for us the mere presence of the telly at school was landmark enough. She was an intense young woman from the English Midlands who wore Dr. Scholl's clogs and seemed to suffer a permanent case of the sniffles. That day she seemed particularly agitated. The set hummed and flickered as she struggled to get a signal. Some wag asked if we could watch *Marine Boy* or *The Flintstones.* Eventually she found the broadcast channel and we settled and fell silent as Neil Armstrong tipped himself back off the ladder to walk upon the moon.

The black-and-white transmission was woolly, the commentary

terse, and there was no grand music to accompany the events before us. Without the misty look in the teacher's eye we might have missed the momentousness of the occasion. But in the street that evening there was no mistaking the importance of what had occurred. The adults of the neighbourhood were fizzing with pride and excitement and on TV the pundits suggested that humans had finally broken free of earthly restraint; the future lay close and undefended before us. We were on our way to the stars.

I was caught in the optimistic uplift of that day, though I didn't feel it the way the grown-ups all around me did. For them the moon landing was the realization of a dream, an achievement they hardly dared to think possible in their own lifetime. But for me, a child of the sixties and of the Cold War space race, the prospect of Americans on the moon was inevitable, and in a sense the lunar landing had already been rendered ordinary by constant expectation. And there was another reason for feeling slightly underwhelmed by the events of July 20: I'd been to the stars already.

The year before, as a treat to celebrate his eighth birthday, the mother of one of my mates from school had taken a group of us into the city to see the big new space film that was in the news at the time. I still have a photo of us at the birthday boy's house before we set off. I'm skylarking about, going cross-eyed for the camera. All of us are in high spirits. It was probably a good thing we got the happy snaps in before the outing, because afterwards the mood wasn't so bubbly.

Having bravely ferried six restless kids into central Perth, the boy's mother wrangled us all into a row of seats at the Piccadilly just as the lights began to dim. The curtains drew back momentously, the way they did in those days, but the screen remained dark. Some very strange music began to fill the cinema, a kind of muttering and welling of voices that grew more eerie and insistent as we sat there in the gloom. The sound made me uneasy. And it didn't let up. Soon

I was truly spooked and I wasn't the only one. A wave of sidelong glances swept along the row. Normally at such a moment I'd have blurted out something 'witty'. Even a fart might have broken the tension. But at the critical juncture I had nothing. My mouth was dry, my throat tight, and I just didn't want to be at the pictures anymore. I was sitting at the end of our row, separated from the aisle by a single empty seat, and I was seconds from legging it to the lobby when somebody sat down and blocked me in.

My new row-mate was older, an adolescent, no less, and despite the conniptions the music was visiting upon the rest of us, he'd taken his seat with a flourish. He gave an ostentatious sigh of pleasure and glanced down at me with an indulgent grin. I had time enough to take in his longish hair and the tassels of his suede jacket before the wretched soundtrack finally backed off. And there, at last, was something up on the screen besides brooding darkness: the African savannah. And a restive pack of apes.

'God,' said the newcomer. 'Don't you just love this?'

I saw his shining face split in a grin. I could think of nothing to say in reply. Things were already weird enough without having an actual *teenager* engaging me in conversation.

'Seen it seven times already,' he said. 'Man, what a trip.'

I looked back at the apes in their desolation. A few picked lice from their fellows' fur. A couple bared their teeth at interlopers. This went on for minutes but it seemed like an age, which may have been the point but it was lost on us entirely. Then, at last, a leopard appeared and leapt down upon an unsuspecting chimp. There was a skirmish, but nothing came of it. More rocks, more apes. The mood along the row grew mutinous. The poor woman who thought she'd taken a bunch of eight-year-olds to see a bit of newfangled Buck Rogers must have been wondering what she'd gotten herself into.

Anyway, enter the Monolith. Or whatever that matt-black thing was. It didn't exactly make an entrance: the sun came up on the primal plain and there it was, parked out the front of the monkey cave, a tall dark rectangle like a supersized version of one of those Cuisenaire rods they were using to teach us arithmetic at school. And when the primates woke, well, they went apeshit. The return of Ligeti's *Requiem* can't have helped. I think we were all as confused and appalled as the chimps. Pretty soon, though not soon enough for my taste, fur and bones began to fly. The older guy next to me snorted with glee. And then, suddenly, and rather beautifully, as the now-famous spinning bone became a spacecraft in the legendary match cut, we were out amongst the stars. I could almost feel my ears pop. It was peculiar. And fabulous. There was even proper music.

For a short while it seemed as if this movie was finally about to straighten up and fly right, but there was plenty more weirdness ahead. For one thing, no one spoke for the best part of half an hour and when dialogue did arrive I garnered from it only the haziest appreciation of the problems at hand. Scientists on the moon had dug up a black slab like the one the apes had danced around, and once disturbed it emitted a noise worse than Romanian art music. It appeared to be linked to strange happenings further out in space, and in order to investigate things properly a craft shaped like a sinister tadpole was taking astronauts to Jupiter. Which was fine by me as far as a story goes, though this affair was like a science documentary whose budget hadn't run to the provision of a voice-over. Still, the machines were ravishing and even the swoony, familiar music they floated upon was sublime. I didn't know what a Strauss waltz was but I knew it made space travel less scary and marginally less boring.

If there was any narrative tension in the film at all it came from the nagging sense that at any moment an alien would appear, as it surely must. I steeled myself, but against the greater anxiety that gripped me I was defenceless, because from the very beginning what was most frightening about *2001: A Space Odyssey* was the experience of being led out into the cold darkness of space and left alone. Things kept happening – or not happening – without commentary, and with the conventional tropes of popular storytelling snatched from me at every turn, I had the child's slowly mounting panic at having been abandoned. I was in several kinds of deep space and there was no one bothering to hold my hand. All I had for support and company was some kid in a suede jacket whose name I didn't even know – and there was something off about him anyway. Still, I was lucky to have him; I was on an acid trip and he was my spirit guide.

On and on the epic rolled, serenely refusing to explain itself as it went. It was hypnotic and opaque. It was eerie in a way that wasn't much fun. And it continued for the best part of three hours. Needless to say, it took the shine off my friend's birthday, and given the reviews bubbling up from the rear of the vehicle on the way home, it would have been a long drive for the boy's poor mother. Of course I had my own withering criticisms to add to the chorus of schoolboy scorn, but in truth the movie had gotten to me in ways I wouldn't understand for many years. Asleep or awake I couldn't shake it off. There were images so singular and so vivid they resonated for decades. That first catastrophic viewing remains the most powerful cinema experience of my life.

Less than a year later, men actually walked on the moon, but the excitement of that historic event soon dissipated. For a few nights I gazed up at the full moon with new wonder, but like most of my peers I quickly assimilated the landing as a fact of life. The mythic, questing aspect that Kubrick's film had helped lend it faded away. The years since have been marked by an increasing obsession with technology. Tools and toys are prized above all else. But every new marvel is on its way to being landfill the moment it arrives, so it's a curious thing to see a work of the imagination endure the way *2001* has. Despite the anachronistic way the film was shot, using elaborate models rather than the computer-generated images filmgoers have become accustomed to, it still outdoes everything of a similar sort that came after it. Rooted in technology and confident speculation, undoubtedly a product of its moment, after nearly half a century it continues to resist obsolescence.

I still return to it occasionally and when I do I can't help but feel I'm watching it in the company of my boyhood self. Wherever I am, in the loungeroom or the revival house, there along the row in his suede jacket and *Midnight Cowboy* tassels sits the spectre of my slightly stoned guide, who endures as companion and intermediary.

But for all that, the experience of seeing it again is never particularly nostalgic. For one thing, *2001* isn't that kind of film. It still expects the viewer to be a voyager, not a popcorn-scarfing chucklehead. And if it has any consolations they are austere indeed. Don't worry, it seems to say, intelligent life will go on, but your entire race will be subsumed: you'll become star people – it'll be great. Little wonder it made me anxious as a kid.

To be honest, love this film though I do, I'm not a Kubrick tragic. Despite the director's reputation, some of his work is just silly. *Full Metal Jacket*, for instance, is an anthology of clichés. During a screening of *Eyes Wide Shut* a friend and I were nearly thrown out of the cinema for inappropriate laughter. So it's not as if each time I return to *2001* I'm dusting off a shrine to the great Stanley. But the impressions his masterwork left in me from that very first viewing have been confirmed and complicated with every subsequent look. I'm not ritualistic or even particularly enthusiastic about revisiting the film. If anything I go back diffidently, nervously, sometimes with many years between viewings, but I go out of curiosity, I suppose, knowing it's likely to set things off in me that will take some time to absorb, wondering if all that strangeness still resonates. And I'm always startled. The film retains its visual power. Its capacity to disturb and inspire is undiminished.

When I saw it again recently I was reminded of Kubrick's brilliant deployment of sound. Not just his bravura use of music, but the way he treats the unbearable silence of space. Many sequences are beautifully, pitilessly quiet, and although we're looking out at the endless possibility of the cosmos, we're conscious, too, that all this volume and distance might suck us out into its maw – like astronaut Frank Poole – as if we'd never existed. In 1968 the sight of the murdered astronaut spinning slowly into oblivion gave me nightmares. Even now the sequence makes me clammy. Fatally unmoored, the helpless man reels out into the silent void. As an image of existential dread it's tough to beat and harder to forget. Kubrick's portrayal of the watchful computer is another masterstroke. HAL's demonic red eye is never more foreboding than when the machine is silent.

Whether dealing with outer space or the operating spaces within buildings and machines, Kubrick overlays many scenes with the fraught and claustrophobic noise of human respiration, like a mesh of consciousness lacing every apparent abyss, and as a result each mute action is threaded with contingencies so great as to be almost unbearable. Since the film's release, this technique has been used so often in the hands of lesser filmmakers it's become banal, but to hear it again in *2001* is to hear it as if for the first time. In his 2011 masterpiece *The Tree of Life*, one of the few films of recent years to rival Kubrick's for ambition, Terrence Malick tries another tack to achieve something similar. He embroiders earthbound scenes and ethereal dreamscapes with mutterings and prayer-like whispers to give everything on screen, human or otherwise, a sacred yearning that builds toward some sort of collective sentience. Kubrick's labouring astronauts, however, are most eloquent when they don't speak. As they struggle to outwit the rogue computer, or as they hurtle through space in mind-warping clefts in time, their every breath says all we need to know about their situation.

As a younger man I never took the *Odyssey* reference in the title seriously. If anything, the nod to Homer sounded a little pompous. But if ever there was an epic journey under way, this is surely it: the crew of *Discovery One* set sail for Jupiter to meet unknowns beyond the ken of any seer. But they have no Ulysses to lead and inspire them: a corporate entity has instead imposed the leadership of a machine. The largest personality on the voyage is the Cyclops that steers the ship, the monster the men must eventually escape. One of the great ironies of the film, and perhaps its most prophetic insight, is the robotic demeanour of the astronauts, who are trained only to submit to the mission. Even as the ship's computer aches to transcend the limits of its circuits, the astronauts endeavour to make machines of themselves. And when the computer asserts itself as skipper and superior intelligence, the last man aboard is cold and merciless in his resistance. The decommissioning of HAL is a murder that implicates the viewer, who badly wants the monster dead. Yet somehow the machine's death is the most distressing in the entire film. It's a terrible thing to see a consciousness destroyed, memory by memory, skill by skill, thought by thought. In the end HAL is too retarded to even beg for his life. As big-screen assassinations go it's deeply shocking and nothing in Scorsese or even Coppola can rival it. Kubrick's long sequence of a man killing a machine is troubling because of its moral force. You ask yourself, Am I witnessing a technical action or a fratricide? Who are the monsters here? Will humans repeat in space what they have done on Earth since Cain decommissioned Abel?

Watching this film in middle age I'm more susceptible to its mythic themes, and the human cost of all this Homeric questing is even harder to ignore. The things men must do in order to sail on. The creatures their treks might turn them into. And the loved ones they leave at home. Mothers, wives, fathers ashore – they are proud and afraid and fatally ignorant of the facts. These peripheral characters are only viewed in passing in *2001*, during stiff and painful transmissions. Like Penelope they have no idea if their voyagers will ever make it home. Nor can they imagine the form their loved ones will take if they do finally drop anchor. All the freaks and monsters of mythology could not possibly prepare them for the beings that might return to harbour, for those who are left haven't just farewelled their loved ones, they've said goodbye to humanity as they know it.

Needless to say, at the age of eight I wasn't taking much of this in. When I wasn't traumatized I was just plain lost. Like the space station, the story was a big, shiny wheel that seemed a little short of hand-holds. And yet the thing that most troubled me – the film's mystifying taciturnity – remains its enduring strength, and the most cryptic sequence of all, the one that really set the birthday boys howling that day, was the part that galvanized my imagination then and delights me still. Having travelled through the psychedelic maze of the Star Gate, mission commander Dave Bowman stands in a room that's all wrong, like something Willy Wonka might have furnished for a man under galactic house arrest. In it the astronaut sees himself as an older man. He seems to age before his own eyes. Moments later, he's a crone alone in his bed. The only sound connecting him to his familiar self is his in-suit breathing. Finally he points, and there, like a new planet above him, hangs a babe in an amniotic bubble. As the sac turns in its orbit the knowing eyes look our way, tilted earthward. It's an extra-human gaze. Startling. And a little chilling. Yet so compelling that even at eight years old I felt something in myself rise to meet it. A greater intelligence, a sense of cosmic promise, an evolutionary turning point? I can never decide. But in this final moment, having famously eschewed the more prosaic elements of Arthur C. Clarke's script, especially its elucidatory conclusion, Kubrick achieves a kind of apotheosis, a wordless mythic suspension that's integral to the film's status as a great work of art.

As a novelist resisting the false shape of 'closure' I find this ending endlessly inspiring and intriguing. It frightened the tripe out of me as a boy and I'm wary of it still. There's a leap of faith inherent in that inhuman gaze, a logic I'm not sure I want to follow. The poet Robinson Jeffers speaks of the necessity to 'unhumanize' ourselves in order to experience what lies before us, but Kubrick and Arthur C. Clarke go much further. They seem to suggest that the next stage of evolution is to leave our embodied humanity behind us altogether. A prospect I find unappealing, even if, in the age of Facebook and flame wars, we're halfway there already.

Now and then I wonder what it'd be like to sit down with an eight-year-old to watch *2001*, but I doubt I'll be road-testing that notion any time soon. I'd probably get arrested. The film was too rich a meal for me at that age; it's a feast I'm still trying to digest. But I'll always be grateful to that birthday boy's mother. She definitely took us to the wrong film. When we wanted gadgets and aliens, she gave us an acid trip, but her little error was a gift to the likes of me. It sent me through a Star Gate of my own into an expanded reality. It wasn't just my introduction to the possibilities of cinema, it was a wormhole into the life of the imagination, where artefacts outlive the tools with which they are wrought as well as the makers who once wielded them. In that parallel universe useless beauty requires neither excuse nor explanation and wonder is its own reward.

Havoc: A Life
in Accidents

I

One summer night, after a few hours surfcasting for tailor, my father and I were driving home along a lonely road between the dunes and the bush when a motorbike roared up behind us. We hadn't spoken much since leaving the beach. I felt snug and a little sleepy in the passenger seat, but it was my job to keep the cooling lantern from tipping over so I resisted the urge to drift off and clamped the gas bottle tight between my heels. We'd gone down at sunset and caught a feed, but at the age of nine I could take or leave the fishing. The chief attraction of an outing like this was the chance to be alone with my father.

The evening had gotten cool and the windows were cranked up. I remember the ordinary, reassuring smells inside the vehicle: the pilchards we used for bait, the burnt-toast whiff of the gas mantle, and the old man himself. In those days his personal scent was a cocktail of Dencorub and Quick-Eze. He hadn't always smelt like that.

For a moment the inside of our car was bleached with light. I saw my own shadow creep across the dash. And then, with a yowl, the motorbike pulled out from behind and overtook us on the long straight into town. There were no streetlights, no other cars. Either side of us there was just bush. The road had only recently been sealed. All my life it had been a limestone track, but now the city had reached the beach. Things were changing.

As the rider blew by, the old man gave a low whistle and I stiffened a moment in my seat. Dad had complicated views about speed. He adored motorbikes; he'd ridden them all his life and he loved to ride fast. As a traffic cop he did it for a living. Half his job was to chase folks and pull them over for speeding; the rest of the time he picked up the pieces when things came unstuck. To me, speed was no thrill and I was especially leery of motorbikes. My father's medicinal smell was a constant reminder of both.

The lantern glass jinked and tinkled between my legs. Out ahead there was nothing to see but the black road and the single red eye of the rider's tail-light. Then it was gone. The light didn't shrink into the distance – suddenly it just wasn't there.

Within half a second the night was jerked out of shape, and in the few minutes that followed I felt that my life might warp and capsize along with it. I didn't see the rider fall but I still think of him and his machine skittering on divergent trajectories across the rough-metalled bitumen. The old man pounded the brake and we came to a howling halt. He got out and with a startling new authority in his voice told me to stay exactly where I was. Not that I needed telling.

I craned forward, stunned; my neck hurt from where the seatbelt had caught me. In the high beam I saw a motionless body on the limestone shoulder of the road. My father strode over and knelt beside the rider. His shadow was enormous; the headlights gave every movement and colour a nightmarish cast. The old man got up again. He dragged the motorbike off the road. When I wound down the window, I could smell petrol and all the salty, minty scents of the coastal scrub. A moment later the old man got back in and buckled his seatbelt. I was rattled by what I'd seen and disturbed by how businesslike Dad was. He was calm and unhurried; this drama did not seem to impress him. He sighed and started the car. He said we had to find a phone and call an ambulance. To my horror we drove away and left the rider out there at the roadside. There was a bus terminal not far up ahead, a lonely floodlit yard full of hulking green vehicles, and a sleepy security guard let Dad use the phone.

When we returned to the crash site the injured rider began to stir. I didn't know it then but he was convulsing. It was as if he were being shot through with electricity. As Dad climbed out of the car, he said he had an important job for me. I was to stamp on the brake pedal over and over again without stopping so the ambulance crew could see our red lights from a distance. The idea made practical sense, but I'm sure it was mostly a means of keeping me occupied and out of harm's way. Many years later, by another roadside, I employed a similar tactic to keep my own kids from seeing something worse. As a nine-year-old it was good to be commissioned, to feel useful for a short while, and as I clung to the steering wheel and jabbed at the brake pedal, which I could barely reach, my father crouched out there in the lights, talking to the fallen rider who kept fluttering in and out of consciousness, trying to get up on his twitching, mutinous legs. Every time the man turned his head I saw that his face was raw meat. Some of it hung off in strips, like paperbark. It was red, white and yellow. His leather jacket was glossy with blood. He tried to haul himself up on his elbows. Then he was screaming.

After a long time a siren sounded in the distance, the distinctive two notes of an ambulance, and the noise seemed to inflame the fallen rider whose yelling and swearing and struggling grew more violent. He needed to go, he kept bawling. Where was his bike? When Dad suggested he stay put for his own benefit, the bloke wanted to fight. Dad held him down by the arms.

I thought once the ambulance arrived everything would be fine, but when it finally pulled up the whole scene intensified, as though some fresh madness had arrived with it. There were suddenly more bodies, more voices, more flashing lights and lurid shadows. And at some point a different man – an even louder bloke – appeared, announcing himself as the victim's father. I don't know how he got there or how he'd been informed but I could see he was staggering drunk, and I felt myself come to a new level of alertness. There was something vicious and unpredictable about him. His eyes were wild. He had the look of a mistreated dog. As he stumbled toward his son, who'd been lifted onto a gurney, he was weeping and blubbering. Then he went crazy. It looked as if he were trying to throttle his son, and when my father and the ambos hauled him off he wheeled, snarling, and began to swing at them.

Though I felt a treacherous panic rising in my chest, I didn't stop pumping the brake; I'd been drafted and I took it seriously. But it was as if I'd woken in a cinema during the final reel of a horror movie. Everything was way over my head. And the mayhem wouldn't stop. I'd never witnessed anything like this before – all the blood, the flashing teeth and fists, the screamed obscenities. I'd been shielded from drunks. I had no experience of violence, domestic or otherwise. I'd certainly never seen a grown man act this way. I couldn't believe he might want to hurt his injured son like that. And I was deeply disturbed by the prospect of him hurting my father. I was outraged as well as terrified, and it felt like I'd been booted with an electric charge myself. A wild man was attacking my dad. He was lurching and lunging at the ambos, too, but they were uniformed strangers, and to me they were just shadows dancing; I barely took them in, I only had eyes for the old man. It didn't matter that he was fending off every blow with an ease bordering on contempt. What I saw was my father under siege. And I couldn't help him. I stayed where I was, lashed to the wheel, in a state I had no language for.

Eventually the police came. The scene quickly resolved itself. Dad dusted himself off and came clapping back to the car in his thongs, chuckling at something the coppers had said. We were late for tea now and he was eager to be on his way. I could still hardly speak. At home Dad did what he could to minimize this lurid little interlude. His account of it to Mum was cursory. But the experience stayed with me. There was something dangerous and outsized about the emotions it had stirred up and the sensation was like being caught in a rip: no purchase, no control.

That scene has puzzled me all my life – haunted me, in a way. It was decades before I understood why I'd been so afraid. Of course it's distressing for any child to see a parent under threat, but what was happening for me that night was a little more complicated. I was being cast back into an older fear, and an accident three years earlier. My father had been taken away from me once before.

By the time I was nine there were things about him I'd gotten used to. The scar on his neck was silvery by then and when he came out of the shower the divots in his hip weren't so livid. The ever-present tubes of Dencorub and the smell of it on his body were just part of him now, as was the roll of Quick-Eze forever sliding across the dashboard. I was so accustomed to all this I'd forgotten what the heat rub was for. Dencorub was the only relief he had for the chronic pain once the quack took him off the anti-inflammatory drugs, and those wretched pills had left him with stomach ulcers, which was why he chewed antacids as if they were lollies. Now I went fishing every chance I could. To be close to him, as if unconsciously I feared he'd be taken away a second time. Clinging to the steering wheel of his car that night, half out of my mind, it was as if someone had kicked the chocks out from under me. The sight of my father under threat again was almost too much to bear. We'd been delivered three years ago, Mum and my siblings and I, and for a long time I'd felt safe. Now, quite suddenly, I wasn't safe at all.

In my fiction I've been a chronicler of sudden moments like these. Because the abrupt and the headlong are old familiars. For all the comforts and privileges that have come my way over the years, my life feels like a topography of accidents. Sometimes, for better or worse, they are the landmarks by which I take my bearings. I suppose you could say they form a large part of my sentimental education. They're havoc's vanguard. They fascinate me. I respect them. But I dread them too.

II

I grew up in safety. In our home in the Perth suburb of Karrinyup there was nothing to fear and no one to second-guess. My mother did everything in her power to give my siblings and me a life free of the disorder she'd known as a child and the violence she'd endured as a young woman. She was determined to provide an environment that was predictable and nurturing. Our father was of like mind. He was a gentle man and he was careful to shield us from the things he saw as a cop. Nevertheless we lived in the shadow of havoc. There might not have been trouble at home, but trouble was the family business, and ours was a house of accidents.

Dad was literally in Accidents. He was a motorcycle cop working in the Accident Branch of the Traffic Office. At the end of a shift he rode his black BSA down the drive, gave the throttle a final *blat* and then propped it on its stand in the carport. When he climbed off the bike in his gauntlets and gaiters and leathers he gave a distinctive creak. His own father, who'd also been a policeman, made the same leathery groan as he climbed down off the horse at day's end. To me, that saddle-creak was precious; it was the sound of safe return.

Around the house Dad was pretty oblique about work. All the same I absorbed plenty of lore and perhaps too much information. As a small boy I knew the lingo. If he was late home it was because he'd had to go to a *prang*. And of course he didn't just go – he *attended*. I knew, too, about the various species of prang. The worst of all were the *fatals*. I knew when he'd been at a fatal because when he came in his mood was strangely subdued. Then the talk between the adults was hushed and the smells were different. Dad's tunic would stink of Dettol and petrol. Sometimes there was no chat at all, just a hug that went on too long. On rare occasions there was muffled weeping behind closed doors.

Any kid with a shift-working parent learns to creep, to be mindful. For a copper's family there are extra weights to bear, unspoken things you experience vicariously. Like the constant physical weariness, and the moral fatigue that accumulates over time, because cops are never fresh and after a while they can't disguise their endless disappointment in people. They become guarded, sceptical. They're always keeping an eye out for trouble. They expect it, anticipate it. And as a kid you sense this. As if by osmosis you learn what humans do at their lowest moments, at their most idiotic or vile, and you register the outcomes, which are invariably awful. Humans, you come to understand, are frail creatures. Yet in a second, from thin air, they can manufacture chaos and carnage. And it was this mortal ruin the old man sought to keep at bay.

But he brought havoc home anyway – on his tunic, in his limbs, and in midnight whispers. When he was out on the road I could read the fear of it in my mother's face.

There's a song in Ry Cooder's back catalogue about a man stalked by misfortune. In the chorus the old trouper sings, 'Trouble, you can't fool me, I see you behind that tree/ Trouble you can't fool me, tryin to get the ups on me.' But the bloke's kidding himself. He can't forestall trouble, and that's the charm of the song. Although trouble loves the careless and the impulsive, first seeking out the selfish and the intemperate, in the end it's pretty democratic; it'll jump anyone, really, for neither virtue nor prudence will inoculate you against it. Just as rain falls on the just and the unjust alike, trouble of some sort visits everyone eventually. But real trouble isn't about inconvenience – it's catastrophic. That's how it felt the year I turned five, when it came to me and to my family.

In December of 1965, as he was riding back from a prang, the old man was hit by a driver who'd run a stop sign. The errant car slammed him into a brick wall with such force it crushed his chest, his shoulder and his hip. He suffered a massive concussion, and because his ribs were broken and his lungs had collapsed the paramedics found him suffocating and close to death. To save him they were forced to perform an emergency tracheotomy as he lay in the street.

When Mum was notified, she was told he'd been in a bingle but that it probably wasn't serious, so she didn't understand the gravity of the situation until she was mistakenly given the blood-soaked uniform that had been cut off him in Casualty. She had two small boys, five and three, and a daughter barely six months old. No one had prepared her for what was coming her way. Her husband, the sole breadwinner of the household, was in a coma. And she didn't know it yet, but nobody fancied his chances.

For days he lay in the resuscitation room at Royal Perth Hospital. There was an unspoken understanding that he would never 'be himself' again, and so traumatic were his injuries that two of his colleagues resigned shortly after visiting him. Even when he finally regained consciousness, nobody could offer Mum much cause for optimism. I was not allowed to visit. I came to suspect he was actually dead and that no one had the nerve to tell me. Mum kept up a brave front, and she was genuinely courageous, but I was there to see the mess she hid from everyone else.

When I think of that long, hard summer I remember the wordless heaviness in the house, the fog of dread we were all trapped in. My brother and sister were too young to understand what was happening. In a sense it was just Mum and me, and a kid in kindergarten can't offer his mother much by way of solace. She must have done a lot of hoping. All the same, there wasn't a hopeful air in the house. Even when they brought him home from hospital, a broken man, an effigy, really, there was no surge of buoyancy for any of us to ride. The grown-ups who visited spoke in riddles and whispers. I had to imbibe the gravity of our situation the way a dog will, reading the smells and the postures and hierarchies, processing them physically.

I knew that a stranger had ruined my father. I was enraged. But I had no idea just how grim the prognosis was and how this might shape our future. My mother never let on but it appeared that the police service was expecting to pension him off. Still breastfeeding her baby daughter, and with two boys not yet in school, she was now married to an invalid. Someone told her, correctly as it turned out, that insurance and compensation would take years to settle. I couldn't know the many ways in which the parameters of her life – and my own along with it – had been radically redrawn in an instant, but I did understand that the world had changed for us. My father's life had been spared and we were glad, but we were no longer the safe, confident people we'd been before.

As a child I was always something of an eavesdropper. I was also an inveterate prowler with a peculiar fascination with the potency of certain objects. Sometime during that long convalescence I came upon the helmet Dad had been wearing when he was hit. Made of laminated cork, it was cumbersome, and it felt unstable in my hands. The crazed pattern of cracks dulling its whiteness gave it an unnerving broken-eggshell texture. For a long time – for years, I think – I continued to seek it out, to turn it over in my hands, to sniff the Brylcreem interior, and try to imagine the sudden moment, the awful impact, and the faceless stranger behind all this damage. The inside of the helmet smelt of my father, but it was as if you could almost smell death on the outside. This flimsy artefact had held my father's living head, his brain, his memory, his jokes; it was all that had stood between him and the void – a crust no thicker than my finger. The older I got, the darker those conjectures became. By most accounts I was an intense little boy. Perhaps it was wise of my parents to get rid of the sacramental helmet when they did.

How quick children are to absorb the unexpressed anxieties of their parents; how fluent they become in the unconscious art of compensation, and how instinctive is their assumption of responsibility. The margins between coping and not coping, between psychological survival and total collapse, are so narrow and often so arbitrary that it's uncomfortable to look back and consider what might have been. The months of my father's convalescence had a lasting impact on me. By these events I was drafted into the world of consequences. I became 'Mummy's little helper'. The little man. I was assigned the role of sibling enforcer and family protector. I was the keeper of grown-up secrets, the compensator, the listener. I had to be 'wise beyond my years', to assume an unlikely authority, to understand what I could not pronounce.

During this time Mum was stoic and subdued. Dad lived in

bed and obediently swallowed the pills that would chew the holes in his guts. He had lost a lot of weight but he was still too heavy for Mum to lift. There was no way she could get him in and out of a bath, so she had to wash him in bed. My parents' bedroom was perpetually dim and the apprehension within it seemed to infect the rest of the house. With the curtains drawn against the heat, the place was infused with a faint amber light, and in that atmosphere of bewilderment there were times when the only signs of animation were the churn and swirl of dust motes.

That summer there were many visits from family and neighbours, but the person who distinguished himself above all others was a complete unknown. He showed up unannounced and uninvited and offered to bathe my father. It was weird. But his unexpected arrival and strange proposal soon brought a new energy to the house. Also a new awkwardness. I didn't know what to make of this turn of events. I took my cues from Mum, who was hesitant at first, even a little resistant. But she was desperate for help and here was a helper, a volunteer from who knew and who cared where. She relented and let him in, and straight away he went to work.

I observed everything carefully, suspiciously. Here was some *bloke* entering my parents' bedroom, introducing himself to my father who consented to be undressed, lifted from his sickbed and carried like a child to the bathroom. There the door wasn't exactly shut in my face but it was pushed to, slightly ajar. My world was already out of whack, but this new set-up was discombobulating, especially when, after a few minutes, my mother decided to leave the men to it and get on with her many jobs. I stood outside in the narrow corridor listening to the sounds of water and the low, deep voices. It was appalling to think of that guy kneeling at the bath and washing my father as if he were an infant. Mum caught me camped by the door and tried to shoo me away, but I drifted back. In the weeks ahead, every time that stranger returned, I was there at the door like a sentry, straining to hear, keeping tabs.

I couldn't really follow what the men said in the bathroom, as they slowly got to know one another. They always spoke quietly. There was none of the hearty blather you heard blokes falling into at the footy or across the fence. I was wary of this soft-spoken interloper. No doubt I was threatened by his presence. And yet his brief tenure in our home helped break down the anxious malaise that oppressed us. His actions taught me something new about strangers – that while they could wreck your life and do you harm they were also capable of mysterious kindness.

By autumn my father began to make progress. His recovery was faster and more complete than anyone had expected. He was a big, strong man but his injuries were awful, and to some the speed of his improvement was unsettling. It was only as an adult that I learnt some of what had gone on in that tiny bathroom. There was a day when Dad's helper brought a bottle of oil with him. Olive oil, I gather, which wasn't common in a house like ours. He anointed the old man with it in the manner of ancient Christian tradition, and 'laid hands on him', as the saying goes, praying that Dad might be healed. Neither of my parents was ever keen to talk about this ritual, and they certainly made no special claims for its efficacy, but after the old man's recovery they became devout and lifelong Christians.

And I've thought a lot about this unlikely turning. Because, like the accident, it had a profound effect on my own trajectory. It's no small achievement to confound a copper's lowered expectations of humankind, for that's a tough carapace to penetrate. Still, being unmanned by injury and sidelined from the world of action had to have been traumatic. Dad was an outdoor, hands-on bloke, a practical fellow. Later he said that during his convalescence he'd had a lot of time to think. Perhaps, like the rest of us in the house that summer, he was left without armour, maybe even without hope – I don't know. I don't set much store by signs and wonders, but I try to keep an open mind. All I can say is that I witnessed Dad's swift restoration and renewal and was grateful for it, and in much the same way that I'd soaked up the fear and horror preceding his recovery, I absorbed the new energy and purpose that came into his life and into Mum's as a result of this stranger's compassion. I think of it as an act of grace. Maybe that's just a fancypants way of appreciating the loving-kindness of humans. But when there's so much opportunity for people to be vile, it strikes me as a miracle that they choose mercy, restraint and decency as often as they do.

III

When he was well enough, the old man returned to light duties at Traffic. For a while he manned the Accident Desk. From there he went to the Plan Room where he drew up schematic representations of major and fatal accidents for use in the courts. What it must have been like to return to such scenes of carnage, gimping out into wreck-strewn intersections with his measuring tape and yellow crayon: the broken glass, the skidmarks, the smells of blood and petrol. He said he was glad he had no memory of the prang. He loved his job and he certainly knew his way around a bingle. But it can't have been easy. At first he walked with a limp. Then he had a bone graft and got fit. He returned to Accidents, and even got back on the bikes. Now and then he rode me to school on his new BSA and I arrived like a princeling. As I waved him off he'd burn away, letting off a lairish blurt of the siren to impress the other kids. I hoped no one saw my legs trembling. I'd always loved the Beezers but now a pillion ride was a secret terror. I never let on.

After all the disaster and uncertainty, we were out of the woods. My dad was back. He was strong once more and I felt safe again. It was the best feeling ever.

At some level every kid knows that his parents' wellbeing is paramount to his own safety, even his sense of self. Mercifully, children are rarely forced to confront the fact consciously. I suppose this is why the minor prang and roadside scuffle I witnessed a few years later were so traumatic. Seeing all that blood and screaming and violence, any child would be disturbed. And I imagine the twisted motorbike, a ghastly echo of the old man's smash, had an effect. But I wasn't just upset, I felt as if I were unravelling. I was in no physical danger yet I feared that everything was about to fall apart again right in front of me, that I might die at any moment.

Fifteen years later, just before my first child was born, I wrote a short story, 'A Blow, a Kiss', about an incident very similar to that night's. In the fictional version the boy behind the wheel can't bear to watch the scene play out another moment. He leaps from the vehicle in defence of his father and king-hits the drunk with the lantern. In a sense I let the character do what I'd been incapable of, and though I doubt it served any therapeutic purpose, I'd be lying if I said I took no pleasure in letting him off the leash on my behalf.

In real life, the events of that night came and went largely undiscussed. The experience wasn't so traumatic as to knock me out of kilter, but afterwards I knew the difference between calm and safety. Family life was good. In many ways we prospered. But now I knew that we were not, and never really would be, out of the woods. Everything you know and see is fragile, temporary, and if there's any constant in life it's contingency. I came to suspect that you don't just relive these sudden moments in your head and in your sense-memories, you repeat them in fresh events, as if ensnared in a pattern.

IV

Barely eight years after that motorcyclist's accident, and just 200 metres from where he fell, I too went through a brick wall.

By then my father was the sergeant-in-charge of the local suburban police station and I was eighteen, the sole passenger in a muscle car that smashed into a girls' school. The first witnesses on the scene said we'd ploughed through the 2-metre-high perimeter wall and the only thing that prevented us from hitting the caretaker's house was the concrete foundation of the rotary clothes hoist in his front yard. The driver, a boy I'd known since infancy, escaped unhurt. But the Slant 6 engine was almost in my lap, and the rubble had crushed the car all around me. I was slumped against the seatbelt, my only visible injury a split chin from the brick that knocked me senseless. Apparently I regained consciousness as people laboured to cut me free, but it was years before I regained any memory of the accident, and when a couple of brief sequences did come back to me, like a brutal ambush, I had cause to wish it had all stayed safely in the vault. Again, the old smells of petrol and blood. And the voices of paramedics, a haze of brick dust, the ghastly hysteria of strobing lights. The whole thing was a garish sideshow, absurd and sinister. In that ugly flashback I heard myself laughing like a deranged clown. I was a university student but I couldn't even tell the ambos who the prime minister was. And in the ambulance I could not move a limb. Some bloke with hairy arms was holding me down. It wasn't a rescue – it was a kidnapping.

Until this nasty spasm of recollection, my only other memory of the night was a brief moment in Casualty in which Mum fainted and Dad caught her. Maybe she was upset by the seizures I was having. Or perhaps it was just the harrowing sense of déjà vu. For the rest I had to rely on the testimonies of others, as if I hadn't even been at my own prang, and their accounts were contradictory. In general terms I know what occurred. What I'm unclear about is how it happened.

After a stint in hospital I came home as weak and doddery as a crone. Weeks into my convalescence I still felt like a ghost in my own body. I shouldn't have been surprised; this is a typical after-effect of road trauma and major concussion. All your organs have been insulted, not just your brain. But while I should have known better, I was unprepared for how long it took me to reconnect with the life I'd been living. I was feeble and mentally stuck.

I wondered if what I was feeling was a little like grief, or maybe shock. I'd seen both at work in others. I knew only too well what they did to a person, swinging down out of a clear sky. All my life I'd heard the old man talk about the dreaded midnight knock that every cop delivers sooner or later, bringing news of sudden death to some unsuspecting loved one. In fact I'd done it myself, been commissioned, you might say. At fourteen, alongside my father, I'd had to help break the news to a close mate that his father had been killed. The feeling is hideous. It's like killing someone. They go down like a water buffalo felled by an axe, and some part of you believes it's your fault.

But as a survivor, what I was feeling was not grief. Neither was it shock, whose physical effects recede soon enough. I just felt diminished. Not unmanned so much as bogged to the boards. Looking back I'd say I was depressed.

It's galling to lie in bed for weeks absorbing the results of some-one else's mistake. But the old man was right – convalescence does focus the mind. I was at that time halfway through my first year of university and drifting along a little bit. For quite a while I'd been thinking of myself as a writer, but I hadn't knuckled down the way I'd planned to. I was in danger of becoming a bit of a pretender. Before the accident there seemed to be plenty of time in which to find my way, but now I thought differently. Suddenly time was precious. So once I recovered I went to work and by graduation I'd written three books. Havoc, it seemed, had leant in and set me running.

But I hadn't emerged unscathed. Everyone told me writing

was a hell of a way to make a living and they were right. Indeed it was hard to think of a vocation more uncertain or less likely, but I'd always figured I could supplement my income with physical work – on the deck of a crayboat or as a brickie's labourer (after all, bricks seemed to run in the family). But in the wake of the accident my back was never the same. I still feel this legacy every morning when I wake – that stiff and fluky spine is the only thing I regret. With my plan B now shot, I had to rely on my wits alone or I was buggered. And in this sense I think the prang was a gift. It shaped my life, which is to say, of course, that it bound me. I was goaded into beginning what I'd dreamt of doing since I was ten years old. Because of that one sudden moment I went harder at the writing game than anybody could believe, myself included. It was as if I had Robert Johnson's hellhound on my tail.

V

As a teenager I flirted with death. It was an irrational impulse, but a powerful one. Risky behaviour of all sorts gave me a buzz. I particularly enjoyed shallow-water apnoea diving, especially beneath low-slung limestone reefs. I'd crawl into underwater ledges, some of them hardly wide enough to accommodate my body and my snorkel, and I'd crab and squirm my way into the gloom, backing myself to eventually find a slim hole through which to shove the snorkel before my lungs gave out. I swam into narrow clefts whose geography was completely unfamiliar. The reefs were jagged and the passages beneath them as spidery and complex as the capillaries carrying the last oxygen in my blood. Pressed into the darkness, I inched along in search of a life-giving shaft of light. It was claustrophobic and dangerous. I got myself into situations that give me the cold sweats when I think of them now. But when I emerged into full daylight and fresh air, half poisoned with carbon dioxide, I felt newly charged. I knew I was truly alive. And the feeling was blissful.

I suppose that by the middle of my adolescence I'd come to feel safe enough to take such risks, even to need them somehow. Of course, the safety I felt was illusory. I'd buried a few memories by then and told myself a few lies.

Those years and that impulse are long behind me. But some of my friends still have that old craving for danger. As they like to say, when you're safe you think you know yourself, but *in extremis* who are you really? By and large, this is not a question that troubles me, because to some degree, thanks to my history, I know. It's odd the extent to which your body remembers things your mind hides from you.

In my experience, at moments of extremity, you often become a person you know very well. Confronted by a kid who's choking, or an adult in distress in the water, you follow a pattern, a role that seems to have already been written. Events swoop down upon you, unexpected but somehow not strange. The sudden, skin-prickling proximity to havoc is creepily familiar, and sometimes its arrival is no real surprise at all. Survivors of family violence talk about being able to sense the approach of savagery. Regular victims become hyper-vigilant. They feel the onset of trouble like a change of air pressure. It sounds peculiar, but you can read a room with your body. If you're attuned, whether you're in a volatile kitchen, a rough sea or out on the open road, you can see things coming unstuck before it starts to happen, and it's an eerie feeling. The problem is that although you may know how trouble begins, you can't predict where it will go or how it will end.

After havoc recedes, the mind often lets the details slip, and that can be a mercy. But the body remembers. When you're tumbling out of control upside down along a dirt road, you think, calmly, weirdly, Oh, this again. Pressed to the seabed by tonnes of roiling whitewater, you catch yourself thinking, Ah, I know how this scene goes.

The sudden moment can come and go in a searing flash or it can settle in to become your day. You're driving home from the city and a pillar of dust rises at the bend and you see the wrecked vehicle with the blood streaming down the door and the familiarity of the tableau turns you into an automaton. There's a small girl running barefoot down the highway. In the blood-spattered van a driver lies crushed at the wheel. You know what this is, how it proceeds. You just don't know how it ends. And as if you're reading from a script you get out of the car. For some reason you have time to note that a Winton always wears thongs to a crisis. You commission the eldest child as you were once commissioned yourself, and when the hysterical girl is safe in his care you do what you can to keep her mother alive until help arrives. There's petrol everywhere. In the summer heat the smell of all that dark, viscous blood is foul. You crawl in through the broken windscreen and register the asymmetrical intimacy of the wreck and it's frightening how calm you are. You're certain that if the woman doesn't go into cardiac arrest before the ambulance arrives she'll lose her arm anyway. It doesn't look anything like an arm anymore and she's turning puce as you watch. There's nowhere to tie her limb off but she's holding herself together by instinct somehow and all you can do is keep her conscious, so you talk to her. You say the kindest things, the brightest things you can summon. And still no one shows up. You consider dragging her out and driving her to hospital yourself, but the nearest emergency room is an hour away and you have a car full of small children. You think of your father whispering to teenaged boys at the roadside as they died in his arms. You wish someone would come along and delete you from this scene.

Afterwards, despite the happy outcome, you are of course a fucking mess. What you have been, all through your moment of extremity, is a casual-sounding robot. Your state has probably been nothing short of hysterical. Maybe *that's* who you are.

VI

Being a copper's son, I've always got one eye out for trouble. I can't help it. But I don't go looking for it anymore. These days I crave stability. I don't like surprises. I have friends who say they love a surprise, but I've travelled with a few of them and I know otherwise. Four seconds of unscheduled plummeting in a commercial aircraft and they're wailing for their mothers. But while I savour routine – I thrive in it – I'm conscious that despite its virtues and comforts the regulated life has its own dangers. Just as an ecosystem requires cataclysmic disruption now and then, the mind and body need a similar jolt. Communities need this too. Eventually a state of seamless predictability – a life without wildness – is a kind of sleepwalking. It attenuates the senses, blunts the imagination. Nobody has written better about this flattened, narcotic mindset than J.G. Ballard. His novels seem to suggest that where there is no wildness humans will create it. In his masterpiece *Crash* his characters, having all but lost the capacity to feel, resort to participating in spectacles so shocking they offend every sense back to life. For them, all other signals besides the grotesque and perverse have grown too faint.

I don't think humans as a whole have achieved Ballard's dystopian state of anaesthesia quite yet. But in the most prosperous enclaves, some have come to believe they've domesticated chaos. Despite having developed social sensitivities that border on the neurasthenic, they've worked up an aesthetic weakness for the gothic and lurid. Some of society's safest citizens develop a recreational need to feel and inflict pain. No longer at the mercy of nature as our ancestors were, we live as if all wildness has been brought to heel. Nowadays people have a kind of agency our forebears could not imagine and on the surface this appears to be freedom without consequence, which is, after all, the consumer ideal. When we set out on a journey we assume we'll arrive intact and on time. We press a button or swipe a screen and receive exactly what we're expecting. The ping of a communications gadget gives us a measurable endorphin shot.

And when we don't get what we anticipated, our reaction is outsized – instant rage. Any interruption to service is received like a blow to the head, an insult, because the consumer is groomed to expect evenness. Such flatness of expectations infects culture, too. Predictability has become a cinematic virtue and a default assumption in literature. The editor of a New York magazine once respectfully rejected a story of mine on the grounds that 'the shark attack came out of nowhere'. The implication being that such an event, insufficiently foreshadowed, is so unlikely as to seem improper, a thought I hold onto some days as I bob about in the surf.

For many, certainty has become the new normal, but it's an illusion. Like it or not, 'old man trouble', as the song has it, 'is laying and waiting on you'. Each of us wades in the swamp of everyone else's actions and intentions. We'll forever be vulnerable to havoc. And no amount of insurance, risk management or technology will keep it from our door. You might not have sharks in your neighbourhood, but there'll always be a catastrophic diagnosis in the wings, or a financial crash, or just some moron running a red light.

My old man survived his career in havoc. He did thirty-three years in the job and got his long-service medal. He's been retired since 1991. He rode motorbikes until he was in his seventies. When I was in my twenties he took me for a spin, though I needed some convincing. Afterwards he said I was a rotten pillion passenger, that it was like carting a hairy coffin.

And now I've been a writer for more years than he was a copper.

All our days, both of us have tried to avoid trouble, and yet it's been our business. Without strife the cop and the novelist have nothing to work with. Perhaps it's morbid to view your life through the prism of violent events, to feel yourself shaped by accidents. Safety is a great gift: maybe it's disrespectful to feel the interruptions to it more vividly than the many peaceful interludes in between. But to be afraid is to be awake. And to exist at all in this universe is to be caught up at the scene of perhaps the happiest accident of all. By now we know how that scene goes. We're just not sure how it ends.

A Walk
at Low Tide

Just before dawn I take the narrow track from the house to the beach and walk the shoreline once more to see the familiar stretch and all its daily surprises. Past the high bund of coarse sand at the foot of the dune and the littoral field of gooseflesh the pebbles become on the long decline, the tidal flats are almost bare, ribbed and fluted from the sea's retreat.

On the face of it there's nothing here to see – an empty beach, a blank ocean. And unless a whale suddenly rises out there in the gulf like a black and glistening hangover from the night's murky dreams, everything before me is unremarkable, event-free. And yet it holds me captive, has me returning morning and evening, high tide and low, because it's never the same place. It holds its secret life close. Every day there are ephemeral stipples and scratches in the sand, divots where euros have stood, and tiny tractor-treads where Gilbert's dragons have come down to cool off. There are tumbled heads of coral, mangrove trunks, an osprey feather, a scorpion in an oyster shell. With every step there is another pattern, a fresh texture, a curving flourish, and when the sun butts up from the sea the palette changes moment by moment, roiling, restless as a spillage. Behind me the spinifex turns gold as baking bread and the stony ranges beyond are washed purple and pink until darkness only abides in the realm of pathless canyons.

Every day I come and most days I learn something new, but only occasionally do I really *see* because while I'm always looking I'm not necessarily paying serious attention. Half the time, in the manner of my kind and my era, I'm looking at shells and stones and stranded jellyfish as though they are objects, rather than subjects. A subject has a life. In its wake and even in its form it trails a story, a journey that can be as brief as that of the cuttlefish that leaves only the foamy hull of its backbone to memory and whose death can be read in the neat curve of toothmarks made by the dolphin that claimed it. The bones of the turtle scattered along the house track suggest a longer story, probably longer than my own, a life of oceanic questing and feats of navigation still beyond human ken. And the pink and yellow boulders pressed up against the coral reef – they are only new in the narrowest sense. The flash floods of autumn ripped them from canyons a kilometre away and rolled them to the sea, but they were ancient and storied long before this, marbled and ground smooth before the world even saw a human.

When you pay attention you feel the presence of the past, you sense the ongoing struggle and the yearning of all things seen and unseen. For the moment, the bleached head of coral that lies face-down in the rockpool is shelter to the tiny and deadly blue-ringed octopus, but before this it was host to half a million lives. Each hole in its aerated cauliflower surface was wrought by an organism straining to thrive, build, reproduce – a minuscule part of what it takes to keep the deeps alive and therefore all life on Earth.

That, I realize too infrequently, is what lies beneath the surface of every sleepy step I take before breakfast: the resonance of a trillion lives, finished or only just begun, subjects that ache to be fed, seek the light and tilt toward increase in a creation that has been burning and lapping and gnawing and withering and rotting and flowering since there was nothing in the cosmos but shivering potential. To tread here and never pay tribute, to glance and just see objects, is to be spiritually impoverished. Things are not just what they appear to be, not even the people and creatures and forms most familiar to us. They are certainly not knowable by how they first present themselves. Looking deeply, humbly, reverently will sometimes open the viewer to what lingers beneath hue and form and texture – the faint tracks of story that suggest relationships, alliances, consequences, damage. If you can ever know something you'll understand it by what it has given, what it owes, what it needs. It has never existed in isolation. And ghosting forever behind its mere appearance is its holy purpose, its billion meetings with the life urge in which it has swum or tumbled or blossomed, however long or however briefly. When you observe long enough, the subject of your gaze seems, eventually, to respond. Or perhaps it's you, the viewer, who is changed; something has stuck, something, in the end, is going on between you and it.

Repatriation

In the great sickle-shaped hinterland of the West Australian wheatbelt, trees have been exterminated. Like embroidered motifs at the hem of a bleached and threadbare rug, a few lonely specimens mark the corners of paddocks. Now and then a remnant stand of wandoos has been spared because of stubborn piles of granite surrounding them, but most of it is a land scraped naked. Today, a late autumn day in 2008, as I drive north from Perth toward the old pastoral lease at Mt Gibson Station, a wicked easterly howls in off the desert and the sky is pink with dirt. Less than a century ago this bit of country was a series of eucalypt woodlands of remarkable biodiversity, but it was bulldozed and burned at the urging of successive governments to make way for cultivation. The ancient soil exposed by all this tree grubbing was quickly depleted; then it was laced with billions of tonnes of superphosphate, which lured two generations of farmers into the delusion that their operations were sustainable. Emboldened by good seasons and high prices, grain farmers pushed right out into the drylands. At the time it must have seemed that nature itself was surrendering to human ingenuity and the vigour of a new settler culture.

I remember driving through wheat country on winter's nights as a boy to see mile upon mile of burning windrows, whose parallel lines were like the columns of an army on the march. Back then the sons of wheat farmers believed they would inherit something precious – this was before the creeping insurgency of salt and the arrival of an almost permanent drought. Farmers have been walking off the land here for more than a decade, and those who hang on to their scorched-earth inheritance are given incentives to plant the very trees their fathers were paid to grub up. For many it's probably too little, too late.

While it still enjoys a residual heroic romance in West Australian culture, to me the northern wheatbelt is the most sterile and desolate country imaginable. As I travel through it today I see kilometres of empty, gentle undulation, taut wire fences, stubble; I see pale dust raked into corduroy grids that run to the horizon, grain silos at lonely rail sidings, hamlets with few signs of life. It's all very orderly, but nothing moves except the flying soil. Heading north toward the semi-arid zone of the goldfields and the red desert beyond, you instinctively resign yourself to the prospect of seeing even less, and for a while the landscape obliges. Fences begin to dwindle and then disappear altogether. The earth turns a deeper pink and the bitumen two-lane of the Great Northern Highway unravels into the wavering distance where country becomes flatter, wider, drier, and hotter by the minute. But then, oddly enough, you begin to see roadkill – emus, cockatoos, kangaroos – bloated and flyblown at the gravel edges. You come to shimmering saltpans around which grow purple, green and salmon-coloured samphires. In time the plains of low mulga scrub become variegated with she-oak thickets, aggregations of pale acacia, and then, rising above everything, bronze and shining, gnarly old York gums.

It takes a while for it to sink in, but the closer you get to the desert, the more life there is in the land; once you're fully beyond the reach of modern cultivation there are trees again, and from their shadows come enough birds, reptiles and mammals to let you feel you are finally back in Australia. Each time I traverse the dead zone of the wheatbelt and reach this territory, my mood lifts – and then I think, What kind of man cheers up at the sight of roadkill?

This far inland I'm way off my patch and I feel it keenly. I'm a coastal person. My home is the white-sand and limestone country of the midwest: grass trees, tuarts, banksia and coastal heath. My abiding interest is in the littoral. Even here in the reddening interior I gravitate to rims and edges, toward a region wedged between farm and desert that has its hooks in me, for past the last big wheat town of Dalwallinu, and before the gold diggings at Paynes Find, is a swathe of country that has taught me a lot about the mistakes of our common past and given me cautious hope for the future. Out here there's a different kind of littoral, where eucalypts and mulga scrub overlap in a wash of unlikely biodiversity. Along a stretch of road where not long ago you'd have seen country so goat-infested, so beaten-down and degraded that you could cry, something new is afoot. Here, in a state whose economy and mindset are bound up in an endless war against nature, private citizens have beheld the paralysis of government agencies and begun taking conservation into their own hands.

If all this sounds a little bleak and dramatic, remember that

Australia has the worst record of mammal extinction in the world: since European settlement twenty-seven species have disappeared entirely. A further fifteen hundred species, mammal and non-mammal, are currently vulnerable or endangered. Marsupials, the mammals unique to the continent, are in particular decline and many of the smaller species are among those gone for good. This is largely a result of land clearing, which devastated the habitat of native animals and allowed their subsequent decimation by foxes and cats. Some scientists estimate that 75 million native birds and animals are killed by cats in Australia every night. National parks and reserves have not provided effective sanctuary because they are exposed to these and other feral predators, and many large and remote parks are either too thinly staffed or not staffed at all.

Some rare marsupials now exist only by chance, in remnant populations on offshore islands. These stragglers are the focus of government breeding programs, but apart from zoos and other enclosures, agencies have few refuges on the mainland safe enough to release bred animals into. The chief sources of safe wild Australian habitat are private. For the past decade, non-government organizations have been acquiring land for conservation purposes. Six million hectares are now held by individuals or associations. None will actually say that they've been doing governments' work for them, but this is more or less the case. Without private participation, habitat conservation in this country would be even more desperate than it is, and the prospects for mammal recovery in particular would be slim indeed.

The chief player in this fight is the Australian Wildlife Conservancy, a not-for-profit foundation that administers more than 3 million hectares of land, making it the biggest non-government conservation landholder on the continent. The AWC runs Mt Gibson Sanctuary, about 350 kilometres north-east of Perth, in the Yalgoo district. I've been coming here since it was acquired, as the AWC's first major purchase, in 2001. A former sheep station of 130 500 hectares, it is transitional country bordering the vast dry saltpan of Lake Moore. The land within its boundaries still supports as many as seven hundred species of native plants in thirteen major vegetation associations, and with every passing year of recovery – since it was destocked and cleared of feral goats, foxes and cats – it gets closer to being a continental refuge for mammal species long extinct in this area and most other parts of the state. My initial visit coincided with the first biological survey of the property, and although I've returned many times to camp and hike for my own pleasure as well as to witness its regeneration, it's been several years since I was here.

In the late afternoon, when the bluish hummock of Mt Singleton shows in the far distance, I pull off onto the dirt drive that runs more than 40 kilometres east to the old station homestead. I bounce past the slagheaps and junk piles of abandoned mine diggings. Already small trees – gimlets and jams – ladder the track with shadows. A mob of Major Mitchell's cockatoos spills, untidy as a closing-time crowd, from a desert cypress. Every few minutes the track changes colour – yellow, pink, black, purple, vermilion, burgundy, gold – as contours and vegetation types vary.

At the State Barrier Fence, commonly known as the Vermin Proof Fence, I stop the LandCruiser and get out to swing back the gate. A desiccated emu carcass stands ensnared in the wire like an inner-city art installation. In exceptionally dry seasons inland, emus head west in search of water, often moving in huge numbers. The fence, which is more than 1800 kilometres long, was initially built to keep rabbits and dingoes at bay, and periodically you still see news footage of the emu 'plague' – hundreds of enormous, thirst-crazed native birds stampeding south or battering themselves to death against the wire, cordoned off as though *they* were vermin.

The fence stands neatly in the centre of a cleared strip of orange dirt. The earth here looks hard-baked but its crust yields to the faintest pressure of my fingertips. How fragile the soil is in Australia. Before Europeans the continent had never known the impact of hoofed animals. When great herds of sheep and cattle arrived they made fortunes for their owners, yet pastoralism may well have cost the nation more than it will ever earn back. The soil erosion and habitat loss resulting from the introduction of these herds (not to mention the millions of feral goats, pigs, rabbits, donkeys, horses and camels that wander the interior) have been catastrophic for native species. As a kid I spent a lot of time outdoors, on the timbered fringe of Perth and later in the rural south-west, and apart from the luckless western grey kangaroos I slaughtered in the company of farmboys, accountants and church deacons on 'family picnics', I almost never saw a marsupial. In the middle of the night, camping on the south coast, I might wake to find a quenda – a southern brown bandicoot – truffling through my foodbox, but of the legendary bilbies, numbats, potoroos and phascogales there was no sign. My biology teachers told me, quite correctly, that these were shy, nocturnal creatures, but the darker truth is that they weren't obscured by the night, nor were they hiding – they simply weren't there anymore. This is not a problem restricted to my home range. When it comes to its famous marsupials, much of Australia is silent country.

From the vermin fence I bash the rest of the way east along the rutted track to the homestead, a modest old place with sagging verandahs and outbuildings. There are stockyards nearby, a shearing shed, and the usual array of once-loved vehicles marking the property's former life as a sheep station. Two new staff dwellings have been built. I note the advent of solar panels, the four-wheel drives with AWC livery, and a mercifully quiet generator in place of the roaring monster you could once hear a mile away at night. For the moment, though, everybody's elsewhere.

Back in the spring of 2001 the same compound was abuzz with zoologists, palaeoecologists and hardy bird folks, and the old shearers' cottage was encircled by utes, swags, caravans, and trailers piled with arcane equipment and much beer. I'd just finished a seven-year writing project and was enmeshed in a wearying public campaign for a coral reef in my spare time, so I arrived depleted, under-briefed and sceptical about this philanthropic venture at the edge of the arid zone.

At that time the AWC was a novel entity and an unknown quantity. One of Western Australia's most senior scientists, Dr Barry Wilson, a man I knew and admired, had suggested I come and take a look while he was up at Mt Gibson with Tim Flannery and other members of its board, but he made the mistake of telling me the whole show was the brainchild of a British-born insurance tycoon who'd developed a late-life passion for Australian native species, so my expectations were not high. I was bracing myself for an encounter with some cashed-up corporate types anxious to redeem themselves with good works – or worse, another pale-green outfit confusing wildlife conservation with the profit motive. Australians are often suspicious of wealthy do-gooders; we don't exactly have a long, proud tradition of philanthropy. Perhaps it's a legacy of the convict experience, and the hard-bitten settler mindset that came after it. Compared with the settlement of America, for instance, which was savage enough on any terms, colonial Australia was specially marked by dismay, hunger and disenchantment: place names like Point Torment and Starvation Bay are common. Here there was no promised land for the interlopers, little milk and even less honey.

The prospects didn't get better as settlers headed west, they got even leaner. When wealth was finally generated, its beneficiaries rarely troubled themselves with old-world noblesse oblige or the ethical gestures that the more religious Americans were susceptible to. Having at last wrested something from the waterless frontier, the colonists of the Australian west grasped hard and long at whatever they got. Along with their war on nature they maintained a stalwart resistance to charity because there seemed to be something effeminate about it; there was no room for softness of any sort. The fixed mind has been no easier to prise open than the clenched fist.

Whether we like it or not, conservation traditionally involves the broke hounding the captive in the employ of the low-minded – at least, that's my experience of advocacy. As for the business of trying to court what we're reduced to calling 'the philanthropic dollar', well, the only metaphors I have are unkind and pornographic. I never held out much hope that the Australian rich might one day enter the fray on the side of nature, especially not our peculiar western breed of mogul. Let's just say that when I arrived at Mt Gibson that September, in the full-blown siege mode of the campaigner, steeling myself for a festival of bullshit, within an hour of meeting its founder and benefactor, Martin Copley, I was disarmed.

In his home counties accent, with an odd mixture of authority and modesty, the quietly spoken Englishman outlined his plan to secure a network of wild refuges for native mammals. Around us, consulting specialists were already establishing which species were extant on the property and how many had been lost since the introduction of grazing and predators. We visited trapping surveys, listened to cross-discipline discussions, and spread vegetation maps across the red-stained bonnets of vehicles. There was a rare sense of excitement in the company. None of the scientists I spoke to that week were troubled by the prospect of their data and conclusions being traduced or ignored, which is common in a mining state where environmental assessments are buried, tweaked, or compromised by conflicts of interest. Copley and his crew treated the scientists with grave respect, as if their work really mattered.

Taking me on a hike across the homestead ridge, the founder pointed out raptors' nests, ancient sandalwoods, and the great pink expanse of Lake Moore. He had a straightforward and unsentimental view of philanthropy. In recent years he'd learnt about native mammal extinction and now had the resources to do something about it – end of story. From the outset he struck me as logical, purposeful and steely. Scrupulously polite, he was impatient with symbolism; his instincts seemed strategic and empirical. Clearly he wasn't a guilty rich man, nor was he anybody's fool. He simply saw a vacuum between government agencies and advocacy groups and decided to fill it. He had committed the AWC to restoring country on an ecosystem basis, unhampered by the artificial boundaries of state and agency jurisdictions. While advocacy groups could only prod and finesse and shame government into enlarging its efforts, Copley's purchase at Mt Gibson dramatically increased Western Australia's reserve of critically important habitats at the stroke of a pen. Having brought a new respectability to both philanthropy and conservation, the AWC has helped spawn something that may become the environmental mainstream in this country.

Meanwhile, literally back at the ranch, I leave a note tucked into the flyscreen door of the homestead and decide to press further into the sanctuary so I can reach Lake Moore before dark. It's slow going. I have to ease the troop carrier up the steep, guttered track of the homestead ridge, whose jagged greenstone surface shifts and slides beneath my wheels. Halfway up I see a telltale mound through the spindly acacias and pull up with a flutter of anticipation. Getting out as quietly as I can, I ease down the scree slope to the hummock of sticks, stones and leaf litter that forms the nest of a malleefowl. In a moment I see there's no bird here, and hasn't been for some time.

Resembling a big speckled chicken, the malleefowl stands up to 60 centimetres tall. It's a discreet and elusive bird. The male constructs the nest by kicking dirt and stones into a circular mound with a central crater, in which he dumps vegetable matter upon which the hen will lay her eggs. Heat generated by the rotting detritus incubates the eggs, and hatchlings must fight their way unaided to the surface and then fend for themselves. Some nest mounds are 6 metres across. There are malleefowl out here at Mt Gibson, but I never manage to luck onto them.

Back in the troopy, I crest the ridge and go yawing and crunching down into a whole new landscape. To the east I can see the treetops of a salmon-gum woodland. Far to the north is the ridgeline running lakeward from Mt Singleton. Before I head down into the valley of trees I make a little detour. I'm anxious about the light, but determined to make what has become a ritual visit whenever I'm here.

I stop the vehicle in a clearing that was once unremarkable to my unschooled gaze. When I first came to this spot, with the station's former leaseholder, Peter Underwood, and the bird expert John Dell, I had no idea what we were looking at or what we might be searching for. Across the hard-packed red dirt there's a plate of exposed rock where I knelt with the two older men to survey a few burrows that opened around its perimeter.

'Rabbits?' I ventured.

Underwood grinned and shook his head. 'Boodies,' he said. 'Boodies!'

'Boodies,' I murmured doubtfully, looking to the bird man for some moral support, sensing a joke at my expense. Boodies? Yeah, right.

'Like a woylie,' said John Dell. 'Closely related.'

Ah. Even I'd heard of the woylie. But like most of my country-men, I couldn't have described one for love nor money.

The woylie belongs to the great treasury of marsupials that we revere and know nothing about. As I learnt that day, the boodie and the woylie are different species of bettong. A bettong is like a kangaroo but smaller than a teddy bear. Its face is more rounded than a kangaroo's, with the protuberant eyes of a possum. While the woylie (*Bettongia penicillata*) nests in the undergrowth of dry sclerophyll forest in remnant populations, the boodie (*Bettongia lesueur*) is the only macropod to shelter in burrows; it digs elaborate warrens under rock lintels that give its redoubts security and unusual longevity. Like most marsupials it is omnivorous and nocturnal. It has a particular appetite for underground fungi.

'Look at that warren,' said Underwood admiringly. 'You'd think they only just built it.'

By this stage I was properly enthralled by the prospect of a boodie encounter. Wondering if we'd have to wait long, I began to calculate the approach of dusk, but before I could embarrass my-self further the others broke the news that, although once widely distributed across the arid inland, the boodie has been extinct on mainland Australia since the early 1960s. The story of this extinc-tion is familiar, involving the catastrophic habitat loss wrought by agriculture and pastoralism. In their native environments, small mammals did not have to contend with predatory ground carnivores like foxes and cats, for which they were easy meat. Under these new conditions the boodie population collapsed quite suddenly.

Still hunkered by the old warren, Underwood confessed to a conviction that somehow, one day, the boodie would return to Mt Gibson. His tone was wistful but also defiant, as if over time he'd inured himself to ridicule on this point. I thought again of the potent space that an absence becomes. The lost boodie is just a part of a wider absence, a pattern of extinction that haunts this continent. Each time I come to Mt Gibson I think of Peter Underwood and his dream of boodies finding their way back to these burrows, like exiles returning to their former homes. With the passage of time that notion has become a little less fanciful. In fact, it might soon be possible, because a partnership of public and private concerns has already seen the boodie begin its long easterly trek homeward.

The last natural strongholds of the boodie are two remote islands, Bernier and Dorre at Shark Bay. A little closer to shore, in the estuarine shallows of this World Heritage Area, squats the smaller Faure Island, another AWC sanctuary. In 2004 I travelled there with Martin Copley, Tim Flannery and the basketball star Luc Longley to help release boodies and other rare marsupials back into the wild. It was a momentous experience. We were there to see something historic.

I remember walking out on Faure into the low mulga just on dark, as stars took over the sky. From a carry cage tagged and supported like a case of impossibly rare jewels came a tiny creature snuggled within a hessian bag. I held it a minute or two while its heartbeat capered against my chest; it wouldn't have weighed a kilo. I was struck by the fineness of its limbs and I wanted to linger awhile, but there were protocols to observe so I knelt in the red dirt between thorny bushes, lay the bag down gently and peeled it open so that the creature might emerge unassisted, and when it did I got my first glimpse of a boodie. When it stood erect on its hind feet it twitched a moment as if to gauge the weight and fit of its radio-tracking collar, glanced about with huge, dark eyes and bolted, zigzagging out into the gloom of the bush. Watching it go free I found it difficult to maintain a dispassionate decorum. One after the other, boodies and then several rare hare-wallabies shot out into the wild while I pumped my fist silently like a mad barracker on his last warning.

Despite their vulnerability to native owls and raptors, the original seventeen boodies released on Faure Island have grown to a wild population of more than a hundred. Mt Gibson's old warrens are hundreds of kilometres south-east of Faure, and there are logistical problems to be solved before the first translocations can be undertaken, but at least with the population thriving on the island, where the mainland is in plain view, the boodie is within striking distance of home.

On this 2008 visit I'm struck by how much better the country looks since it was destocked. There's more vegetation, so much less broken ground, and after a little rain the colours are vivid. Driving slowly down the valley through the shadow matrix of the woodland, I startle a euro, and then a red kangaroo as tall and insouciant as a footballer. Each pauses a moment to sniff the air before launching itself effortlessly out of sight. The euro has a distinctive upright posture, even on the move. Shaggy and auburn, it tucks its elbows in and hitches its shoulders back as if, conscious of its own diminutive stockiness, it's trying to seem as imposing as its big red cousin. Small macropod syndrome.

Here and there are remnant sandalwoods and clumps of gimlet but the dominant tree of the woodland is the silvery, lithe salmon gum, whose trunk has the luscious sheen of oiled flesh. This tree seems perennially youthful, especially in the presence of York gums, which are heftier and only half barked, as if suffering male pattern baldness. The asymmetrical Yorkie is mildly shambolic, scrofulous and hulking, but its gnarls and wens offer cover and roosts for birds, tiny mammals and reptiles. All about on the red dirt are fallen trees, flat on their faces with their guts spilled open by termites that are gradually reducing them to the very soil they grew in. They've become horizontal habitat. During the original

AWC survey, palaeoecologist Alexander Baynes identified, in a single hollow salmon gum, 283 jaws of half a dozen native mammal species, mostly dunnarts, many of which were recovered from owl pellets. His work at this and other sites has helped create an invaluable picture of the creatures present at Mt Gibson before the arrival of feral pests. The list he produced is a rollcall of troubled species that includes not just the boodie and the woylie, but the elusive wambenger, the chuditch, the short-beaked echidna, and several species of dunnarts, bandicoots, bats, wallabies and mice.

Animals with names like these would be at home in a satire by Jonathan Swift, so it should be no surprise to discover that the dean's co-ordinates put Gulliver hereabouts. At the time Swift was writing there was indeed an austral island teeming with creatures more strange and marvellous than even he could imagine, but so quickly have they disappeared from view or from existence altogether that they can sometimes seem a product of mere fancy. The sad fact is that the citizen on the street in Sydney will have as little idea about what a dunnart is as his counterpart in London or Chicago. For the record, it is a carnivorous mouse-sized marsupial with huge ears. There are about twenty species of them.

Eventually the valley becomes a rutted old delta and eucalypts give way to jam and other kinds of acacia. Conscious that it would mean an all-night walk back to the homestead should I stake two tyres or get myself bogged beyond recovery, I take the sketchy track slowly.

Finally, with the sun gone beyond the western ridges, I come out upon the great and terrible expanse of Lake Moore, at whose dry shore I'll make camp for the night. I've driven all day away from the coast in order to roll my swag out on the edge of a ghostly body of water. There are better campsites back in the salmon gums or up on the quartz ridges but the eerie blankness of the saltpan fascinates me. I've never slept here before. I want to be present at dusk and dawn to see what comes in from the shimmering distance.

Just on dusk, I walk a little way up the scree slope behind me to a low ridge where a quandong – such a shapely, mild-looking tree for a landscape as austere as this – lays down its decaying shade on the samphire edges of the saltpan. A close relative of the sandalwood, the quandong produces a red stone fruit keenly sought by emus, who are responsible for spreading its seeds in their scat. Quandong fruit was a favourite bush food of Aborigines and in recent years has enjoyed a minor vogue as a preserve. Beside the pale little tree I stare across the dimming lake. In the far distance the last of the sun hits a solitary dead eucalypt. The skeleton tree flares like a beacon for a few seconds and fades to nothing. From the edge of the breakaway below me, another euro bounds out into the open and sets off south along the shore.

Back at the vehicle, I tip my swag onto the stony ground and cook a meal on the little propane stove. In the gathering dark bats flit overhead. A creepy, egg-like moon squeezes up out of the interior. The stiff easterly breeze begins to blast across the gritty surface of the lake and somewhere behind me a tree creaks. I climb into my swag to get out of the wind – I can see just as well from there.

At midnight I wake, surprised to have slept for almost four hours, startled by the passage of some emus. Later other creatures will move by unseen, thudding south. I snuggle back down but sleep eludes me. The moon overhead is almost oppressive and I hadn't anticipated how intimidating the luminous expanse of the lake would be. The broad wash of the Milky Way begins to look like a reflection of the saltpan below and after a few hours I have the discomforting sense of being pressed between two fierce fields of light.

I twist down into my canvas cocoon and cannot help but think of the three small girls who trekked alone through this country back in 1931. Theirs is a legendary journey, recorded by Doris Pilkington and made famous by Phillip Noyce's film *Rabbit-Proof Fence*. Molly Craig, Gracie Fields and Daisy Kadibill spent nights hiding in hollow logs and walked all day for nine weeks at the mercy of forces crueller and more implacable than landscape. They were up against the blind and pitiless logic of institutionalized racism. And here I am, a big pink grown-up with a LandCruiser, beginning to feel – well, a little uneasy in the moonlight.

Just before dawn cockatoos begin to shriek in the trees on the ridge, and as light comes up I roll out of my swag to make coffee while spinifex pigeons clatter past.

As I set off along the shore the first pinprick of sun is at the horizon. I veer out from the rocky breakaways that separate lake and land to walk amid the hundreds of animal tracks impressed into the soft crust of the saltpan. Lying north to south, Lake Moore is well over 100 kilometres long. Here, at one of its narrower points, it's still several kilometres wide. It's bigger than a city, yet except for me the only thing that seems to be moving on it this morning is the easterly.

I walk south until a dark mass appears in the distance. A newcomer could be forgiven for mistaking this smudge for a group of people, or a mob of kangaroos. It takes quite a few more minutes for the gathering to reveal itself as a long, winding alignment of upright stones. The stones are green-black hornblende schist from the breakaways back onshore. They vary in height from about 15 to 60 centimetres and have been embedded in the saltpan in a distinctly serpentine pattern that tightens at its western end into concentric coils, like a fish trap. Yet there seems never to have been any fish in hypersaline Lake Moore.

When American archaeologists visited this site in 1966, they measured the startling stone configuration at more than 80 metres in length, and counted 437 upright slabs and ninety-one that had fallen over where they stood. They noted the remains of a footpad across the lakebed, a track that still leads directly to this site. The visitors were in no doubt that this was an Aboriginal ceremonial place, and in the spirit of the era they set off in search of 'informants' who might explain it to them. Forty-two years on, it's impossible to know how good their information was, for even back then traditional folkways had long been catastrophically ruptured by pastoralism and government policies of dispersal and abduction. By the time the Americans arrived local people were a sad diaspora, living hundreds of kilometres apart in settlements with meagre traditional association or none at all. This site is difficult to get to, and very little has been written about it since 1966, but it's generally agreed that it was an important meeting point for Noongar people from the south, Wongai from the desert and Yamatji from the coast. On the opposite shore there is an ancient dance-ground, a women's place related to this one, part of a series linked to ceremony, dreaming and trade.

Although the site on the lake is protected under federal legislation, its custodian is a frail old man who lives nearly 200 kilometres away, and upon his passing there is small prospect of the place having a new guardian with the full authority of traditional law.

There are human sites in this country that thrum with power, places whose ancient presences intimidate and confront, but this is not one of them. This feels like a monument to lost songs, languages, connections and clans, and a place without its people is bereft. Across Australia, many of the 250-plus Aboriginal languages have disappeared since the colonial era, and too many folkways have fallen away in our own time. The coercive paternalism of earlier eras has been replaced by a paralyzing and infantilizing regime of cradle-to-grave welfare. And to be blunt, the journey from cradle to grave is scandalously brief – it is the measure of our nation's great shame, for despite significant legal and political advances, there are likely now more Aboriginal Australians in ill health, without education or employment than in the years of my childhood, more adults without agency in either tradition or modernity, more young people illiterate in every sense. In some Aboriginal communities the funeral has become the dominant form of social gathering.

On previous visits to this ancient site I have walked away consumed by sadness and anger. But my conviction that it was a lost place, another bit of silent country, was presumptuous. In recent years Aboriginal people have been coming to the lake and its environs more frequently, either seeing these sites for the first time or revisiting them in an effort to revive the old and educate the young. Separated by great distances, some Aboriginal people are looking to the internet as a tool for the encryption and propagation of secret and sacred lore, and although cultural connections are sometimes as sketchy as the register of extant species of marsupials hereabouts, the will for recovery and restoration gives some cause for optimism. When the surrounding country bore all the disheartening marks of degradation, it was harder to sense much human promise in this place. The old war on nature, for too long our prevailing mindset, seemed unassailable. It was evident in every bullet-riddled sign, every bleached paddock, every redneck bumper sticker and depressing roadhouse conversation. But this year, in a landscape speckled with new growth, hope for the cultural and the environmental future of the region is just that little bit easier to cling to.

Something has definitely shifted. There is a new attitude to country, a sense of responsibility and respect evident in the language and actions of land users and custodians. The neighbouring sheep station, White Wells, was recently destocked and is now Charles Darwin Reserve, under the management of Bush Heritage Australia, thanks to a bequest from Darwin's great-great-grandson Chris. On the northern boundary of Mt Gibson, within sight of where I stand, Ninghan Station has become an Indigenous Protected Area. Its stewards, the Bell family, are of Badimia descent. The Badimia are the Yamatji clan with closest traditional links to Lake Moore, and the Bells have responsibility for conserving indigenous sites and restoring natural heritage on their lease. Alongside the AWC sanctuary at Mt Gibson, these properties provide vegetation reserves and a crucial wildlife corridor in a region that has been flogged for years.

These projects are all private concerns, the labour of mere citizens. The native flora and fauna under their protection belong to the state, but the operations are leaner and nimbler, and can be more immediately responsive than most government agencies, which are politicized and bureaucratically inert. Faithful public servants working to protect the environment have to endure vacillations of policy, infuriating budgetary constraints, and the sick reality that every other arm of government is hostile to their efforts. The advent of this new movement will hardly make the work of government agencies redundant. Nor does the welcome emergence of philanthropy in this part of the world mean that strident advocacy has become unnecessary – far from it, for most significant gains in conservation must still be won in the brutal, sapping rhetorical arenas of the courts, the parliament and the media. But the arrival of a quiet and respectable third way is a critical part of the cultural change needed in Australia if we are to restore our scorched earth.

Up on the ridge, above the barely perceptible tracks of the ancients, I look out on the bewildering expanse of the lakebed that here and there manufactures the illusion of water as the day's heat gathers. It's hard in all this dazzling light to separate wishful thinking from something more substantial. The far shore, like the past itself, looks foreign indeed, swimming off behind countless interleaving blurs and mirages, but around me in the trees and schist and termite mounds, in the buzzing air and crackling leaf litter, the recovering world feels close and familiar, animated; or as the great Ngarinyin lawman David Mowaljarlai would have it, you see 'everything standing up alive'. You can sense the country regaining strength, fighting back, and on a fresh morning like this you really can imagine boodies bunkering down in their old warrens, forward scouts dug in ahead of a wider repatriation.

* In the years since this visit, Mt Gibson has become the largest cat-free area on mainland Australia. In September 2015 radio-collared woylies were reintroduced after an absence of fifty years. A number of other marsupials, like stick-nest rats, have already been repatriated and numbats, bilbies and banded hare-wallabies are slated to follow. Perhaps I'll live to see the boodie's return after all.

    Martin Copley died on 30 July 2014.

Betsy

My dad's father was the only one of my four grandparents who ever drove a motor vehicle. Les Winton was a pastry chef and shopkeeper and his chief mode of transport was the '35 flatbed Chev he used for deliveries. But he was also a muso and pater-familias and for his off-work activities he favoured the Harley. The ancient bike had a sidecar the size of a zeppelin's gondola and could accommodate his band and instruments or his family and camping gear, including firearms and tackle. As a kid I loved to hear stories of him riding home from a gig at the Blue Room while his ventriloquist dummy rode shotgun, gums flapping in the wind, beside him. For a few years after the war he sported a Depression-era Rugby tourer whose side curtains were X-rays salvaged from the repat hospital around the corner – a vehicle worthy of his vaudevillian spirit.

So I never understood why he purchased the dour little sedan he called Betsy, for it was an inexplicable departure. It was as if he'd suddenly surrendered to convention. Perhaps this was the point at which he realized it was time to put away the nose flute and give up his shadow life as an entertainer, because a conveyance more dowdy than the 1954 Hillman Minx could hardly be imagined. By the time I knew Pop most of his japes and jalopies were the stuff of myth. The only thing ever I saw him drive was Betsy. Heavy of haunch and whiffy at close quarters, that car was an aesthetic travesty and an offence to youth, but she was a family fixture, like an embarrassing relative who lingered dismally and could never be quietly seen off.

The Hillman was a dumpy colonial sedan of unmistakably English provenance, a testament to modesty and low expectations. Its duco was cardigan grey. Introducing a later model in 1955, the manufacturer crowed about the two-tone paint job called 'the gay look', but Pop seems to have spurned this zany innovation and resigned himself to the sobriety of the model at hand. On a good day the interior smelt like an abandoned cinema. The bodywork was bulbous and cumbersome. Under the hood, like a cowering cockroach, lay a tiny 1300 cc engine. At the other end a lofty back seat afforded passengers an excellent view of the driver's balding pate, a glimpse of the gunmetal bonnet and little else. To port and starboard there were toy-like signal arms with which to semaphore turning intentions. These last accessories should have been charming. Now, of course, I smile at the memory, but back then they were badges of family shame.

I always dreaded being seen in the Minx. Slotted into her low asbestos shelter behind the chookhouse, Betsy was beautifully camouflaged – grey on grey, quite hard to see, which was just how

I liked her – but on the streets of Perth she felt all too visible. And Pop's antic driving didn't help. On the road, as in religion, he was a trenchant nonconformist, and being his passenger certainly kept you protestant and prayerful. Was I the only kid to wince in recognition when *Mr. Magoo* came on the telly?

Old people were bores and obstacles. I didn't see the point of them, and so I prided myself on my forbearance. Some dull Sunday afternoons, if I were feeling righteously indulgent, I could work up a spasm of interest in oldish things. Behind Nan and Pop's shop, for example, there were many ancient marvels: prehistoric tools and weapons, prostheses, musical instruments. You could encounter these in private. You weren't required to sport them in public, so they couldn't trap you and define you. Which is not to say that every old car was a threat to one's reputation, but in matters of carriage a fellow needed to be discerning and I knew style when I saw it. My cousins from Margaret River had a '38 Ford Coupe called Henry that exuded gangster swank even as it squeaked and belched along a dirt road. Uncle Bill in bogan Carlisle had a '59 Chev Bel Air the size of an aircraft carrier, surely the most glamorous vehicle to ever grace the bitumen – not even the Batmobile could shade it. I'd learnt a few things about cars by then, many of them through a gap in the fence at home. The sociopath next door had a grease pit in his garage and a street rod that he and his mates liked to work on day and night. That jalopy was chopped, pinched, ported and polished. Some evenings it sounded like Satan clearing his throat. Even though my parents were unimpressed I thought his hot rod was deadly. It later transpired that he was too, but that's another story.

The point is, I understood old cars were not to be dismissed out of hand. Driven the right way, some could be cool. Within a few years, it'd be nothing to see a beaded hippie at the wheel of a '55 Wolseley or a punk moll lurching from a '59 Anglia. But I knew

Pop's Hillman would never be cool. To this day no beardy hipster will go there, for even irony has frontiers. The tragically misnamed Minx would never outlive her homeliness. I didn't just hate riding in her, I was offended by her very existence.

You'd be drawing a long bow in trying to give Betsy a pass on the grounds of eccentricity. I was conversant with oddness – after all I was a Winton. My nan had a certain local reputation. She lived in a tent in the backyard while Pop shared the bedroom with the kids and the in-laws. She tied 20 yards of twine to Pop's big toe so she could be alerted to developments indoors. All he had to do was yank on the string and his crash cymbal would shimmy cacophonously along the path. I guess you can't run a family and a business without a communications system. Every Sunday as we left their place after the ritual visit, Nan stood in the street and waved us off with a long and jaunty waggle of her right leg. Always and without fail – it was her signature move. Knee stockings and all. The neighbours were inured to it. To my mind such behaviour was unusual, but not actually disgraceful. Owning a car like Betsy, though – that was crossing the line. It put a dent in the family's honour.

The Minx was no kitten when Pop bought her but she managed to outlast him. Once he was in his seventies even a carriage as sedate as Betsy was too much car for him to manage. For a while she brooded undriven in her asbestos hutch, and not long afterwards Nan and Pop were forced to give up the shop and 'go into care'. That was a sad day. But there was worse news to come. Nan and Pop thought Betsy should move in with us.

Such were the giddy means by which we became a two-car family. Dad drove the Minx to work and left the Falcon at home with Mum. When we moved to Albany and I began high school, he insisted on driving me, even though I could see the grounds from the front verandah. He thought a lift in the mornings might steady my nerves in the first few weeks. Which was kind, I know, but the gesture was wasted on me. I spent those brief trips finding new ways to slide so low in the passenger seat as to become invisible. I didn't know a soul in town but I was still making sure no one would recognize me. As the old man hoisted the natty indicator-arm and set sail for school at a pace that was plausibly nautical, I'd press my lower back against the seat springs and take a passionate interest in the inner seams of my bag. As if the choice of ride weren't shame enough, Dad always expected a kiss goodbye at the school gate. This was delivered in-car at great speed and very low altitude.

Eventually I broke free of the morning delivery. I did everything in my power to distance myself from the Minx. When I finally made friends and brought them home I denied all connection to the portly conveyance in the drive. Months later, when my mates took to squatting in the front yard to howl at their distorted reflections in Betsy's double-D hubcaps, I was still huffing and bluffing, but no one bought my excuses. That car was a perpetual laugh at my expense. I feared it would do me permanent damage.

Unlike most country boys, I wasn't anxious to get my driver's licence. For one thing, I had ghastly forebodings about having to learn in Betsy. While other kids kangaroo-hopped their mums' Datsuns and dads' farm utes up the main street, I'd be trundling along in something that looked like a slow-combustion stove. I was in no hurry to experience that.

I wasn't alone in my antipathy to Betsy. It was a rare patch of common ground between my younger siblings and me; we mounted a years-long campaign to convince Dad to put her out to pasture. I suggested we take her to a friend's farm and give her a real Sam Peckinpah send-off: expend a couple of boxes of shotgun shells, maybe a Molotov cocktail if it wasn't fire season. But Dad said Betsy was no trouble. In all these years he hadn't had to spend a cent on her. No, it'd be a waste to let the Minx go. At the mere mention of her name a dreamy smile came to his face. I don't think he had any special affection for the old bus – he'd come to enjoy the discomfort she produced in us, the goad to our youthful vanity. And it was true that car kicked on: you just turned the key, pressed the old-timey starter button and she sputtered to life.

My last vivid memory of Betsy is of the day we moved back to the city after three years of exile. Before we left town we had a rare nosh-up at a Chinese joint. Then we hit the road, Mum and my sister and baby brother in the Falcon, my other brother and I hostages as much as passengers in the dreaded Minx. The day was brutally hot. It was a five-hour trip in a decent car, but in Betsy you could add another hour. The harvested paddocks either side of the highway were brown. We were shirtless. Dad wore his signature singlet, a saggy old thing whose days of whiteness were but a memory. The wind through the open windows was dry and fleecy and as the seats heated up beneath us they released the stench of church halls, courthouses, railway waiting-rooms: odours of weariness, boredom and advanced age.

From boyhood I had known my father to be a man of kindly nature but irritable bowel. And for him, Chinese was not ideal road fodder. So it was no surprise when, about three hours into the journey, he pulled over, snatched a handful of tissues from the glove box and vaulted across a farm fence for the shelter of some piled logs. Accustomed to this sort of behaviour, my brother and I sat in our customary bovine silence as the engine ticked and the pong of old people rose from the upholstery. Eventually our father returned at a jog, trailing a comet-tail of flies, tucking the singlet back into his shorts as he came. He got in, turned the key, pressed the endlessly embarrassing starter button and off we went, at 36 miles per hour. Which may have been quite a clip in the days of Menzies, but not so impressive to a teenager in 1975. It certainly wasn't enough to blow the flies clear of the cabin.

A few metres down the road I caught a whiff of something

vile. Worse than old people, this was the smell of death. It seemed
that four hundred flies were onto something. I tried to bring this
to Dad's attention but, like his gaze, his mind was fixed firmly on
the road. The stink got worse. My brother began to whinge, but
the old man wasn't having any of it. Once he was on the bitumen
he was hard to stop. He drove on with the baking wind in his face,
squinting through the blowflies, noticing nothing, conceding less,
until my brother began to gag. Even then Dad smelt nothing, but
the prospect of a puker had him standing on the brakes. He reefed
Betsy to the road's edge, and given the stiffness of the suspension
and the trolley-like steering, it was a manoeuvre as jerky and sped-
up as a scene from an Ealing comedy.

The moment Dad got out the offending stench went with him.
Which seemed significant. A rapid examination of his person –
conducted, of course, in full view of the rural motoring public –
established the unpalatable facts, the finer details of which needn't be
gone into here. Suffice it to say that in the event of an unscheduled
roadside comfort stop, a long and saggy singlet is not helpful at-
tire. Dad had brought a stowaway aboard. It will surprise nobody
to learn that with a shortage of water and no more tissues available
the remainder of the trip was a test of character for all.

To this day my father refuses to attribute the disappearance of
the 1954 Hillman Minx to this little misadventure. But I believe that
after it he saw Betsy in a different light. The rest of us had always
associated that car with foulness, ridicule and lingering shame, and
it was as if the scales had finally fallen from his eyes – or perhaps his
nose. While he denies this, the vagueness with which he speaks of
Betsy's retirement is telling. Neither he nor any other member of
our family can fix a date to her demise or the circumstances under
which she left our employ. She certainly didn't get the paddock
shoot-up I'd dreamt of. For all her sturdiness, her grey, implacable utility, she faded away without valediction. Her replacement,

a pinky-brown '59 Austin Lancer, was no filly either but at least, as everyone agreed, she had some poke. Betsy had been supplanted by a frisky cousin, a dame with colour left in her cheeks, and daggy as she seemed, the Austin was a bit of a giggle. Old, yes, but not socially catastrophic.

Still and all, even if in her dullness Betsy epitomized the Menzian era whence she sprang, she saw out the Malayan Emergency, the Vietnam War, the space race and the Whitlam revolution. In our time of instant obsolescence, her endurance is sobering, and as I age I wonder if perhaps I was a little hasty to spurn her. We're such merciless judges in our youth. And she'd be a vintage ride now. But I have to admit that if I came upon her tomorrow, abandoned in a cow paddock, I'd set fire to her in a heartbeat. Provided, of course, it wasn't fire season.

Twice on Sundays

Where Mercy, Love, & Pity dwell
There God is dwelling too.
WILLIAM BLAKE

And like the sea, God was silent.
SHUSAKU ENDO

I

When I was a kid Sunday evenings were melancholy. With the precious weekend spent and school looming, it was as if a sea mist had rolled in. An otherwise boisterous household grew reticent. Sunday tea was always the most desultory meal of our week. With soup or mince on toast balanced in our laps, we ate in languid silence in front of the black-and-white TV. For all their homely gags and canned laughter, shows like *Green Acres* and *Petticoat Junction* barely raised a chuckle from us. It wasn't that we were too sophisticated to laugh at this fare, or such good Calvinists that laughter had gone the way of beer and cards, it was just that the epic effort of Sunday had begun to take its toll. We weren't sad or sullen, we were conserving energy, because by six p.m. we were all out on our feet.

Tea was little more than a ringside squirt and a flick of the trainer's towel because, knackered though we were, Sunday had plenty of fight left in it; there were more rounds to contend with. There'd be no Sunday Night Movie for us. We had the evening gospel service to stagger through yet – always a strenuous affair. Then there was Fellowship Tea, ostensibly a social occasion but in truth another opportunity to 'witness' to newcomers and bring them to the brink of salvation. Which was nobody's idea of a casual warm-down. So we were a long way short of putting Sunday to the canvas. Any kid who senses the weekend slipping through his fingers knows this creeping sense of loss. Ours was complicated by knowing so much more was still required of us, for in order to finish the job, fight the fight and run the race, you had to give your all. And we'd have blown an O-ring for Jesus.

By the sixties, churchgoing was no longer a mainstream practice in Australia. If you were more than a weddings-and-Christmas family, it was something you were expected to do discreetly, without bothering anybody, which was difficult if you were evangelical fundamentalists because the cosmic meter was running and we were geared to spreading the Good News while there was still time. So, as a twice-on-Sundays outfit, we definitely stood out. We were unaccountably and unreasonably churchy, and given that some of us did Sunday school and pastoral visitation on the Sabbath as well as church, the twice-on-Sundays label probably sold us short. We were odd bods, and knew it. Still, our neighbours, who were typically squeamish about God-botherers, were mostly quite tolerant. They had us pegged as weirdos, but the persecution we'd been trained to expect never seemed to materialize.

Of a Sunday morning we were up early – a locally distinguishing feature in itself. At eight-thirty, dressed in our best, we rounded up kids from the neighbourhood, packed them two by two into the back of the station wagon, and Dad drove them uphill to the local church. It wasn't as if any of them were that excited to be going, but their hungover parents were grateful to have them out of the house for an hour, and the knowledge that my old man was a cop seemed to engender a rare compliance amongst these luckless junior heathens. From the church you couldn't quite see the ocean but you could definitely smell it. Foregoing a morning at the beach was never a small sacrifice in a surf-mad suburb like Scarborough but in the summer, when the swell was up and the seductive briny air danced its seven veils through the foyer, there were mutinous mutterings in the pews.

Sunday school began with communal singing. Which was a little like the warm-up we did at football training – hard laps done from a dead start. We arrived as a sleepy, resentful rabble and shambled into song without pleasure or discernible melody, but after a couple of numbers we were rolling; we had a sweat up, and we sounded like contenders. For some reason the species of rollicking tune we sang was called a chorus rather than a hymn. A hymn was a more complex affair and generally reserved for the church service proper. Of course tunes such as 'Wide, Wide as the Ocean' and 'Give Me Oil in My Lamp' were shockingly uncool. They belonged to an era as distant as the penny-farthing and the horsedrawn bathing machine, but somehow they grew on us, and momentarily liberated from our Anglo-antipodean reserve, we bellowed them until our faces glowed. If this wasn't always a spiritual experience it was at least genuinely aerobic. The resulting endorphins helped get us through the bout of self-criticism and textual analysis that lay in store as we turned to our bibles.

Scripture stories were my imaginative bread and butter. The best, of course, were from the Old Testament, though for all their colour and action they were morally incomprehensible. The violence of these ancient fables was darkly appealing, but beyond imagining myself as the plucky goatherd David with his giant-killing slingshot, there was rarely much in them for a boy to aspire to. I knew the first, very Jewish, bit of the Bible was sacred, but it hardly fanned the embers of idealism I felt smouldering within me before the onset of puberty. Only the Jesus stuff would do, because the Nazarene was the hero of all boyhood heroes. He wasn't just good and brave and kind – he was mysterious, confounding, anarchic. I badly wanted to emulate him, but that was a rough road. Turning the other cheek, for instance – this was harder than killing giants. Harder, perhaps, because there were no legendary qualities involved. Nonviolence required ordinary human capacities, powers you already had but would rather not use. The parting of seas and chariots of fire seemed to happen in an impersonal and permanently exotic realm that could never make claims on you. But Jesus was another matter. He didn't want the impossible – that was what was so awkward and yet so inspiring about him.

Once we'd gotten through our communal exegesis and a bit of prompted pondering, there were prayers of abject supplication offered on our behalf, most of which I tuned out of or couldn't follow. Finally the hour was rounded off with another rolling mawl of choruses that salved the troubled spirit, like a musical rub-down.

With its debt to revivalist enthusiasm, our hardy Wesleyan singing generated a rare noise. You could have lit the city grid with it. The songs we bellowed were full of longing, triumph and giddy devotion, but their chief consolations were sensual. At eight or ten years old it's tough having to crunch ethical and cosmic dilemmas as we did every Sunday morning. For example, if you had an evil thought, did that mean you'd already done something wrong? Was Jonah a good guy or a bad guy? Why did crazy-drunk Noah curse Ham for seeing him naked when it was obviously his own fault in the first place? And how come he could drink beer when our dads were supposed to be better than that? And who calls a kid Ham anyway? Some mornings my brain ached and my spirit fizzed with the strain. So it was a joy to close ranks in mutual shortcoming and ride the simpler wave of feeling in the hall. We were all hopeless failures and numbskulls, but when we sang hard enough we saw spots, our limbs tingled, and we managed to feel huggable and beloved. We were a team. Even if we were rubbish players, Jesus would give us a gallop around the paddock and we'd have a crack for Him.

And so, at the end of Sunday school, we were let out into the sunshine panting. By this stage there was just enough time for Dad to return the neighbours' kids to their breakfasting post-coital parents, collect a few pensioners who were without transport, and get back in time for the eleven-o'clock. Left to my own devices I usually spent this period courting a girl I fancied. My method involved a lot of stone throwing. It was quite successful; we wound up married.

Just on eleven a.m., moments before Mum had to come scouting for me, I drifted in with all the other kids and slid up beside my parents and siblings as the electric organ warbled the intro for the opening hymn, whereupon we stood as one to sing:

> *Praise God, from Whom all blessings flow*
> *Praise Him, all creatures here below*
> *Praise Him above, ye heavenly host*
> *Praise Father, Son and Holy Ghost.*

Written by Thomas Ken in 1674, this simple doxology had a strange and calming effect on me and I wasn't alone in feeling its gentle force. Sunday by Sunday, the moment we began to sing it, a pacific mood descended on the hall. There were other hymns to follow but this one was special; it was a steadier. There was a lot to get through in a morning service – Scripture readings, prayers of intercession, sundry announcements, communion, the occasional baptism or musical interlude, and of course hymns aplenty. We rocked on our heels and swayed in rows, rubbing shoulders, friends and strangers alike, gorging on song like sailors victualling before a long and uncertain voyage, because the entire service thus far was but a preamble to the main event – the sermon.

Our tradition measured itself by the quality of its preaching. The 'message', as we called it, was not a homily. Nor was it a cool collation of encouraging thoughts. And it certainly wasn't a slice of scholarly insight wrapped in a homely reflection. It was a verbal reaming, a coach's spray, a physical and mental ordeal you needed to endure and survive for your own good. Once the minister got to his feet and took the pulpit in both hands like a man at the wheel of a windjammer, we were all pilgrims and wayfarers in his hands. We sailed with him in search of enlightenment, heavenly treasure, and, in cases of epic length, deliverance by any means. Over the years I suppose I experienced every conceivable form of oratory. Some preachers whispered and cajoled. Others walked the boards, clawing the air. Many sweated and crooned, some wept. It was all the theatre I knew and it was quite a show.

Some of these talks were inspirational. They could be haunting, even lyrical. They featured tales of degradation and courage, moments of searing illumination, and the best were masterful feats of Dickensian digression packed with outrageous sentimentality. They softened you up, stalked you around corners, and ended up as muggings of the first order. They scrambled your wits, reduced you to rubble, and left you to assemble yourself again as best you could in the aftermath. Not every sermon soared and roared; we heard our fair share of duds. Wallowing in the horse latitudes of doctrine, the worst of them were like tax seminars, or PowerPoint presentations about occupational health and safety. During some of these clunkers – on the mechanics of the Trinity, say, or the fun parts of predestination – time became as elastic as the limpets of gum I liked to prise from beneath the pew and revive by means that don't bear repeating here.

After church we dropped everyone home, ate the roast lunch we called dinner and set out for an afternoon of family visitation. While not strictly parish business these visits were nevertheless occasions of intratribal witnessing. Every week there were various cousins and grandparents to be seen and few of these were believers. And if that wasn't hard enough, they all seemed to live at a pioneering distance from one another.

Farthest away were my mother's parents who lived at Belmont, between the airport and the racetrack, where they were unknowns at the former and stalwarts at the latter. That side of the family thought we were a bunch of wowsers, a complete joke. And one Sunday when she'd drunk almost as much as Noah, my dear old Nanna Miff told me as much. Having caught me alone in the kitchen she dished this news up with relish. I was about nine at the time. I'll never know why she picked me out for a bollocking, nor could I have any notion of how we'd trodden on her corns that particular afternoon, but she gave me a pasting. We were Jesus-creepers, fucking idiots, and why in God's name couldn't we have any fun? Sadie Mifflin was generally a stranger to remorse, but later that day, piqued by conscience or softened by subsequent beverages, she went rooting through her giant handbag to fish out a sagging Cherry Ripe, which she offered in silence as a sacrament of peace. And all I can say is that for a staunch puritan I was easily bought.

After all these family visits, it was another hour in the car back across town to wash the stink of fags from our hair before we sat down to soup and mince in front of the telly.

The evening session was the gospel service. This was goofily upbeat and catered to a younger crowd, and in later years featured guitars and drums. Sermons were incandescent, the music relentlessly emotional, and the service always ended with an altar call that could last twenty minutes or more. While 'Just As I Am' trundled on, verse after wheedling verse, like a rag-and-bone cart that wouldn't leave the neighbourhood until someone brought out their reeking junk, we sat tight until a tormented soul cracked and went forward to surrender his or her life to Christ. Whereupon we all cried from joy or relief and then limbered up for cake, witnessing and a bit of flirty fellowship. We rarely got home before nine or ten at night.

When I was a kid the Day of Rest required grit; it was a marathon, a test of character. Looking back I wonder if we only went to school on Monday for a breather. Compared to church, school was easy; the demands it made were relatively inconsequential.

II

Even if the Australian society of my childhood was militantly irreligious, the church was my first and most formative culture. It was in effect the village I was reared in, and in many senses this meant I grew up in a counterculture, although it was the sort in which beads, feathered hats and granny glasses were worn without the sense of performance that arrived a little later with the hippies.

Churchgoing was my introduction to conscious living. Nowhere else was I exposed to the kind of self-examination and reflective discipline that the faith of my childhood required. I'd be surprised if anyone at my boyhood church had read even a page of Tolstoy, but it seems to me now that the question that ate at him so late in his life was the central issue for us, too. *What then must we do?* Preoccupations of this sort may well have bubbled in the suburban life around us, but it's fair to say they were not immediately evident. In retrospect we had more in common with the anarchists and Trots the state was so fearful of, for our loyalties were unfathomable to outsiders. We were reaching for something beyond the ordinary. Any striving impulse at school or in the sports clubs was largely a matter of surfaces, a competition for glory. Being a God-botherer marked you out. Even the word 'glory' meant something different. And strange as it might seem to a Brit or an American for whom churchgoing has always been respectable, religious life was like a childhood inoculation against social conformity.

Thanks to my churchy upbringing I began to learn what a civil life might be; how crucial it is to cultivate disinterest, to free oneself from tribalism. These core Christian teachings are liberating and civilizing but they are rarely thought of as legacies of evangelical fundamentalism. Similarly, the dour nonconformist assembly is not conventionally seen as a crucible of democracy, as it surely was in the nineteenth century, nor as a nurturer of culture in the twentieth, but church life was my introduction to politics, high language, story and music. We were doers. If we stood for anything it was for 'love with its sleeves rolled up'. Our calendar may not have been latticed with high days and liturgical seasons but the year was busy with eisteddfods, concerts, clubs and camps. There was always a study group to join, a working-bee to attend, a sports competition to enter, a song or poem to learn, a picnic to wash up for. And at a time when our suburb was literally being hewn from the bush in front of us, when even the street itself was still a rough work-in-progress, there was in church life a sense of coherence and communal spirit unmatched elsewhere. The nearest library was fifteen minutes away by car. There was no community hall in our suburb, no concerts. The state concerned itself with material improvements, but the intangible chemistry of community was not yet a priority. Citizens toiled and played in a dispensation of relentless pragmatism, a mindset bequeathed to many by settler forebears.

That hardy, incurious and unreflective outlook has been a long time dying, but in the 1960s it was still going strong. Patrick White had been railing against its prickly, philistine defensiveness for decades. In his greatest novels, the nascent mystic and the dowdy pilgrim labour under the weight of its thoughtless certainties. I doubt our scowling laureate would have warmed to the cardigan-wearing seekers I looked up to as a boy. They were poorly educated and their life experiences were narrow, but they were the bearers of more culture and civilization than even he could credit. They were not drawn together by some gnostic destiny, hardly White's shambling 'elect', just plain folk trying to follow the Way, but when I read *The Tree of Man* and *Riders in the Chariot* at nineteen I heard their voices and saw their faces. They had their sights set higher than many of the sleeker people I came to know.

III

I was the child of converts. My parents came to faith in the crusading era of Billy Graham and joined the local Church of Christ. Churches of Christ had their origins in nineteenth-century American revivalism and their first congregations appeared in Australia in the 1840s, not long after the Baptists. The new arrivals were primitivist dissenters with a history of disputation and schism that made Baptists seem laid-back by comparison. One of the sect's founding fathers, Alexander Campbell, described the Bible as 'a book of facts' and while his Australian co-religionists had mellowed somewhat in the century since his day, theirs was still a denomination in which Scripture was the prime and unimpeachable source of revelation, and the reading of it remained doggedly literalistic. This was a theological line in the sand. Verse by verse and line by line, the Bible was the actual Word of God.

So our tradition was a bare-knuckles, no-frills affair. There was in its history a deep suspicion of clerical authority, a visceral reaction to the structural snobbery and 'spiritual dilution' that a uniformed class of religious professionals had brought to more mainstream outfits. We guarded our unmediated access to the Almighty with a vigilance that could seem paranoid. We disdained received forms and sought personal authenticity, which meant that except for The Lord's Prayer all prefabricated invocations and entreaties were rejected. Sunday prayers were raw and improvized and they had about them a jazz element of anxiety and freedom that produced everything from the profound and sublime to the painfully banal. It was not uncommon for the congregation to find itself captive for many minutes to an intercessor's fervid verbal inspiration: like a soloing sax player he or she might follow the cryptic logic of their riffs and runs to their farthest imaginable limits, and like the smoky hepcats of bebop the rest of us were trained to abide and endure with murmurs of appreciation. Even if it was incomprehensible tosh. With a sensibility like ours, the thought of swapping extemporized prayer for its liturgical form would be like giving up Coltrane for Roger Whittaker.

In our church there were no robes, no funny collars, no bells nor smells. All ritual was ritually discouraged. We did entirely without creeds – apparently our little motto 'No creed but Christ' didn't count. The parish was governed by elected lay members, some of whom bore the added authority of eldership, and although the minister might have been the most visible and influential member of the congregation, his tenure was subject to the lay leaders and the collective vote of the membership. Parishes of this tradition were therefore not dependent on diocesan management from elsewhere. They were associated but essentially discrete. It was a form of syndicalism whose anarchistic tendencies were never really acknowledged.

Like many evangelical outfits with dissenting origins, our lot restricted baptism to penitents of responsible age. There would be no tribal baby-sprinkling for us. And by baptism we meant full immersion; nothing else was sufficient. If you weren't entirely submerged it didn't count. Not that we entertained any magical notions about the water; it was just that if it was good enough for Jesus, then it was good enough for us. There was a tank set into the stage for this purpose and that's where I was baptized at age twelve.

Baptism was the only unreservedly sacramental aspect of our worship, although we wouldn't have spoken of it in such terms. Words like 'sacrament' made us anxious. But as rites of passage went, baptism was unrivalled. Not even a wedding was as important.

Sunday worship was conducted according to a rigid order of service from which we rarely deviated. Scripture readings were delivered as if the verses contained not simply a sacred meaning but an inchoate power that bordered on the magical. Communion was celebrated every week with water crackers and grape juice – ours was a strictly teetotal affair. The 'bread' was handed along the pews on wooden plates and the 'wine' distributed in tiny individual shot glasses on purpose-built trays. We spurned the unsavoury common cup. Defiantly backward we may have been in many senses, but we were modern enough to know about germs. We didn't pretend to conjure up any spirit by this ritual, either, as Catholics and High Church Anglicans did – the idea of that was scandalous. This was a 'memorial feast', not a séance.

As befitted our sectarian aversion to ornament and elaboration, the interior of the church building was austere, the sole concession to iconography a wooden cross on the gable wall. Yet for all this bareness and lack of liturgical flim-flam, the services were not solemn. Somehow there was room for good-natured joshing and laughter. Along the pews, women grinned at one another and men winked. Infants said things that brought the house down. Dogs wandered in and babies were passed from lap to lap. Piety was one thing, but few of us could forsake our ingrained working-class ethos with its scorn of bumptious ceremony. And of course, there was all that lusty singing. Nevertheless Sunday with us was only for the hardy.

IV

Ours was a yeoman farmer's religion, the province of humble folk and autodidacts. Its mindset and temper were rooted in a pre-industrial era. At church blokes often wore the only suit they owned. They were manual labourers, factory hands, farmers, tradesmen. Their wives worked in the home and frocked up in floral themes for Sunday worship. These parishioners were frumpy but forthright, hospitable and cheerfully communal in their instincts, and although their theology was extremely conserva-tive their politics didn't necessarily follow. Like their parishioners, most ministers were men of very modest education. Outside of military service few adults in the congregation had ever travelled. Most had left school by fifteen and some had been pulled out at twelve. Education was revered and suspected in equal measure.

The people I grew up with were socially uncertain but they were not cowed by the contempt of unbelievers. They were hungry to improve themselves and to be of service to something larger.

Jeanette Winterson was an alumnus of a sect far more severe and lurid than ours. But she can still credit the 'camaraderie, the simple happiness, the kindness, the sharing, the pleasure of some-thing to do every night in a town where there was nothing to do' against the miseries and cruelties she later fictionalized in her most acclaimed novel, *Oranges Are Not the Only Fruit*. In her memoir *Why be Happy When You Could be Normal?* she writes: 'I saw a lot of working-class men and women – myself included – living a deeper, more thoughtful life than would have been possible without the Church. These were not educated people; Bible study worked their brains. They met after work in noisy discussion. The sense of belonging to something big, something important, lent unity and meaning . . .'

Winterson's rough-handed Pentecostalists could just as easily have been card-carrying communists or members of a repertory theatre group. Had they been held together by some broad purpose other than spreading the Gospel they would still have been weirdos to their neighbours: they sought to liberate themselves and transform society. Such dreams take courage and solidarity, personal sacrifice and no small measure of pig-headedness. Like Winterson, I saw the fruit of all that striving and self-improvement at the midweek Bible study. Church members were a bookish lot. They certainly knew their way around the Scriptures. Their mnemonic capacities were often breathtaking. It was common to see heavy concordances and commentaries in people's homes. In an era when workingmen's institutes had long since faded away, churches like ours provided a rare opportunity for civil debate and intellectual enlargement.

It was in church that I learnt how perilously faith depends upon story, for without narrative there is only theological assertion, which is, in effect, inert cargo. Story is the beast of burden, the bearer of imaginative energy. My favourite stories were endlessly repeated and learnt by heart. Behind them all – from Jacob pulling a hamstring in his struggle with the angel to Elijah fed by ravens, or the Nazarene overcome by crowds at the lakeside – lay two great mysteries: the unfathomable presence of the divine, and the perennial enigma of human behaviour.

And it was church that taught me the beauty and power of language. Recited and declaimed from the pulpit week after week and year upon year, these stories and their cadences, in the King James and Revised Standard versions, were deeply imprinted. Until I was sixteen and had Shakespeare rudely thrust upon me, I knew no other high language to rival it. *Hamlet* didn't exactly make my spirit glow – it was confusing and yet eerily familiar. I can still remember the hot summer classroom, the droning flies, and the dread of being called upon to read aloud – I just knew I'd balls it up – but as each of us took our turn, halting, sullen, mortified and sceptical, I heard the sound of a thousand Sundays, the voices of balding men in Pelaco shirts quoting Saint Paul, riding incantatory rhythms toward the stifling reaches of noon. *What a piece of work is a man, how noble in reason, how infinite in faculties . . .* At sixteen I was hard-pressed to keep up with what the Bard was actually on about but I recognized his sound from the get-go.

Once I was old enough to attend the Bible study groups hosted in members' homes, I began to see how potent words really are, how thrillingly they could unite people but how quickly they divided us. I was in the livingroom of a senior parishioner one evening when the gathering stumbled over the word *wine*. When Christ produced wine at the wedding at Cana, were those jars really full of an alcoholic beverage or did his miraculous provision only extend to unfermented grape juice? A lot hung on that single word, as it did later upon *slave*, *demon* and *men*. That was before we even got to the prickly business of *fornication* or what it meant for a man to *lie with mankind*. For some of us, though we didn't know it yet, there were family traumas lying buried like landmines in those words. Matters of social organization, justice, mental health and sexuality could depend on the interpretation of a single biblical term. Expressing faith is not unlike expressing love, for both involve fraught searches for exactly the right phrase when it often seems there are none good, true or safe enough to do the job, and a wrong word at the wrong moment can be catastrophic.

Many of those evenings of soulful study and pedantic debate were tedious. Some scarred me for life. But they weren't wasted. Over time, by a process I don't understand even now, the occult power of metaphor revealed itself. I was still years away from thinking of the Bible as a library, a storehouse of experience and longing rather than a discrete document that was the product of some sort of divine dictation; however, I grew increasingly enthralled by the paradoxes of its imagery. There was truth there. Somehow Christ was our *rock*, but he was also *water*. And by his account we doughty believers were *salt*. Even Paul, the apostle who spun so much mystery into dry doctrine, could pull me up by reminding me that the whole of creation *groans in travail* like a woman in labour. These constructions weren't just apt, there was something organic and sustaining in them.

Language, I was to discover, is nutrition, manna without which we're bereft and forsaken, consigned like Moses and his restive entourage to wander in a sterile wilderness. As a novelist I seem to have spent every working day of my adult life in a vain search for the right word, the perfect metaphor for the story or sentence at hand, while so often writing about characters for whom words are both elusive and treacherous. I didn't catch the bug at school, I picked it up in church.

What church and school had in common was how damned boring they could be. You were a captive in both. But while kids in class and in the quadrangle blanked you out, and some teachers, recoiling from your adolescent mulishness, gave up and deleted you from their consciousness, at church whatever I did or said I was not made to feel inconsequential. I was never rendered invisible. If anything I was endlessly noticed, sometimes to a wearying degree.

Still, during a service I fidgeted and giggled like any other kid. I drew tits, peace signs and swastikas on the endpapers of hymnals and let off farts that could have justified a rush for the emergency exits. During epic prayers of intercession I liked to keep count of all the Thees and Thines and run little wagers on the tally with my guffawing mates. We developed alternate lyrics for famous hymns: 'My chains fell off, my heart was free/ I rose, went forth, and took a pee.' Brilliant, I know. Poker-faced we belted out our feats of lyrical resistance, but as heads began to swivel we were helpless against our own laughter.

Older folks were remarkably patient. It was only after puberty, when I grew surly and sarcastic, that senior parishioners started to lose patience, and whenever someone pulled me aside to straighten me out the experience was always worse than a roasting from a schoolteacher. Somehow it mattered more that you'd disappointed a fellow member, especially an elder. And unlike teachers, who came and went, an elder was in your life for decades, sometimes forever; he was in your home some nights during the week, you went camping with him and learnt your first guitar chords off him. Besides, you often fancied his daughter.

There were certain old people, including those with whom I locked horns occasionally, who took a particular interest in my spiritual progress, my 'walk', as it was known. For some of them this began when I was a small boy and continued long after I reached middle age. It was rare to have a schoolteacher take a similar interest. Some of those old folks knew me better than my grandparents did.

When I was six I approached an older gentleman called George Smith to ask him about the size of my soul. I sidled up to him after church one morning and stood at his side until he registered my presence. He was younger then than I am now but to me he was a man of wise and ancient mien. Maybe it was the specs. I don't remember why, at that age, I required soul dimensions, all I know is that my need was urgent. Mr Smith took off his glasses and gave them a bit of a buff. Eventually he took my hand, closed it and pressed it against my chest. He told me he'd never actually seen a human soul but his best guess was that mine was about the size of my fist. I considered this sceptically; I may only have been six, but I wasn't stupid. Then I thought how sometimes my spirit ached like the aftermath of a sucker punch, burning right there where old George Smith had his hand and mine, like a thump in the chest whose afterglow left the feel and shape of a fist. And so his answer rang true.

In the years since, my satisfaction with it has only deepened. Not because it convinces me in the literal sense it once did, but because there's such humanity and imagination in the image. What moves me most is that he bothered to answer my question at all. In a society where relationships between generations are increasingly rare, here was a grown man who was neither relative nor paid supervisor giving his full attention to a young boy. At his funeral a few years ago I thought about that precious encounter. I wondered how I'd measure up in such a situation. Should ever a questing child come to me with a similar question, how would I deal with it? After all, it's a real googly and I'd have no better explanation than the one George Smith came up with. Perhaps the answer itself isn't paramount. I'd be grateful if I could summon the kind of grace he found in the moment, so as to offer a child half the gravity and good faith he showed me.

V

Being a full-immersion sect was one of our distinguishing tenets, but it wasn't only on the day of baptism we were fully immersed. Parish life was all-encompassing; it took in everything from cosmic wonder to sport and romance. In it I rose to adulthood on a tide of story, and having lived in an era of social atomization I will always be grateful for the communal existence it provided. But like all countercultures, ours was an enclave, and its limitations could not go unfelt forever. There were a lot of decent people in our parish, folks who had, thanks to their faith, striven for their higher selves. Of course there were episodes of mean-spiritedness within the congregation, outbreaks of gossip, clashes of ego, grudges barely suppressed. Mostly, though, I saw care and kindness, and an impulse toward mutuality. The default setting people aimed for was some sort of loving self-control and it resulted in a civility that would be the envy of any community. But in the face of growing social complexity, that discipline seemed to stale and then curdle.

The seventies were an unprecedented challenge for our church. Overnight the lives of parishioners became less predictable and more problematic. In the world beyond the pale an explosion of ideas and new trends had arrived and suddenly it was a struggle to meet the needs of believers, let alone match the concerns of those outside the fold. What did we have to contribute to the nationwide debate over Vietnam? What was our position on gender equality? The new no-fault divorce laws had begun to produce what felt like an epidemic of marital dissolution. And for some reason, nothing could now exercise us so much as the sex lives of others. Our pietist theology sprang from a simpler, more static world. Our thinking was cautious and faithful but hopelessly flatfooted. Confronted with the upheavals of the time it was quickly exposed as insufficient.

Overtaken by an anxious nostalgia, parishioners began to look back to an imagined golden age, or forward to Glory. What they didn't want to look at was what was happening beyond the ghetto. So the communal mindset shrank and hardened. Some reverted to an incipient millenarianism and became obsessed with prophecy and conspiracy. At fourteen, under the careful supervision of youth leaders, I was parsing the chiliastic lunacies of Hal Lindsey's *The Late, Great Planet Earth* and crunching the numbers on the imminent Rapture. It was exciting in its way, reefing through the Scriptures to uncover secret codes as history's clock ticked toward the End of Days. Nixon was in disgrace. Oil shocks and wars had broken out. It felt for a while as if the wheels were coming off our earthly wagon. The church thought it was safe from all this frenzy and hysteria, but it wasn't. If anything it was especially vulnerable.

Where once it had been a beacon of community, engaged in the affairs of the neighbourhood, the parish became insular and its siege mentality grew oppressive. At the age of six my coltish curiosity was honoured and welcomed, but by the time I was sixteen a spirit of inquiry was a threat to moral hygiene. The civility and empathy within the group grew thin. In Bible studies I began to be chided for being obtuse. Apparently I'd become a 'stumbling block' to others. In fairness, this accusation wasn't simply a result of the new mood in the congregation. During my adolescence I'd mislaid my old compliance. Less creditably, I'd lost my manners as well. Now that I was reading widely I was charged with excitement. Compared to thinkers like Bonhoeffer, Barth, Tillich, Hans Küng and Jacques Ellul, the homely devotional guides we still cleaved to were backward and myopic. But I was painfully clumsy in my new enthusiasms, and bewildered by the reactions of my comrades. The sophomoric thought bubbles I let off during group discussions were hardly as objectionable as the farts I'd let loose as a boy in church, yet it was a marvel how quickly I could empty a room by simply brandishing a new idea, a fresh metaphor. As theological propositions these notions were old news but the brethren recoiled from them in fear and disgust, calling them heretical and *worldly*, and by worldly they meant dangerously profane. Concerns were expressed about my spiritual welfare, but when push came to shove it was the health of the group that counted most. Fear of contagion overtook any distress about my personal trajectory.

Frightened by the spirit of the times the church did what it could to quarantine itself against change, but an epidemic of anxiety had broken out. Many younger members of the congregation nursed misgivings but only a few openly rebelled and rejected the faith of their fathers. More lapsed discreetly but continued to pay lip service for the sake of status, family harmony or tribal safety. During these years I was a mouthy youth and a know-it-all, but I remained a passionate believer. It stung to know that my belief was more offensive than the sly apostasy of others, for some parishioners toed the line without a shred of sincerity. Under the ancient mantle of political correctness, they prospered while I became the wayward son.

In a letter to the early Christian community in Rome, Saint Paul gives an impassioned account of the fervour of his conviction: 'For I am persuaded that neither death, nor life, nor angels, nor principalities, nor powers, nor things present, nor things to come, nor height, nor depth, nor any other creature shall be able to separate us from the love of God, which is in Christ Jesus our Lord.'

At our church this passage was a perennial favourite. I loved the chanting repetition, the lofty chain of negatives. There was a whiff of greasepaint and footlights about it, a bit of Elizabethan ruffle that I couldn't resist. But what moves me now is the desperation in it; Paul is brimming with devotion and defiance. As a boy I knew those lines by heart: I could never have foreseen a time when the principality most likely to threaten my faith was the church itself.

I'd always been a natural believer in more than one sense. Although I treasured Scripture I didn't need to be convinced by it. Similarly, the church enriched my instinctive apprehension of a divine element at play in the world, but I didn't require the parish organization to inspire faith or sustain it. Like the twelve-year-old mystic Ort Flack in my early novel *That Eye, the Sky*, I felt from infancy that I belonged and was known to more than just the people about me. Even in solitude Ort feels accompanied, as if observed and sustained by something larger. I, too, felt a benign force in the natural world; I saw it in the higher instincts of people. Creation wasn't some kind of cruel divine experiment, the world was the body of God, the life force expressing itself. I still couldn't say what God was, but I had an inkling as to what He was about, and that was love and liberation.

As a teenager I struggled to break free of the smothering codi-
fication of this mystery; everyone seemed determined to domesti-
cate it beyond all recognition. I know my resistance puzzled and
hurt some members of the community. At times my parents were
embarrassed and dismayed; it appeared their eldest child's membership of the congregation often hung by a thread. And I didn't
want them to fret. I knew what a deliverance their conversion had
been; it truly was the making of them, raising their sights beyond
suburban self-interest. They'd said *yes* to life, *yes* to love, and the
fruits of that assent were what distinguished them at work, within
the neighbourhood and in their own families, and I had no intention of spurning it.

Amidst the church's growing obsession with right thinking and
self-censorship, one thing above all others drove me wild. Not the
sad reversion to tribalism, nor even the neurotic preoccupation with
sex, but the contention, as many a chorus had it, that *this world is
not my home*. This phrase left the confines of churches a century ago.
You can hear it, sprinkled in like a noxious seed, in many bluegrass
songs and country tunes. Once or twice we've heard its nihilistic
echo in an American presidency.

There were plenty of things to kick against at church, so why
rage at *this* particular idea?

For one thing, I'd grown uncomfortable with the repudiation
of human life implicit in it. The contempt for creation bothered
me. It was as if the natural world were either inconsequential or
insufficient. This seemed profoundly dismissive of the great gift of
life, and for humans to be pining for a superior existence beyond
the world of matter – well, that struck me as absurd, especially in a
subculture like ours where no one went hungry and our sufferings
were not exactly of the highest order.

I suppose what intensified my repulsion was the spectacle of fellow parishioners who'd drunk so deeply from this poisonous notion

that they were now thirsty only for death. Some were anxious to see the End of Days. During the Cold War they welcomed the eve of destruction as an opportunity to 'go home' and as a result they turned their backs on temporal concerns. The poor and all structural injustice could be ignored. So too the planet's ailing health. Tough luck – not our problem. It was bitterly ironic, given how often we all intoned our favourite Bible verse. Even the little kids could recite John 3:16 by heart: 'For God so loved the world that he gave his only begotten Son, that whosoever believeth in him should not perish, but have everlasting life.'

But in their rush to greet the apocalypse, some of their parents had forgotten, as Marilynne Robinson reminds us, that 'God so loved the world, this world, our world.' I didn't see the point in feigning virtue in this sorry existence only so as to prosper in the next. As W.H. Auden writes, 'Eternity is the decision *now*, action now, one's neighbour *here*.' I wanted to live in a community where matter still mattered, and I was saying so, but I was doing it without elegance or diplomacy.

Initially the elders humoured me. When I kept pressing this point and others, they politely declined to engage. At first this tactic puzzled me. In time it made me furious. To generate discussion I provoked them, but they grew defensive and high-handed. Some questions seemed to strike them as improper. Eventually they barely spoke to me at all, and I read their retreat as spineless evasion. Although I was accused of being variously a communist, a pantheist, a humanist and a lukewarm liberal, I was never formally shunned. No one saw me off in a blaze of anger. There was no fire and brimstone. I kind of slunk away and that was that. Hardly even a whimper. My exit from the community was neither sudden nor dramatic. I was never denounced from the pulpit as friends from similar traditions were. There was no excommunication and thankfully no hideous ordeal of exorcism like the one Jeanette Winterson depicts in *Oranges Are Not the Only Fruit.*

But for years I remained perplexed by the behaviour of the elders I'd tried so hard to confront and convince. With the benefit of hindsight I see that I was completely blind to a crucial dynamic we were all at the mercy of but unable to express. From a position of generational privilege that I couldn't even recognize, let alone acknowledge, I was arguing with men dragged out of school at twelve or thirteen to drive horses and ride tractors. There I was, a university undergrad, pounding these old geezers into rhetorical corners, hurling all my ten-dollar words and half-digested book learning at them, thrusting and parrying excitedly, oblivious that every challenge was a judgement of them and the poverty of their origins. I don't resile from the youthful instinct to question and dispute, to call bullshit on ideas that are unexamined or oppressive, but I do regret the fact that every time I argued my corner I shamed them for things over which they had no control.

I spent my twenties in other, somewhat more progressive church communities, determined to find a synthesis of ideas that was watertight and definitive, but in the process I wore myself to a theological standstill. In the face of mystery, it seems no language is sufficient. Every expression is partial, contingent, as if written in sand. If I discovered anything it was that theology is speculative, not descriptive. At its best it's poetic, for any discussion of the divine rests on metaphor, but what a peculiar task it is to try to describe silence. Even the grandest poetic language is hard-pressed to contain or carry an intimation of grace. Language is not experience itself. Reminding the faithful that the great mysteries of life cannot be brought to heel by theological assertion, Dietrich Bonhoeffer said: 'Where God tears great gaps we should not try to fill them with human words.' In matters of the spirit words are poor cousins to music. At best they remain muted echoes.

I still hear from stalwarts of my childhood church now and

then. Old folks I fought with as a youth send cards and letters prompted by fond memories and abiding concern. When I see them at football games or asylum-seeker rallies they discreetly ask about my 'walk'. At their funerals when I stand to sing the doxology in the company of their dwindling peers, the hair stands up grey at the back of my neck.

Nearly all my best friends are refugees from evangelical fundamentalism. Some are atheists, more have become agnostic, but the closest are still believers and some wear dog collars. I hasten to say this is not the result of any policy; it's actually slightly mortifying. But it's as if, when we first met as strangers, we recognized something familiar: a turn of phrase, a musical reference, the same queasy fascination for the work of Paul Schrader or Stanley Spencer. Perhaps it's the do-gooding energy so carefully cloaked in irony – it can't simply be the cardigans and the dissenter's posture. Whatever it is, it's kept us entertained. Our common pasts provide a reservoir of jokes and horror stories that soften our middle-aged bewilderment.

Like some of my post-evangelical friends I seem to have developed an irrational fondness for liturgical worship, and the more bells and smells, the better. Oddly enough the fixed forms are liberating and the repetition something I can lose myself in. Following along with the crowd, incanting what is essentially a long poem, I find a rare privacy. I do this, to misquote Auden, 'in company, for solitude'. The sacrament of the Eucharist has become the central focus, the still point, if you will; I receive it on my knees and cross myself like a papist – spectacles, testicles, wallet and keys – but there's no magical thinking in it. Sometimes the music is lovely, though a sung mass, like a musical, makes me fidget. I quite like a choir. I just wish the solemnity of choral music wasn't so relentless. In truth I miss the brawling choruses and supercharged hymns of my youth. There's nothing quite like the mad, joyful, erotic abandon of evangelical singing. The genteel wheezing of Anglicans and Catholics will never do. So used to being sung for, they seem to lack faith in their own voices. And the white-bread bump-and-grind of the charismatic mega-churches is just showbiz in the temple, the sound of money being made. My mother was right all along, there's no pleasing the likes of me.

Which brings me to the point I'm always avoiding, the question strangers and some friends continue to ask: What brand of believer am I now? You'd think I'd have worked up an answer beyond the admission that I'm still a practising Christian but clearly getting no better at it. The thing is, I'm worn out with the labels and definitions people seem to be expecting, bored by the forensic nitpicking I was caught up in for so long. Besides, I'm no good at this stuff anymore, a feisty teenaged doorknocker can snooker me inside ten minutes; I've come to learn that matching a perky fundamentalist requires the certainty, memory and bladder control of a much younger person. To me, the rhetorical detail is no longer paramount, and like the poet Christian Wiman, I've come to see that 'so much of faith has so little to do with belief, and so much to do with acceptance', by which he means the acceptance of grace.

In the company of Protestants I feel rather Catholic, and a roomful of rockchoppers certainly brings out the Calvinist in me, even though, with the exceptions of Bonhoeffer and Martin Luther King, all my heroes 'belonged to Rome': Thomas Merton, Dorothy Day, Julian of Norwich, Leonardo Boff. My politics tend toward the collectivist, but like a lot of former fundamentalists and survivors of totalitarian regimes, I'm leery of conscripted solidarity. The bad faith of political correctness, what John Updike calls 'coercive self-righteousness', is too horribly familiar. And, having been so comprehensively inoculated in childhood, I find I'm immune to sermons, or maybe just allergic, though that's not something I'm proud of.

I remain a believer and even a churchgoer, though I am in more than one sense irregular. Church was my village, but I doubt I'll ever be truly at ease there again. All the same, on a Sunday evening, wherever I am, I feel that tidal pull, the old melancholy descends, and it's as homely and as unsettling as the smell of the sea.

High Tide

Late in the day we step out into the withering heat. Most of the sting has gone from the sun but the air is still so hot it's like trying to inhale a fluffy towel fresh from the tumble dryer. The hard red dirt is radiant. The spinifex sweats its oily musk. At noon it was 53.3 in the sun and 49.9 in what little shade there is out here on the floodplain. Even now it's hellish but both of us are half wigged-out with cabin fever and we can't sit in the aircon another moment; time for a swim.

The heat here is dry. Perspiration evaporates in the desert wind before you have a chance to notice it. Within a minute or two my eyeballs are so parched the lids begin to stick and grate. The mask and fins feel like jelly in my hands.

The sea's only 100 metres away but by the time we reach the shore we're half knackered, and it's not much relief anyway – in the shallows the water temperature hovers around 30 degrees. Still, if you dunk yourself and stand in the gale you feel coolish for a moment or two.

Neither of us has the energy for a big swim. We content ourselves with a visit to the rocky bar at the mouth of the dry creek. As we kick toward that little reef, the top layer of the water is so warm it's hazy, and to keep our masks from fogging up we haul ourselves along the rubble-strewn bottom whenever we can; it's cooler there. Besides, the tide is turning and the current is tough, and crabbing along the seabed is easier than kicking up in the heat.

Ahead of us bluebone and garfish peel away and head for shelter. A big turtle clocks us and veers off. Near the rock bar, a hunk of coral-encrusted stone no bigger than a badly bogged LandCruiser, we pause awhile to get our breath. At low tide, when it stands proud of the pebbly shore, this is an unprepossessing bit of littoral. It's neither completely of the ocean nor of the land. In one of its crevices there are giant clams whose jaws are filled with petrified desert soil and stones. But on a high tide during a full moon, the sea overwhelms this chunk of range country and for an hour or so makes the place its own.

The trick is to get close to the bar and then swim hard enough at the last moment to grab hold. You're only in a metre of water but it's difficult to maintain position and you can barely keep your feet against the torrent. At the surface it's just a boil of retreating water over a dull bit of rock, but underneath it's all colour and action. You hang on, let your legs wallow behind you in the current, and the first thing you see is dozens of blue-spotted lagoon rays with their heads tucked under the ledge, their tails wafting beneath you. Once you get your bearings you clamber sideways until you're wedged beside one of the clefts through which the traffic pours on the current.

And the traffic is hectic, ceaseless. In columns three and five deep baby emperors and bream and coral trout fly past, parting and merging to avoid colliding with you in flashes of silver, gold, blue, bronze, white, in stripes and spots and chevrons and blazes. Hundreds of them, streaming past silently in their mad splashes of colour. It's like an acid trip from which you can exit at any moment by simply lifting your head. Ashore there's a wary osprey astride a bleached stump and beneath him the charred remains of a bonfire from last winter. Drop your face back in and it's something out of Kubrick, all hurtling colours and shapes and patterns so intense as to be slightly mind-bending. It's like standing in the middle of the freeway, addled and awed and happy as a loon.

I count them off – fingermark, Spanish flag, trevally, honeycomb cod – and soon lose track. My arms ache but we stay as long as the current lasts and the water with it, and in the end we have to wade home the way we swam. By the time we're up the sandy track and back on the doorstep we're dry again and the hair stands up on our heads in spiky shocks as if to signal the level of our childish excitement. It might be there again tomorrow. But the day after the spectacle will be gone. For another month the rock bar will be high and dry. We'll walk past it and I'll stop as I do nearly every day and look at the desert packed into the mouth of the clam that sprouts from its brow like an improper thought.

The Wait
and the Flow

On the beach one day, as I was sliding my board back onto the tray of the ute and trying to clear my sinuses of salty water, an old neighbour who was passing by with his dog told me he didn't know what people like me saw in surfing. He said, 'I see youse blokes out there day and night. Any time I go past you're just sittin there, bobbin around like moorin buoys. Tell me, Timmy, what's the point?' And I didn't know how to answer. Almost every day of my life is shaped according to the weather, most acutely to swell, tide and wind direction. After surfing for fifty years, you'd think I'd be able to give a better account of myself. But there wasn't much to tell him, because there *is* no point. Surfing is a completely pointless exercise. Perhaps that's why I'm addicted to it. But he was right, my neighbour, God rest him. We go to the water every day and every hour we can. And most of what we do is wait.

I grew up near Scarborough Beach in the sixties where surfing was the local culture. At the age of five, when my teenaged cousins, both girls, pushed me out on a big old longboard, I was more scared than excited. The physical details and sensations are still vivid and fresh in my mind. Like the greeny tint in the board's resin and the weave of the Volan cloth beneath it. The deck was bumpy with paraffin wax. I remember the stolid symmetry of the three wooden stringers under all that fibreglass. Everything about the trek out to the break was overwhelming: the light and noise, the sheer heft of the board, the nervous anticipation. I wasn't paddling, I was being ferried out there in my Speedos. Then, without warning, I was spun around. The air roared all about me. Suddenly I was rushing shoreward, flat out. And that was it. I was gone from that moment on. I wanted more. I wanted to be a surfer.

I began riding Coolites, the way you did as a beginner in those days. They were stubby styrofoam demons without fins and I skated about on one for a year until someone showed me how to cut a hole in the hull and wax in a bit of plywood for a skeg. The rashes we got from those foam boards were horrendous; it's a wonder I've still got nipples. The best thing you could say about the Coolite is that you could surf it between the flags and keep your mum and those pesky lifesavers happy all at once. They were pigs to ride but you couldn't kill anybody with one when you fell off and it went bouncing and fluttering beachward through the wading throng. I did a lot of falling off; it was my specialty.

These were the primary school years. I surfed for hours at a time, until my face and back were roasted and my little chest was

a grated, weeping mess. I'd spend the final hour studiously avoiding eye contact with my poor mum who'd be madly waving me in
from the shore.

My first glass board was a 7-foot egg with a radical raked fin.
This was 1973. By then the shortboard era had well and truly arrived
and this thing was already a relic. It rode like a longboard, and
though along with everyone else I soon progressed to shorter and
shorter craft, I never forgot the pure, gliding feel of those old-school
boards and the graceful way good surfers rode them. These were
the guys I watched most, the blokes who'd quickly become uncool
in the seventies.

The most obvious attraction of surfing is the sheer momentum,
the experience of rushing toward the beach. It's a buzz. And though
you might repeat the experience millions of times in thirty or forty
or fifty years, the prime thrill never fades. It looks repetitive but no
ride is ever the same; it feels like a miracle every time you do it and
I'd hate to lose that sense of wonder.

Surfing has its origins in Polynesian ritual and play. At one
level it was a display of power and caste: kings and princes standing proud and insouciant on their *olos*, commoners bellying in on
alaias. But it was also about grace and beauty. Early illustrations
and accounts depict scenes of boisterous celebration and physical
prowess. Surfing was fun; it was liberating. It was this spirit of
freedom and grace that *haoles* witnessed in Hawaii, from Cook
onwards. They marvelled at it and they wanted to emulate it. Jack
London was hardly the first, but he's a notable convert. You might
say that in this instance the missionary impulse was reciprocal. With
their *aloha* spirit, the Hawaiians let the rest of the world in on one
of life's great pleasures and it's hard to overestimate the cultural
impact of surfing since it spread from the Islands. Here in Australia
it helped shape people's sense of themselves; since the forties it's
gradually become an identifiable element of our national culture, an

expression of youthful vigour, engagement with nature, lust for life. In the fifties surfing became a form of individual expression, too, an act of rebellion. When most Australians seemed anxious about sticking out in a crowd, surfers wanted to distinguish themselves. They weren't exactly gracious in going their own way, they were brash and selfish, ensnared by a beatnik resistance to conformity that's easy to ridicule now, but it's worth bearing in mind just how rigid the social mores were at the time. Surfing and beach life offered an alternative to local orthodoxy – which was to submit to the group, join the club, buy the stuff. In an era of shiny surfaces, new appliances and suburban indoor order, surfers were heretics. And they liked it that way; they celebrated the rebel. While their mums and dads still venerated dominion over nature and separation from it, surfers were, consciously or not, in the vanguard of those who sought to honour the natural world; surfing is done at the mercy of the elements and requires an intimacy with them beyond the ken of a golfer or a tennis player. To surf, a person foregoes timetables and submits to the vagaries of nature.

The late sixties and early seventies were surfing's Romantic era. I came to it at the peak of this period and it had a lasting impact on me. Back then we thought we were special when we were just lucky. We surfed with a sense of kinship with each other and with the sea that marked us out, if only for a while. We spoke a lingo that puzzled our parents and not all of it was hippie nonsense. What we craved was *flow*. The activity influenced our conceptual framework in ways that aren't always credited. Non-surfers, it seemed to me, strove for symmetry, linear order, solid boundaries. Waiting and flowing were anachronistic notions, they'd nearly become foreign concepts, but to me they were part of an imaginative lexicon, feeding something in me that had to do with more than surfing. The child of a pragmatic, philistine and insular culture, I responded to the prospect of something wilder, broader, softer, more fluid and emotional. It sounds unlikely but I suspect surfing unlocked the artist in me.

Of course this was all before surfing became yet another occupied territory. By the eighties it had been colonized and pacified by the corporate world, and its language and attitude reflected its captivity. How eager surfers were to surrender their freedom! Suddenly they needed to be *respected*. Board riders wanted to be sports stars and millionaires. So began the years of dreary contests and sponsor-chasing, the chest-beating and swagger, the brawls in the surf. Surfers distinguished themselves by their machismo and their ultranationalism. The dominant mode was urban, aggressive, localized, greedy, racist and misogynistic. Out with all that touchy-feely shit. Surfers became jocks, defiant morons who trashed beaches and scowled at each other on the break. I wonder how many five-year-old boys were introduced to surfing in the eighties by girls. By then women were almost entirely absent from the surf. Driven out by the bellicose mood, they were consigned to the beach. *Gidget* made way for *Puberty Blues*. What I knew as something soulful was now the preserve of violent thugs like the Bra Boys. I gave up and walked away for shame. I put on a mask and snorkel. It was quiet and solitary underwater. You weren't at the mercy of the big swinging dicks.

But I missed surfing badly. After a couple of years abroad I moved to a coastal hamlet where there were waves and a few surfers with an attitude mellow enough to suit me. It was a treat to paddle out again, to wait, to glide, to flow. There were others like me, who came back to surfing in the nineties when pure fun was valued again. They were past all the aggro, they'd outgrown their self-consciousness, and they were sick of the belligerent conformity that had overtaken the 'sport'. They rebelled anew and rode strange craft unseen for decades, glorying in eccentric board shapes and retro designs. Sitting on the break you'd see people smiling, speaking to each other once again. The slit-eyed surf punks were still out there, slashing and snarling and scowling, but they were no longer the only tribe afloat. And the women were back, thank God. Within a decade girls were a constant, active and growing presence in the water.

To me surfing has always been a matter of beauty and connectedness. Riding a wave to shore can be a meditative activity; you're walking on water, tapping the sea's energy, meeting the ocean, not ripping anything out of it. Few other water pursuits are as non-exploitative. Humans exist by creative destruction; there's no evading that reality. So having some major interactive pleasure in the natural world that comes without mortal cost – that's precious, something to celebrate. The physical sensation of sliding along a wall of water, vividly awake and alive, is difficult to describe to the non-surfer; it feels even more beautiful than it looks. And for some men – men in particular, whose lives are so often circumscribed by an exclusively utilitarian mindset – surfing is the one pointlessly beautiful activity they engage in. There is no material result from two hours spent surfing. All the benefits are intangible, except perhaps the calibration of mood. Everyone close to me knows that when I come home wet, I'm a happier man than when I left. Think of the Prozac I've saved.

I credit surfing with getting me through adolescence. When I was lonely, confused and angry, the ocean was always there, a vast salty poultice sucking the poison from my system. If surfing's addictive, and I'm bound to concede that it is, all I can say is there are so many more destructive addictions to succumb to. Even in my middle age it continues to provide respite. When I get in the water I slow down and reflect. That's the benefit of all that bobbing and waiting. I wait and wait and then I glide and flow. I process problems without even consciously addressing them. The wider culture expects you to hurl yourself at the future. Surfing offers a chance to inhabit the present.

The wait and the glide have become a way of life. Strange as it might seem, the life of a novelist is often like that of a surfer. I come to the desk every day and mostly I wait. I sit for hours, bobbing in a sea of memories, impressions and historical events. The surfer waits for swells, and what are they but the radiating energy of events across the horizon, the leftovers of tempests and turmoils already in the past? The surfer waits for something to turn up from the unseen distance and if he's vigilant and patient it'll come to him. He has to be there to meet it. And when it comes he has to be alert and fit and committed enough to turn and ride that precious energy to the beach. When you manage to do this you live for a short while in the eternal present tense. And the feeling is divine.

That's how I experience writing, which is its own compulsion. I show up. I wait. When some surge of energy finally arrives, I do what I must to match its speed. While I can, I ride its force. For a brief period I'm caught up in something special, where time has no purchase, and my bones don't ache and my worries fall away. Then it's all flow. And I'm dancing.

In the Shadow
of the Hospital

In 1995 veteran folksinger Loudon Wainwright III released a typically mordant song in which he catalogues the births, breakdowns, deaths and near misses of friends and family. Somehow, in 'That Hospital' all the health campuses of memory coalesce as a single monolithic entity, a site of inescapable mortality. That hospital, Wainwright senses, will never be done with him; it will always be there, waiting.

Hospital. The word itself carries historical notions of shelter, respite and hospitality. The modern institution remains a refuge, a place of deliverance. It's often a bulwark against chaos. Anyone who's ever needed a hospital in a hurry knows the otherworldly sanctuary it promises. One afternoon in the Greek islands thirty years ago I sat in a small boat holding my infant son's scalp together with my thumbs as we beat into a gale toward the prospect of harbour and hospital. Although the clinic we were trying so desperately to reach was a seedy little affair my wife and I had little faith in, during that rocky passage it became in my mind a citadel of hygiene and expertise. *In extremis*, we yearn for the hospital, and yet the rest of the time, if you're anything like me, the very word brims with dread. Like the aging Canadian strummer, I have a lifelong preoccupation with *that hospital*, an aversion I'm too proud to call a phobia.

In my earliest apprehensions of hospital it was a mysterious reservoir of bounty. This was where mums and dads got their babies. And though I'd apparently come from there myself, I'd never been back to see. Grown-ups spoke of it as a place where broken arms were fixed, where sick people went to get better; it was amazing what they could do these days. On visits to the city when a parent pointed out some bland tower and said it was a hospital I struggled to match this with the miracle factory I'd imagined. But by the time I was five I knew better. Hospital was trouble. You didn't want to go there because if you got out at all you came home in ruins.

I was still a small boy when my father suddenly disappeared. It took a long time for me to understand that there had been an accident. My mother tried to reassure me. So did the policemen who came to the door every day. They all said my dad would be okay – he was doing fine, the folks in the hospital were looking after him, it was incredible what they could do these days, and he'd be back in no time. We just had to sit tight. But he wasn't back even in a long time, and all those other words of comfort began to sound like lies. Our little brick-veneer bungalow in the outer suburbs had never felt so empty and isolated. As the weeks went by I began to suspect hospital was a place from which people could not return. If Dad was doing so well there, why was Mum crying all the time? And if this was the best place for him right now, why couldn't I visit? He was sleeping, they said. But I knew that was what they told kids when people were dead and they were too scared to say. Even after someone came by with the startling news that Dad was finally awake, there would be no visits. The weeks rolled on.

Then one day a big white armchair appeared in the lounge. It seemed to take up half the room. Mum said we were having a special visitor. And that afternoon a pale and wizened creature was carried into our house and carefully lowered into that new chair as if made of glass. His eyes were the colour of broken red bricks and he breathed through a hole in his neck. If I squinted a little he looked a bit like my dad, but he was so much older and too feeble-looking. My father was a big, strong, vigorous man. And yet everyone in the room – the off-duty coppers, the blokes from the hospital and even my mother – kept saying his name over and over: Johnny, John, John! They shook their heads in wonder and joshed with him, laughing as if this were a great day indeed. Though I didn't really recognize him I took everyone's cue and played along. If anything I was a little afraid of this husk in our midst. If this was my dad, something awful had happened to him. He'd been carted off to Royal Perth and sent home as a wreck.

After that there were always crutches by my parents' bedroom door, pills on the side table, bandages on the coverlet. Under the bed lay a slippery carpet of X-rays and some days Dad looked as ghostly and indecipherable as them. There were endless doctors' appointments, visits to this specialist or that therapist. Finally the crutches gave way to the awful walking stick. And then the stick disappeared and he was suddenly plausible again. We had him back.

But now and then during my primary school years, Dad would have to go in for more surgery, and anytime he returned to hospital I felt a chill of panic. That lingering doubt was always there. What if he didn't come back? What if he came home a stranger again?

As if picking up on my anxiety Mum eventually took me to visit him during one of these sojourns. At the time he was recovering from a bone graft, and that visit is my first memory of the inside of a hospital. I remember being nervous, but the reality was worse than I'd imagined. It was like a descent into the netherworld: the grand entrance, the high desks and hard lights, all those flat, stern faces peering down at me. I shrank against my mother as she led me through a maze of corridors. Nurses' shoes squawked on the lino. The opaque windows had threads of steel in them, as if the patients were captives. In the long, open ward with its ranks of steel-framed beds, there was a gauntlet of horrors to be traversed before I could see my dad. It seemed there was a price to be paid for visiting.

In the sixties an orthopaedic ward in a big public hospital was a confronting environment for an adult, let alone a child. Visits by children were discouraged. For patients there was no privacy, and even those ghastly curtains the nurses ricked around beds at crucial moments allowed precious little discretion. On that long walk, with coughs and moans and pulleys and pins and plasters at every turn, I felt the first onset of the weird tunnel vision I still get in hospital wards. It was as if I were walking down my own tiny hallway from which the lurid tableau of men in traction and wing-headed matrons were excluded. But what I could not see loomed larger in the mind. Behind the death rattle of curtains I envisaged limbs plastered into gothic contortions, hypodermic needles the size of bike pumps, bandaged heads in which black mouths gaped and pulsed like anemones. With all those horrors, real and imagined, it seemed quite a distance to travel. I pressed so hard to my mother's leg she could barely walk.

After this ordeal the eventual sight of my dad with tubes snaking from his hip wasn't quite so bad. Beneath his bed bottles collected a tawny liquid like the juices of a lamb roast. Dad hoisted me up and showed me the plaster and the gruesome antiseptic stains on his skin. He pointed out where the pipes went in. It was gross but it was nothing like the charnel-house I'd just been through. When our time was up I didn't want to go. I bawled and said I missed him. But the truth was I didn't want to walk back down that ward.

Years later I saw a movie by Dalton Trumbo that brought all that childhood horror back to the surface. *Johnny Got His Gun* is about a quadruple amputee, a soldier reduced to a helpless trunk. Blind, deaf and mute, alone with his fevered thoughts, he lies on a bed encased in plaster, just a silent screaming mouth. From the first glimpse this character was like something bursting in from the banished periphery. Trumbo no doubt meant him to be exactly that, a reminder to the culture that boys pay the price for the wars of old men. But to me he was personal: a memory and a nightmare, one of the images that once danced out of bounds beyond the walls of my panicky tunnel vision. Man or boy, whenever I've visited someone in hospital a version of that suffering gothic effigy has lurked at the edge of consciousness.

As a family we had our share of waiting-room nights and long days in carparks, at Princess Margaret, King Edward, Osborne Park, and Albany Regional – puncture wounds, fractures, births and miscarriages, episodes of pleurisy, osteomyelitis, asthma and meningitis – yet somehow I managed to avoid admission all the years of childhood. Sometimes it seemed I was paying for this apparent immunity with traumatic visits to others. My infant brother emerging from a coma, his mouth a nest of ulcers. My grandmother writhing and raging after her catastrophic stroke. The day I stumbled into the burns unit by accident. Hospital seemed like a constant presence. But I was only visiting.

And then one morning when I was eighteen I woke up on the inside. Royal Perth Hospital. I had no idea where I was, though, or how I got there. There was a bloke gurgling and moaning beside me. I tried to get up but there was no power in my body; it was like a nasty dream. I tried to speak – to the man in the next bed, to anyone really – but all I could produce was a croak. For a few moments I lay there taking the room in, trying not to panic. Every surface had a ghost. I couldn't focus my eyes. My roommate sounded as if he were dying. My hair was full of biting insects, my head hurt, my face hurt, my back and legs hurt, my belly felt as if it had been perforated with something blunt. I really needed to piss but I couldn't get up. I knew I wasn't paralyzed but I was stuck. I felt ruined. Frightened, angry, I began to cry.

Eventually someone arrived to see what the fuss was about. A glass of orange juice appeared. The drink was cool but it stung my chapped lips and I spilt some down my chest, unable to lift my head sufficiently. Soon afterwards I puked it all back up.

By all accounts I was lucky to be alive. My convulsions were gone but I was still badly concussed and there were ongoing tests on my innards. Those weren't whiskers on my chin, they were sutures. And the bees in my hair were thousands of fragments of windscreen glass.

The guy next to me died, or was moved elsewhere; it wasn't clear. Nothing looked right, nothing felt right. If I dropped off I couldn't tell, when I woke again, whether I was still in the same day. It was like being a very old man, feeble, confused, at the mercy of others. I couldn't think straight for long but all I could hold onto was the idea of fleeing. Yes, hospital was awful to visit, but it was far worse on the inside.

If you're an inpatient, acute illness does you the oddest favour; it takes up all mental space and serves as a buffer between you and the institution. Once the worst of the pain and fear have receded, however, your ordeal is not over; it merely changes shape. Of course nothing is more hellish than extreme pain and ungovernable terror, but nobody can prepare you for the challenge of recovery. That's the long game.

For one thing, unless you're out of your head on drugs there's no rest to be had in hospital. When the trolleys aren't crashing and scraping in the hectic daylight hours – all those drug carts, food wagons, theatre gurneys – the noises they make at night are both sinister and cruelly promising. As you lie awake in the wee hours the squeak of castors in the distance telegraphs the certainty that something is coming, coming, coming. Something better, something awful, some food, some unspeakable procedure. You're hooked up to machines that whirr and burp and chirp and the same nurses who sternly tell you to get your rest will bellow and gossip outside your door all night. You're exhausted, and on top of that you feel like a captive, so you're agitated. Whatever you want is perpetually unavailable: better pain relief, a pillow that hasn't previously done service as a sandbag, an open window, a view, some news, some better news. The only thing worse than visitors is other patients' visitors – or no visitors at all.

In hospital you become needy, greedy, callous. While you'll concede the necessity of tapering off the painkillers, you'll always find the decline too steep, too sudden. Even knowing how hard it is to be a hospital visitor you glory in showing friends the sutures and staples and you laugh boorishly when they lurch away in horror. Suffering is supposed to be ennobling, but being in hospital could make even a saint cruel and peevish. Perhaps it's the enclosed world, the infantilizing effect of being confined to your room, ordered to bed – wearing *pyjamas*, for goodness sake – having baby food served up and sometimes spooned into your mouth.

So many great novels have been set in hospitals. From the paralysis and recriminations of Solzhenitsyn's cancer victims to the pettiness and moral vacancy of Endo's lung patients and their doctors, or the murky circus-world of Kesey's mental ward, the healing institution harbours the bully, the whiner, the snitch and the cowardly accomplice. Wars and hospitals – it's a surprise we write about anything else. Hospitals make rich fictional settings because from the inside they are such chillingly plausible worlds unto themselves. They have their own surreal logic, their own absurd governance, their own uncanny weather, and the power-lessness and boredom they induce is hard to match anywhere else but prison or the military.

No wonder so many terminally ill patients prefer to die at home. Perhaps it's not the prospect of expiring in the company of loved ones and familiar surroundings so much as the thought of being a civilian again, with some command over the immediate environment.

As fate would have it, I married a nurse. I don't know what that says about me, but there it is. After every shift at Sir Charles Gairdner she brought the ward home with her – in stories, in bruised silences, in the smells and stains of people suffering and dying day in and day out. That was all the hospital I needed in my life, though now and then I relented and met her for lunch in the cafeteria. But I was rotten company, forever distracted, fidgeting, flinching at the clash of trolleys and the sight of patients wheeling their IV stands between tables. My wife worked until a few weeks before our first child was born. It must have been strange for her cancer patients, being ministered to by such a young and hugely pregnant woman, and perhaps no less startling a few months later when she was back at work while still breastfeeding. Once or twice a shift, I drove our son in to Charles Gairdner so she could feed him on her breaks. I spent many hours lurking in the carpark, spooking the security guards as I waited with him for her to emerge from Oncology. When she came rushing out into the fresh air she was as hungry for our baby as he was for her, and as she lay back in the passenger seat with him at her breast, she discreetly kept me up to date with the progress of patients I felt I knew but would never meet. She smelt of antiseptic and sweat and things I didn't care to guess at and it was odd to be with her in those minutes when she fed our baby, with those strangers struggling and mostly dying a few floors above us.

For five years we lived in the very literal shadow of a major metropolitan hospital. Like all institutions, Fremantle Hospital managed to be bigger than the sum of its parts. It wasn't just a health facility. At times it was more like a furnace or a power plant. In summer the air around it was thick with screams and sirens and the drone of cooling towers, and in winter its beige mass blocked out the sun. It was a constant, implacable presence. Because we'd just moved from a rural community too small for a pharmacy, let alone a doctor, the proximity of a hospital was supposed to be reassuring, even for the likes of me. After all, we had three small kids now and I'd done more than my share of driving through the roo-infested night to get medical help. I told myself, This is great – really – we can walk across the street to Accident and Emergency.

As it turned out the hospital didn't just offer safety, it provided a startling amount of free entertainment. It was a 24-hour soap opera. Whether their problems were large, inconsequential or totally imaginary, the people who visited the building functioned in an unrelievedly histrionic register. It seemed as if the hospital brought out something peculiar, something that altered folk from their workaday selves, as if hospital didn't just license them to behave differently, it required it. And the variety of people a public hospital draws into its orbit hour by hour is hard to credit. In the time it took to get the groceries from the car to the house, you could see a football star, a weeping woman with a painted moustache and too many fingers, and a man with a steel bolt protruding from his forearm.

Fremantle Hospital was not the discrete health campus of the suburbs, set in awesome isolation like a hyper-mall and bounded by a vast moat of carparking. This was the inner city, a neighbourhood of narrow streets and workers' cottages, and the establishment had long outgrown its original footprint. The old Victorian building was buried amidst hulking modernist slabs. It didn't just tower over the surrounding streets, it projected outward. And the over-spill wasn't simply physical. With A&E opposite the local primary school, and the new mental health unit directly opposite our house, the hospital dominated the environs. Around a medical precinct some institutional colonization is unavoidable – the nasty signage, the ever-present uniforms and flashing ambulances – but there were occasions when overzealous security guards or high-handed management gave locals like us the feeling we were intruders in our own neighbourhood.

The place had its own microclimate. But it ran to more than just the steaming and the shimmering and the roof-rattling down-draughts. Within a block or two you could feel the atmosphere around it become feverish and the closer you got to the foot of those towers and their yawning electric doors, the more you noticed the vortex of suffering and need that sucked and boiled around you. There was electricity in the air, latent havoc. Within a few moments our street could change from being a circus to a battlefield. With its aura of hope and dread, it was peculiarly volatile, especially at night and on weekends. Negotiating it required vigilance.

On any street in any city, there's a human story walking past you every moment but it's usually withheld. In the lee of a hospital the social camouflage slips away, and what's usually disguised is on display. Where else do people bear their own narratives so openly? Body language is heightened, almost balletic. Patients who step out for a fag by the taxi rank will pace and smoke and weep like actors in a *film noir*. Down on the forecourt, visitors, frightened relatives and self-admitters exist in a zone well outside their usual reserve. All discretion deserts them, and their basic competencies forsake them, too: they drive as if in a trance, park like rubes who've never been at the wheel before. At times they don't even park, they simply abandon the car across or even in your driveway, keys and all. People literally carry their troubles on the pavement before you: their sick and shrieking child, their disoriented parent, the demon hissing in their ear. From all those sliding doors – the locked ward, the A&E, the palliative unit – the anguished spill onto the street in haunted shifts, dazed by news good, bad or incomprehensible. They stagger into the traffic, they stumble, they faint. At the kerbside shocked and grieving families unravel in public, sometimes erupting in vituperative brawls. I've seen people flog each other with cardigans, shoes, bunches of flowers.

The A&E entrance was like the door to a bright-lit hell. On the way home some nights, I crossed the road to avoid it. The sick and wounded came in ambulances, taxis, shopping trolleys. In the small hours of the weekend patients and their supporters beat at the windows, threatened and bashed the staff, or crawled bleeding and intoxicated through the hedges around the ramp, until eventually the hedges were removed. I woke one night to the sound of an outpatient ramming the doors of the mental health unit with his car in a desperate bid for admission. I once stood at an intersection waiting for the light to change as a woman sat in a vehicle a metre away, screaming without pause. She was right beside me at eye level in the passenger seat, flailing and writhing. She gripped the seatbelt with both hands as if it were the only thing preventing her from flying from the car and bursting into flames. Her face bore the clenched solitude of untouchable suffering. It was as palpable as radiant heat. At the wheel the woman's friend wept. They were 50 metres from help, at the mercy of a single red light that seemed as if it would never relent. Just standing there, healthy and pain-free, I felt ashamed. I wanted to turn away, walk in another direction, but finally the light changed and they were gone.

Sometimes, around the hospital, you see the worst in people. It's a surprise to sense how quickly your tolerance and fellow feeling are eroded. You can still find some pity in your heart for the woman who regularly defecates in public because you know she's at the mercy of impulses beyond her control. But for those querulous supplicants whose derangement is entirely recreational you end up feeling only disgust. As you step around the puddles of blood and the shitty nappies and the needles and broken glass and the pools of piss of a standard Saturday night in the hospital carpark, it's hard to spare the emerging wounded much sympathy; you just want them to bugger off and take their squalid fun elsewhere.

Despite all that bad weather, kindness still endured in the lee of our hospital, even if it sometimes took a little concentration to notice it. It was both tonic and lesson to see how strangers comforted one another as they waited to be collected on the forecourt, how they dandled the babies of weary mothers and offered the unexpired time on their parking tickets. The forbearance of nurses and paramedics was remarkable. Beneath their brusque drollery there was great care and courage. Every morning on my way to the office I saw nurses and doctors emerging into the light wearing the long night on their faces and in their scrubs, and I felt frivolous heading off to my safe, dull day's work.

All the years I lived next door to Fremantle Hospital I barely crossed the threshold. But in time its influence grew too oppressive for me. Like the grey noise of the cooling towers, its grim presence was unceasing. Even my wife admitted that the precinct was wearing at her nerves. We didn't move far. Still, the distance of just a few streets was telling.

But the shadow falls wherever you are.

I got a message one day from an old friend. We'd been estranged for some years. He shocked me by announcing he was in hospital and that he could see my roof from his room. The silver flash of corrugated iron was like something burning in his mind, he said, and he needed to see me. Would I come?

It was only as I walked down the ward, feeling that ancient flutter of dread, that it dawned on me just how ill my friend must be. Even so, when I was allowed into his room I thought I'd made a mistake, like the time I bumbled into the burns wing. Sitting on the bed, staring out the window and dressed only in a nappy, was a tiny bald man. Wrong room. What a dunce I was. I'd half turned to leave when he called my name.

I didn't need to be told how close to death he was. He said what a provocation to conscience it was to be trapped here staring at my roof and how glad he now was that he'd been assigned this room. Before he grew too weak to continue, we made our peace and said our goodbyes. Afterwards I often looked up at that dreary building as the sun lit its windows and thought of strangers staring out in hope and regret as the rest of us went about our day oblivious. It was sobering to think of all the yearning that spilt down amidst the treetops and roof ridges, a shadow I'd never properly considered before.

Such overspills of yearning came to mind the day I paced the halls of the Royal Women's in Melbourne awaiting the birth of our first grandchild. The circumstances were novel but the building felt only too familiar. Even before we were presented with the prospect of complications, I was agitated. The air was all wrong – well, there *was* no air. The place gave me the creeps.

This, I told my wife, is why we had our babies at home.

Actually, she said, glancing at her phone, it was about more than just your phobias.

She was right, of course, and I stalked off, chastened, determined to reprioritize my anxieties. For hours there was no news at all. I couldn't sit still, couldn't eat, couldn't relax, and going for a walk outside felt like a dereliction of duty. Every few seconds the lifts in the corridor chimed festively, and after a while that demonically chirpy sound drove me down to the end of the hall where I pressed my hands and face against the glass, staring out at the strange city below as if there might be relief down there. What a sight I must have been, with that hopeless imploring look I knew so well from the faces of others. Eventually my longsuffering wife relented and took me out to an astroturfed courtyard where the air was real and the open sky merciful. And that's where he found us, our eldest son, the colicky boy we'd nursed in the hospital carpark all those nights a lifetime ago, holding his tiny squinting daughter in the sunshine.

I still have to steel myself for a hospital visit. Sadly I need to do it now more often than ever. People have breakdowns, heart surgery, they get cancer or simply wear out. And they're still having babies, God bless them. The wind bloweth where it listeth, as the old book says, and the shadow falls likewise.

'Here,' my father said one afternoon, pressing my palm against the egregious new lump in his grizzled chest. It was his new pacemaker. 'They can do amazing things these days,' he said.

They can. And they do. In an earlier era he'd have been long dead. They brought him home next day. From that hospital.

The Battle for
Ningaloo Reef

On 4 July 2003 the Premier of Western Australia, Dr Geoff Gallop, flew north of Perth to the tiny settlement of Coral Bay to announce his government's rejection of a controversial resort proposal at nearby Maud's Landing. Further, he said he would be pressing for World Heritage listing of the area. 'Today,' he said, 'we have drawn a line in the sand and declared that we will not accept developments that threaten this precious and fragile coast.' His unequivocal decision ended a bitter and very public battle over one of Australia's most precious wild places.

For the Coral Coast Marina Development it was the end of a business opportunity. But for the motley bunch of citizens who'd fought to stop it going ahead, the announcement promised a fresh start. Only the day before, Purnululu, otherwise known as the Bungle Bungles, had been added to the World Heritage register, and with Shark Bay already listed and Ningaloo Reef now mooted, it suddenly seemed that Western Australia, mostly known for being the nation's quarry, might soon become a world leader in the preservation and management of fragile places. It's a massive state, blessed with natural assets, and a new generation was pushing for a more prudent stewardship of all this bounty.

While the premier stood on the beach with his trousers rolled up, a group of community organizers and volunteers huddled around a speakerphone in an office 1200 kilometres away, straining to hear the announcement. What they heard coming down the fluky line in Perth were words they often thought they'd never hear. And before the premier had even finished his announcement, phones started ringing all through the room. The fax machine began spitting paper. Within minutes wellwishers and news crews were jamming the corridor outside. It was pandemonium.

I was one of the stunned campaigners in that stuffy room. And right then I was supposed to be preparing for a press conference but I couldn't quite take the news in. Gallop's decision and his language went much further than I'd dared hope for. He was using phrases I'd written myself in speeches and opinion pieces and repeated in public so long they'd begun to make me nauseous. I'd met Gallop a couple of times; he was someone I'd come to respect. But having been schooled by the past two or three years of advocacy, I was steeling myself for some dirty trick, the usual mealy-mouthed compromise that even a so-called conviction politician is forced to make. Now, with Gallop's high excited voice piping from the speaker, I needed to see the decision on paper, on Department of Premier and Cabinet stationery, before I would believe it. And a few minutes later there it was, curling from the overheated fax machine, followed by something from the government website and more requests for interviews. Apparently it was real. I sat down with my comrades and tried to fashion a few words for the press conference.

As part of the Save Ningaloo Reef campaign I'd often felt like a bit player in the low-budget movie *The Castle*, the story of hapless Darryl Kerrigan doing what he can to save his home from compulsory acquisition. Like the Kerrigans, those of us who went up against the big end of town to prevent the resort from being built were always outgunned. The difference was we knew it. Our hearts might have been in the right place, and our cause just, but the forces of money and influence were massed against us. We were a fart trying to fight a cyclone. As in that now classic Australian comedy, we too had our ideas men and women, our spurts of inspiration and some unexpected friends, but half the time it seemed to me that most of us were simply dreaming. Because the little people don't win in real life – that stuff only ever happens in the movies. And yet it had happened to us.

So how *did* we fall across the line?

In 1987 the West Australian Labor government invited the Coral Coast Marina Development group to submit plans for a tourist development at the tiny beach settlement of Coral Bay. Brian Burke, the state's premier at the time, is remembered for an administration with close ties to business and notoriously lax standards of governance. He was later found guilty of rorts and went to prison. During the WA Inc era, development deals could 'progress' very quickly, and with a government so obliging and eager, an invitation such as this must have looked attractive. But plans came and went, governments rose and fell in Burke's wake, and the project seemed to go nowhere. In 2000 it resurfaced, a $200 million proposal for a 2000-bed resort at Maud's Landing with a 240-boat marina, a golf course and 250 residential blocks. And that was just for starters. It was a classic white-shoe behemoth, a major imposition on the landscape and a danger to Australia's longest fringing coral reef, the Ningaloo. At the time, coastal planning in the region was ad hoc; the implication seemed to be that they'd build the marina and see to planning and environmental issues later, and that was just how things were often done in Western Australia. Not exactly a handshake and a wink, but few defenders of the environment were under any illusions as to which way the wind usually blew out west.

Unlike the larger and more famous Great Barrier Reef on the east coast, Ningaloo is very close to shore and therefore especially vulnerable. At many points you can wade out to it, flop onto your belly and be instantly amongst it. Home to endangered turtles, dugongs and three hundred species of coral, the 260-kilometre reef is known mostly for the whale sharks that visit it every year. These and all Ningaloo's other natural wonders are the basis of a sustainable and well-run ecotourism industry, most of it concentrated at Exmouth, at the reef's northern extremity. Between Exmouth and Coral Bay – about the same distance as from Sydney to Newcastle – there's nothing but red ranges and empty white beaches. Along that stretch of coast you'd be hard-pressed to see a building, and the hinterland is a semi-arid mix of dunes, spinifex and rugged gorges. Ningaloo's isolation has helped it remain Australia's healthiest coral reef.

For these reasons, it is an irreplaceable piece of our natural heritage, but in 2000 few Australians really understood this, not even those in the west. The reef's remoteness isn't just a challenge to tourists – it's a thirteen-hour drive from Perth if you go full bore and don't stop along the way – but to scientists as well. But what researchers in the field were learning at the turn of the millennium was that the reef and its adjacent terrestrial wilderness were so rare and precious they needed much greater protection than they were being afforded, and the idea of digging a marina in the midst of all that was cause for alarm. The construction phase alone would be destructive enough to rule it out. The marina was designed to open onto Cardabia Passage, through which humpback whales, whale sharks, manta rays, dugongs and turtles enter the inner lagoons to seek refuge. Once they saw the mooted plans, architects and urban planners concurred with the marine scientists: any tourism benefits the resort and its marina brought would come at a drastically disproportionate cost to the very things that drew people to the region. By any measure it looked as if the proposal was a dud – wrong plan, wrong place – but any time these concerns were aired in Perth they were buried by the developer's PR machine and the faithful barracking of the local media.

The fight for Ningaloo turned out to be more than just a squabble over a tourist development: it was a battle of worldviews. In one corner, the lingering settler ethos, the colonial assumption that nature exists to be exploited – it has no intrinsic value, there will always be more. And on the opposing side, the idea that nature has value in its own right – it needs to be studied, nurtured and used with great care to increase its chances of enduring, because all its systems are finite. At the time of the campaign the old view was still respectable establishment thinking, and to the powerbrokers on St Georges Terrace the stuff defenders of the reef began to say was fanciful at best, seditious at worst.

But there was a generational change afoot in Western Australia. While the issue of Ningaloo was barely a minor rumbling at the margins, a long and traumatic struggle over the future of the state's old-growth native forests was reaching a climax. The Gallop government came to power on a platform of sustainable development and a policy of ending old-growth logging. Gallop seemed keen to distinguish himself from the quarry mentality and spiv ethics of

previous administrations, but in a state so traditionally conserva-
tive, with a media culture still caught up in the provincial boos-
terism of the 1980s, there were real doubts his aspirations could
come to much. As we were to discover, and as Gallop himself was
to learn at his personal cost, the old frontier alliances are not to
be challenged lightly.

In late 2000, during the last days of Richard Court's Liberal government, six people met to talk about the marina proposal. We were
all from different backgrounds – a former fashion boutique owner,
a hardened forest campaigner, a commerce graduate who'd served as
an adviser to a Liberal member. I only knew a couple of them. Dave
Hannan, a wildlife cinematographer from Queensland who'd just
spent thousands of hours filming underwater at Ningaloo, pleaded
with us to get word out to the public. He wrote a cheque for $1000
while we sat there. He wasn't sure he had the funds to honour it, but
the gesture was telling – and as it turned out the cheque was good.

At that stage I'd been quietly involved with marine conservation
for about six years. As a lifelong angler and spearfisher it seemed to
me I represented the redneck wing of the movement. I'd had to learn
to find common ground with corporate types, nervy scientists and
dreadlocked vegans alike, and heartened by the camaraderie I found
amidst all these disparate members, I was determined to bring new
people to the movement, to broaden it even further. Our long-term
objective was to see a responsible proportion of Australia's waters
protected as marine parks. A skirmish like the one at Ningaloo,
promising all the divisive rhetoric and petty political rivalries that
I hate, was not an attractive prospect. I was interested in the bigger
picture. Besides, from what I could tell, this marina development
at Maud's Landing looked like a done deal.

I really admired Dave Hannan's films and I was moved by his

passion for the reef, but I wondered if he realized what we were up against. The plan was to form a campaign and seek to strike a coalition of NGOs. But all the state's environmental groups were preoccupied with fighting for forests and none of them had funds. They were throwing everything at woodchipping. So we'd have to find money of our own, people of our own. We'd be starting from nothing. The prospect was nightmarish. But I'd loved the reef since the day George King took me out to it ten years before and sent me over the side of his boat *Nor-Don* to see my first whale shark. After that encounter I was a victim for life. I signed up anyway.

But how could we defend the place from such a distance? What did the locals of Coral Bay and Exmouth think about the issue? And given the odds, how could our campaign be anything more than a gesture? Maybe it was necessary to make it, but it felt like a doomed gesture all the same.

We borrowed an office, sought the advice of seasoned campaigners, and began to attract an increasingly diverse team of helpers who wrote submissions, answered phones, inspired a little following. With the input of the Australian Marine Conservation Society and the imprimatur of the local Conservation Council, we formed alliances with the WWF, the Wilderness Society, and the Australian Wildlife Conservancy. None of these organizations could spare us much cash but what they gave us served as seed money for the endless grind of fundraising, and their expertise was invaluable. Seven years into a book I couldn't seem to finish, I fidgeted through many meetings, struggling with acronyms and talk of political players I'd never heard of. I was the wrong man for the job. I looked for ways out.

Apart from being broke and inconsequential, our newborn outfit was truly up against the tyranny of distance. Nobody understands this like a sandgroper. The Australian media establishment lives in Sydney. Even the Perth news media is 1200 kilometres from Ningaloo.

For most Australians, Western Australia was obscure enough. But Ningaloo? Ningaloo *what*? Because of its devoted diving clientele, the reef was better known in Europe. So there we were, with some serious cultural, financial, political and spatial gaps to contend with.

On top of that, our enterprise got under way during a low moral ebb in our nation's history. A federal election distorted by lies about asylum seekers throwing their children overboard. News that radio's most powerful political personalities were taking 'cash for comment'. And all this as the churches' widespread culture of child rape was finally bubbling into view. There was a palpable disgust at what seemed like an endless parade of public officials and business leaders in collusion against the majority who had little or no access to influence. In canvassing support I was often confronted by how contemptuous young people were of civic leaders and politics in general. Across a spectrum of age and class, people told me there was absolutely no point trying to make a difference in society because nobody was listening, everything was corrupt, the fix was in. And in such an atmosphere of betrayal and deception you could hardly blame people for feeling cynical and disaffected, but this nihilism and disengagement really worried me. A bumper sticker of the time read: IF WE STOP VOTING, WILL THEY ALL JUST GO AWAY?

Luckily there were people out there angry or optimistic or just plain desperate enough to see things differently, and my time with Save Ningaloo exposed me to such a range of views and people that I still think of it as a significant part of my education. What the political comfort class and the pliant journos hovering around them see is a reality that conforms to their own limited interests; it's confined and shaped by their shared cynicism. They see an electorate made up of beasts and babies, people who want to be fed and stroked, who are passive, greedy and suspicious. When necessary, you can inflame them by frightening them or making them angry, but the best thing to do is to leave them alone and let them shop.

But I found that many people were curious and generous, happy to volunteer their time, their expertise – even their car or their house – for a good cause. I discovered that despite the consumer current of selfish insularity, there were still those interested in the common good. Many, many volunteers busted their boilers for Ningaloo. Some were there running off flyers, donning goofy turtle costumes, grinding out FOIs, showing us their scientific research, briefing us in hallways and carparks and airports for nearly three years. These folks were my midlife postgrad course in civics.

Our first public meeting, in September 2001, filled a 200-seat auditorium. From the wings I saw lots of grey hair and older faces, which surprised me. I'd been drafted to speak, pitched as the headline act, but I felt like a bit of an imposter. I was bait, really, something to attract the crowd so others could present the science and outline the politics and the challenge ahead. Here was my first major lesson in activism: we didn't just need to fill an auditorium, we had to get media coverage. And in order to bring the sharks, you need blood in the water. Without an eminent person or a crazy stunt to present in the hours before the daily deadline, there's next to no chance of getting a journo or, heaven help you, a TV crew to show up and give your cause some attention. It felt to me that I might be both – an eminent stunt about to fall flat. The second lesson in activism is to pretend this bait-and-switch routine is not really happening, and you must act as if it isn't because journos despise 'celebrity activists'. And gimmicks. The fact that they'll only show up if the celeb is wheeled out or the gimmick deployed is something they'd rather not have rubbed in their faces. The third lesson is not to take any of this personally, because they don't. Except the part about having the rules of the game openly acknowledged. Apparently that's offensive.

The evening turned out to be a bit of an organizational shambles. One journo turned up, got my picture and left after my little speech. He wasn't there long enough to see how passionate the audience became when scientists and planning specialists spoke, how the sudden availability of what was, in the end, pretty dry information, ignited them like a flame given oxygen. Afterwards we were inundated by offers of help from marine science students, pensioners and young parents. We were still only an idea but at least now a few hundred people shared it.

A tiny trickle of money came in. While the committee got on with the grinding procedural business of seeking out bureaucrats and experts and sifting through masses of government papers, a few bumper stickers were printed to give the campaign a public focus. Right from the start we could never print enough to keep up with demand.

As it slowly gathered momentum, Save Ningaloo began forming alliances with people in the Gascoyne region, in the communities closest to the proposed resort. Campaigners flew if they could, but often as not went up four to a car and shared motel rooms or tents. In Coral Bay the public bar was the only available meeting place. The locals may have looked like roughnecks – they could have been characters from a novel like *Dirt Music* – yet many of them, deckhands, divemasters, workers from the caravan parks and backpackers', were passionate about the environment and they knew more about the reef and the developer than anybody.

In Coral Bay and Exmouth, opposition to the resort ran at well over 90 percent. We were invited to speak at chambers of commerce and progress associations and I was apprehensive about how we'd be received, but a truly unexpected coalition was born. Rural business and urban greenies? Commercial fishermen and greenies? You bet. Outside every meeting, from the North West Cape to Cottesloe, there were Kombis and BMWs, bicycles and utes. Suddenly we had a movement wherein you'd find the facially pierced and the bark-knuckled. All preconceptions were pointless, though I was once kicked out of the Coral Bay pub for being barefoot after six p.m. There's a limit, I guess. On occasion I shared a plane with one or more of the developers. We made awkward but good-natured conversation; they seemed like decent enough blokes.

Newspaper and television stories about us began to appear. Radio presenters got curious. Even one of Perth's right-wing shock jocks gave us a fair hearing at first. The campaign's early success was piquing people's interest. And it seemed to me that ordinary sandgropers were getting to know Ningaloo by proxy. Better than that, they were starting to understand an ecosystem like this for what it is, a piece of the family silver, a common asset held in trust by government, one that did not automatically belong to speculators and developers. And soon people came to see that before such natural assets are given over to business concerns, an orderly, coherent process of evaluation must be gone through.

Very slowly, departmental advisers began to take meetings with us and then cabinet ministers graced us with a hearing. Our spokesperson, Paul Gamblin, was steely and concise under pressure. Behind the scenes, Dennis Beros and David Mackenzie agonized over every strategy and the crushing weight of detail. We knew we'd never have the access to government that business people routinely enjoy, so we tried to make the most of it on the rare occasions we got it. I shut up whenever possible and tried to look intelligent. I avoided every meeting I could. I learnt what a PowerPoint presentation was. Later, as we pitched to curious or sympathetic civic leaders and even captains of industry, I came to realize that PowerPoint is the lingua franca. The media wants grabs and so do the movers and shakers. Grabs and pictures. No details, no time!

There was a period, probably up until the moment we were taken seriously, when local media treated us with a mild, indulgent interest, partly because of my involvement as a minor celeb and failed recluse, and partly because it was a soft story – we were harmless. After we started to make some headway things got harder.

So we learnt to stage 'actions' on slow news days. Our signature stunt involved a troupe of vollies called the Ninga-turtles who gussied up in blue body stockings and wore plastic laundry baskets on their backs. They camped outside banks, MPs' offices, wherever they were needed. We learnt about timing and placement, to judge the career situations of journos and take account of the egos of their all-important editors, for they, not the public's right to know, are the crucial factor in deciding what is and what is not news. We had moles in newsrooms, friends who could warn us about the moods of certain news directors. I discovered more about some of these people than I ever wanted to know. Thankfully there were always a brave and curious few who covered the Ningaloo campaign impartially, but by and large, from the moment ordinary folks began to listen, we had to contend with a headwind.

The media is an ecosystem. Like the local political scene it's a food chain comparable to that on a coral reef. Smaller fish are afraid to upset the big swimmers. In a city as small and incestuous as Perth there are sharp lessons to be learnt. The news world is as toothy as it is twitchy. Beware the journo trying to distance himself from the idealism of his youth. Take note of the youthful reporter for whom idealism sounds like an art movement. Never forget how welcome mediocrity is in such a profession in such a place. But don't assume that the cynicism on view is held with any more sincerity than the utterances of parliamentarians. I guess I learnt these things on the job.

Having said all that, there are a lot of decent journos and hardworking pollies who want to do good but who are hopelessly constrained by circumstances beyond their control. If public advocacy teaches you anything, it's to find out who has real political responsibility and who is owed a favour. Learn who the idealists are in cabinet, and by that I mean people with genuine conviction. Watch out for those who will only ever jump the way the numbers are likely to fall. Don't assume that party politics are coherent. As with the media, make it your business to know who each member's real boss is. And never underestimate the role of paid lobbyists: they're the mercenaries in the mix. They make journos and backbenchers look like romantics. These are the people you're never told about at school. Sometimes, in Perth especially, they are not content to be the conduits of power, they aspire to be power itself.

Don't make assumptions about anyone based on their job or their clothes or the suburb they live in. The stockbroker in the Jag could be an ally. The lady in the twinset and pearls might be weary of being misunderstood and secretly ashamed of what her husband does for a living. Don't give up on the shabby older journo hoisting his gut from the company car; he might have a memory and a soft spot for the little people.

Running a campaign, I discovered, is not just a community-building exercise but also a short, sometimes brutal lesson in your own personal prejudices. At a remote station in the midwest I met a wealthy gent who was curious about what we were up to. We walked for an hour or two through a eucalypt woodland and agreed to meet in Perth a few weeks later. At that meeting he brought along a friend. They were men of industry who loved nature. They each cut us a very big cheque and kept us alive as a group.

Our second public meeting crammed the Fremantle town hall in April 2002. Fifteen hundred people came. National newspapers, TV and radio covered it, and afterwards citizens peppered the press and pollies with letters. Vollies ran fundraisers, auctions and stalls. They painted banners and took up positions at railway stations to hand out flyers. MPs from every party wanted to meet us and offer discreet advice. Members of unions, clubs and churches gave quiet support. Perth streets were awash with our blue bumper stickers.

But as the response from local media cooled we were forced to do more and more of our advocacy online. In the days before Twitter and Facebook the internet was a fresh field for activism. Save Ningaloo was one of the first environmental campaigns to harness some of its potential. Without the website that Dave Graham, a Queensland volly, set up and maintained in our name, it would have been impossible to get information out fast enough and often enough to keep the enterprise going.

In response to our progress the developer's PR company began to crank out the spin in earnest and they gained real traction in the Perth press and on radio. The shock jocks gave them a handy platform. Things started to feel rocky.

And then we had a few strokes of luck. The novel I'd published the year before won several literary prizes. These brought media interest and I was able to turn that attention to Ningaloo. When the book won a WA Premier's Prize and Geoff Gallop was booked to hand the cheque over in person, it was too good an opportunity to miss. But miss it I did. I was working overseas at the time. Nevertheless I accepted the money by proxy and donated it to the campaign. A stunt, of course, but by then I'd learnt how these things work. The money and momentum bought the campaign a few more weeks' grace.

But for much of late 2002 stunts were all we had. Anneke de Graaf was our stunt-mistress and pied piper. The Ninga-turtles ambushed pollies with friendly and comical actions and sometimes TV crews showed up. People sculpted huge turtles on city beaches for press photographers. Feeling the cool wind from the *West Australian*, the state's monopoly daily, we took our story to suburban newspapers and community radio. By then we were nearly broke, flannelling away and holding on for the decision of the Environmental Protection Authority whose recommendation would probably indicate which way the political cards were to fall.

This was our lowest ebb. We were jittery and exhausted. People's families and work lives were under awful strain. Several folk were working sixty hours a week for nothing. We were scrounging, pleading for money, fed up, obsessed, not sleeping. Ningaloo dominated our lives and we were close to the burnout that every developer counts on. In desperation, we wrote dozens of letters to prominent Australians at home and abroad to beg for help. The response was astounding. First to put his huge hand up was NBA star Luc Longley. Then other sportspeople, actors, scientists and rockers signed up as supporters, lifting the morale of the faithful and exciting the curiosity of the public.

Toni Collette offered herself as media bait and the scornful press came running. We took Toni north to Ningaloo, and with the help of awestruck locals gave her a long swim with manta rays a few metres from where the enormous hole would be dug if the developer had its way. Toni spoke passionately about the reef and against the resort. Images of that encounter went national and overseas.

Within weeks, the EPA brought down its recommendation on the proposal, but its language was so choked with bureaucratic doublespeak that nobody knew whether it meant yes or no. The developer claimed victory. The *West Australian* editorialized in favour of the resort and took the time to brand those citizens opposing it as part of 'a presumptuous . . . self-proclaimed environmental elite'. We hadn't been imagining the antipathy. With the emergence of that weasel word, 'elite', I thought the jig was up. The shock jocks loved it. Finally someone was talking *their* language again.

But the campaign now represented so many diverse people that the slur never stuck. In retrospect, the furore over the EPA's decision and the baldness of the *West*'s editorial did us a huge favour.

It mobilized supporters we didn't even know we had. It aroused indignation. People helped buy time on FM youth radio. An email campaign began and in the weeks to follow twenty thousand people wrote to Gallop. T-shirts appeared and eighty thousand stickers went all over Australia and abroad.

On 1 December 2002 fifteen thousand people marched through the streets of Fremantle. The local mayor said it was the biggest public demonstration there in living memory. This was no shadowy, mythical elite. This was rate-paying Australia, school-going Australia, suburban Australia. A phalanx of marchers a kilometre long brought the city to a standstill. Famous footballers walked alongside teachers and retirees and schoolkids. The same day, hundreds of like-minded souls gathered in Coral Bay and Exmouth. In all three places it was a peaceful, colourful, passionate gathering. The whole of Fremantle's Esplanade was a mass of faces and banners. I'd never spoken to so many people at once before. I felt a terrible responsibility, that I'd helped give them hope for something I was by no means certain we could deliver. But the day was a triumph. It was clear people wanted their natural heritage safeguarded.

And it was soon obvious that public passion about the reef was not ephemeral. A couple of months after the rally, when the Seattle grunge band Pearl Jam came to town, lead singer Eddie Vedder took time during the performance to mention the plight of Ningaloo. Vedder said ruefully after the concert that the crowd responded to mention of the reef more intensely than to any of his songs. But would anybody in power listen?

In the end, sensing the mood, the premier undertook direct responsibility for the Ningaloo decision. In June that year, in the space of two days alone, he received more than eight thousand emails. Each of those was copied to his entire cabinet and the government's computer system felt the strain. It was bigger than anything we could have expected.

Despite vicious smears generated by the developer's dwindling supporters, including some choice things said under parliamentary privilege, I began to believe we might actually have a chance. Each of us fluctuated on this point hourly. It was torture.

Things came to a head in a hurry. The EPA appeals process finished. The information gathering was done. The countless all-nighters by unheralded and so often unheeded scientists were over and the verdict was imminent. When to massive acclaim the premier canned the resort once and for all the *West* editorialized approvingly. Those mythical elites were forgotten.

One of the first emails of congratulation to reach our office that morning was from an outer-suburbs panelbeater. There were jubilant and sometimes tearful calls from all over the world, and weeks later the deluge continued. On the night of the announcement a stranger with a biker beard kept kissing me. There was a kind of delirium in the air. The streets were full of Camrys, delivery trucks and tradesmen's utes bearing emblematic blue stickers. Within days the government launched an impossibly lavish advertising campaign to publicize its decision.

Something quite out of the ordinary had happened. A bunch of amateurs with the help of a couple of battleworn campaigners had inspired citizens to get involved in a decision about their common wealth, their natural heritage. At least a hundred thousand people had taken part in some way, almost every one of them a volunteer.

How did we succeed when most community campaigns fail? I am not really sure. And it would be naive and foolhardy to think that this battle has been won for all time. We didn't save Ningaloo Reef, we just improved the odds of its survival a little. We encouraged the state to redraft its coastal planning regime and perhaps emboldened a few other Australians to preserve their natural estate. Our efforts were sometimes raggedy, but they were always inclusive; we sought to be the broadest possible church, marrying sober science and the passion of citizens defending their country. We had the strange new power of the internet to bring people together cheaply. And we were lucky to be mounting a campaign that began as a new and relatively idealistic premier came to power and which peaked as his government passed its mid-term point and became vulnerable.

Perhaps our success had something to do with the rise of green politics in this country and abroad. It seemed to me at the time that this movement might have been named after the wrong colour, that nothing was as likely to stir the imagination of Australians so much as the sea. With Save Ningaloo we stumbled onto the only sacred site in the mind of mainstream Australia – the beach. Somehow the childhood memory of clean seas and the workaday longing for respite in salty air and the dream of retiring to a still-living coast resonate in the suburbs like nothing else.

Every civic struggle is different in its details and its timing, but I learnt that to give itself half a chance and make itself heard, the advocacy group needs both visionaries and hard-arses, fetishists for detail and broad-stroke types, community builders and political animals alike. You need generous people, rich and poor – kind ones, too. Like it or not, you'll require some thick-skinned celebs and a few silly stunts. Perhaps most of all you need group discipline. The luck required to pull off something lasting cannot be so easily sourced.

Not everything I learnt as a rabble-rouser was welcome information, but one thing sticks out. You can still appeal to people's better instincts. People do believe in the common good. For that they will make sacrifices. They'll blossom as comrades and do difficult things for love. And in the face of every ugly revelation that pours from the news day and night, I'll hold onto that.

---

* In 2004, 34 percent of Ningaloo was gazetted as sanctuary. In 2011 the entire reef was added to the World Heritage register.

Letter from
a Strong Place

In memory of Peter Bartlett

After dinner these days it's still light enough to walk down through the ash wood behind the cottage, climb the stone wall of the old bull paddock and spend half an hour checking rabbit snares along the hedges. If the evening's clement enough I'll ramble through other fields and into the lanes that wind up to where the Slieve Bloom Mountains float behind the mist. All along the way choughs will be trafficking in the hawthorn. Down at the swampy bottomland the sweet smell of peat fires overcomes even the reek of silage, and house lights are coming on here and there. Dogs bark and cattle bellow in their barns. As I make my way up from the valley floor, the grim shadow of Leap Castle is always in sight, plain against the marbled sky. I climb stiles and slip through hedges, crossing soaks and pastures until I reach the Hanging Tree in the field beneath the ramparts of the estate where I turn for the Gate Lodge that's been home to us for the past five months. Coming up the freshly gravelled walk I see the slate roof through the trees and think of the night ahead: a cottage full of books, a turf fire, a strong pot of tea.

I never planned to be in Ireland, the opportunity arose by chance. I was home in Perth one evening in 1987 when a stranger phoned to offer me a few months' residence in his castle in County Offaly. He'd read about me having been granted a travel bursary and thought I might enjoy the experience. I tried to explain that the Marten Bequest probably wouldn't run to the renting of gothic castles, but the caller went on to say his pile was a ruin; what he was really offering was the Gate Lodge and its library of rare books and first editions, somewhere to live and work for a while. I'd have the place to myself for half a year, all I needed to do was kick in some money for the power and heating – how did that sound? To me it sounded preposterous, but I accepted his generous offer and I've been here all winter with my wife and small son, and now it's spring and we're already mentally getting ready to leave.

Leap is a vivid place. That's what stays in my mind as I go through the accountancy of settling up, shedding paperbacks and heavy coats and boots that will be no use in Greece, our next destination. While I gather I have Irish ancestry somewhere on my mother's side I certainly don't feel any Celtic pull. But I like strong places. This has been an exceptionally damp one, strange as well.

Each morning after breakfast I gather my writing kit, pull on my wellies and make the short climb to Spencer's Cottage. The Gate Lodge is a snug and comfortably renovated place, but the bothy at the crest of the hill is a far more rustic affair. In the mornings its stone floors are like the bottom of a freshly drained swimming pool, and despite the coats of whitewash I've given the inside, the walls are going back to the creeping shades of green that greeted me when I first arrived. For the past few months the kitchen at Spencer's has been my workroom. At the beginning of every day I light a fire in the hearth, straighten the damp-curling pages of the novel I'm writing and wait a few minutes until things dry out a little. Spencer was a gardener at the estate, and from his front door you can see his former master's domain, from the Gate Lodge pressed up against the old estate walls to the ruined stables, the roofless gothic wing and the castle keep looming over it all.

I'm conscious that everything I see from here is named and storied, not just the wells and wishing trees and cryptic dirt mounds, but every hedge, it seems, every wood and boreen. All of it heavy with a past that's palpable and rich, moving in its way, even if it doesn't quite mean anything to me personally.

When the mixture of turf, coal, larch and oak burns hot enough to cheer the room a bit, I sit at the little deal table and get down to the daily business of coaxing a thousand words out of the ether. There are Aboriginal bark paintings on the wall, first editions of Randolph Stow on the spindle chair by the fire, all the property of the estate's Australian owner, Peter Bartlett. A former diplomat who seems to be in London one day and Chicago the next, he has amassed quite a collection in his travels. The Gate Lodge is packed with art and books. Above our bed there's a framed letter in James Joyce's hand, on the sidetable a rare edition of Yeats.

The words come steadily, as they have since Paris when the story began to feel as if it wanted to be told. In January and February when the weather was bitter, the work was arduous; the words presented themselves faithfully enough, but the cold made them hard to form on the page. My hands ached, the paper was boggy. Some mornings I headed uphill to Spencer's in sleet or snow. One day my wife arrived at the door in a flap, too breathless to do anything more than point back toward the Gate Lodge where the chimney burnt bright orange against the grey sky like the flare of an offshore gas platform. This year we've seen our first snow, experienced our first chimney fire, and come to understand the virtue of the wellington boot. And all the time I'm writing about hot, flyblown places like Geraldton, Margaret River and Perth in another hemisphere. I spend half the day in two places at once, which is to say no place at all. But whenever my concentration lapses, or I need to step behind the stone barn for a pee, my eye will be drawn to the castle and there's no mistaking where I am.

The sight of Leap is not neutral. This month the keep has an uncanny sheen to it, not so much a result of the turning of the season as the work of the glazing team who've finally finished up and gone. For the first time in sixty years or more, the tower has glass in its windows and this has confounded the local rooks and jackdaws which have been roosting in the mighty hulk for untold generations, wheeling and swooping through its many orifices without obstruction. For a few weeks now we've been collecting their broken bodies from the grounds, and new blood smears show up daily, like spring blossoms. The windows are too high to wipe clean, so the stains remain. We bag the birds and bin them with a wry acceptance. It's a macabre domestic routine, but we've been here long enough to find it bizzarely fitting. Leap is like that; you can't look at the place without feeling ensnared by it. The estate is probably more entangled in myths than it is in rampant ivy, but even if you're entirely ignorant of its past the castle evinces a brooding presence, the sort that leans on you a little. Like all strong places it will, I imagine, leave a mark on me. It's certainly had a peculiar effect on others over the years.

In *Dance of the Quick and the Dead,* a frothy compendium of horrors he published in 1936, Sacheverell Sitwell said: 'The intensity of this strange place exceeds in its details anything that the most dramatic mind could design,' and the excitable Sacheverell should know. When he wasn't being charmed by Oswald Mosley's fascist prognostications he spent his considerable leisure time chasing spooks and poltergeists. His accounts and many others by ecto-plasmic enthusiasts like him line the shelves of the Gate Lodge at Leap. They're tosh of course, but there's no question that the castle has been a troubled place.

The initial keep at Leap is said to have been built by the O'Carrolls in 1380 to guard the pass from the Slieve Bloom Mountains into Tipperary. It was consolidated and extended as a tower house in the 1500s and over the centuries gothic wings were added. Redoubts of this sort often have spotty histories, but the O'Carrolls were a rugged lot and Leap's annals are particularly lurid. Mercenaries murdered rather than paid, prisoners thrown from the battlements. Rivals were poisoned and awkward family members bricked into the tower walls forever. The family's most legendary assassination was a fratricide. In 1532 Teige O'Carroll murdered his brother Thaddeus in the chapel of the great hall. Thaddeus, a priest, was reportedly before the altar saying mass as he was dispatched, and thereafter that chamber was known as 'the Bloody Chapel'.

When I arrived at Leap that room, the size of a dance hall, was knee-deep in twigs and nesting detritus. Rooks whirred from its darkest corners. Wind howled through the open windows and rain misted through in eddies; it was like something out of a Monk Lewis shocker. The room has been cleaned out in recent months, but it's still not a pleasant place in which to linger. In one corner there's an alcove you need to approach with care to avoid stumbling over a precipice, because the trapdoor that once covered it is long gone. The gap in the floor drops away to the oubliette, a dungeon into which unsuspecting victims were pitched and left to die. In the late nineteenth century, three cartloads of bones were removed from it and buried in consecrated ground. According to local chroniclers, 'bits of several old watches were found among the remains'.

I've spent a good deal of time in the castle keep. On fine afternoons I sit out on the battlements and when the rain mists in across the valley I poke about in the halls and chambers below. And I don't mind admitting that on its day the place can give me the yips. Perhaps because it's open to the sky, the gothic wing seems more melancholy than eerie. We probably shouldn't even go in there, it's the least stable part of the castle, but my little boy and I spend hours clambering through its vine-snarls, marvelling at the ash trees that have twisted their way up through its windows. He also loves the nook on the second floor of the keep that features a rudimentary toilet. We take turns sending imaginary 'parcels' to the yard below, putting the long-lost O'Carroll pigs into a frenzy. The only place I find myself hurrying through at all times of the day is the spiral staircase. Even with its new electric lighting it's both cold and close, an uncomfortable place in which to be alone.

So I admit that there's a distinct atmosphere about Leap. All the gothic tropes are present and accounted for, and of course locals have been in my ear about its legion of ghouls and ghosts since the day I arrived. There's no doubting it's been the scene of many horrors, and those that can be verified are lurid enough, but I'm impatient with all the breathless mythmaking, the buffing of the place's reputation as some kind of occult hotspot. Ireland seems haunted enough without succubi and shrieking shades.

Lots of Leap's tall stories have taken on the treacherous smoothness of the tale too often told. All the kinks of plausibility have been ironed out of them; they begin to sound like every other spook account you've heard. Many have their origins in real events and characters, and like so many stories of the 'weird and unnatural' they're what gossip turns into. People hereabouts are fervent storytellers and brilliant embroiderers. Most of them have been hearing and telling stories about Leap since infancy and they spin yarns with an unsettling combination of peasant guile and gullibility. The place and its legends have had a long roster of enthusiastic promoters over the years – including Daisy Bates who was born in nearby Roscrea and is said to have told stories of the castle's spectres – though few tale spinners were as influential as Mildred Darby, the mistress of the house in the late nineteenth and early twentieth centuries.

It seems odd but also oddly fitting that so much of Leap's paranormal reputation should have been burnished so faithfully by a hardy no-nonsense Protestant of some education. In fact the castle was an anti-papist stronghold from 1649, when Jonathon Darby, a Cromwellian soldier, was granted it for services rendered. Two hundred years later his descendant and namesake, John Nelson Darby, was one of the founders of the austere evangelical sect the Plymouth Brethren. Having concluded that the advent of the telegraph was a signal that the End of Days was imminent, J.N. inspired the apocalyptic obsessions that have kept many fundamentalists busy for a century and more. Despite, or perhaps because of, having married into such a family, Mildred Darby was a keen dabbler in the occult and wrote febrile accounts of having seen the famous 'Elemental' with her own eyes. Writing as Andrew Merry in the *Occult Review* in 1909, she claimed: 'The thing was about the size of a sheep. Thin, guanting, shadowy . . . its face was human, to be more accurate inhuman. Its lust in its eyes which seemed half decomposed in black cavities stared into mine.' And so on.

Leap soon outgrew its local reputation and was often spoken of as 'the most haunted castle in the British Isles'. This seems to have become a source of pride to the locals. In the pubs and front rooms hereabouts they remain eager to tell of their own encounters, which invariably entail things seen at a distance – an unexplained illumination, a pale figure in the field beneath the Hanging Tree, an unholy stink by the well – but rarely require the witness to have actually been on the premises. The closer to closing time these tales are told, the less truly felt and more high-toned they sound. They seem to be drawn from a universal pool. Mostly I'm reasonably sure the locals are just engaging in their favourite entertainment – getting drunk and frightening themselves half to death – but most of them are genuinely wary of the place and plenty believe it's cursed. I've heard eerie accounts from sober women, Legion of Mary types, whose stories feel like burdens rather than party treats. I've met people who swear they wouldn't set foot in the place in a million years. And I have to admit I've seen and heard some things in the past few months that I'm not sure I can explain. Like the time all the taps came on in the Gate Lodge. All of them simultaneously, in the wee hours. And the time our son reported hearing voices in the roof space. People, he said, were laughing and farting up there half the night. The former was genuinely unsettling. But the latter sounded to me like a regular family haunting.

But not all Leap stories are about ghosts. The seancer Mrs Darby also wrote an account of the Sunday in 1922 when the IRA bombed and burned her home to a ruin. She wasn't there, as it happens, but Richard Dawkins, the caretaker, was. Until a few years ago the rebel who led the eleven-man 'raid' was reportedly living just down the road. I've spoken with people who claim to be the children and grandchildren of the bombers. All of them are keen to see the castle restored 'to bring life back to the area'. Many played around the grounds and in the ruins as children – but never at night – and though the castle was thoroughly looted soon after the bombing, they were forbidden to take anything from the site. Earlier this year, my son's little friends from a nearby farm found two candles that had been burned in the newly renovated tower for Saint Brigid's Day. They showed me the stubs and asked if they could keep them. They were melted candles – no odds to me. I sent the kids home but they were soon back. Their father had forbidden the candles to be brought into the house. 'Daddy says there's the divils in em,' one said. Maybe it was their father's way of making sure they didn't get light-fingered. If not, one wonders who the Republicans thought they were burning down in '22, the Proddies or the Divil himself. I guess they weren't too keen on that distinction, then or now. In any case the Darbys never lived at Leap again. Its care fell to the gardener, Spencer, whose cottage I work in every day and whose personal effects were still in the place when I arrived.

In January the little bothy was a reeking ruin. Joe Sullivan, the Banagher builder who's helping restore and remodel the castle for Peter Bartlett, helped me clean the hovel out and patch it up for a work space. There's supposed to be a secret tunnel linking castle and cottage, but I've never looked for it, perhaps for fear of finding it. Anyhow, I have a novel to finish.

But in the afternoons I have a kid to amuse, too, and in recent weeks there's always been something going on at the castle, more tractors and machinery to entertain him with, more glint-eyed men in cloth caps for him to pester. Some days we watch the cellars being emptied of rubble. Other times we stand in the freshly timbered gallery and watch Joe swing huge beams through the curves of the vaulted ceiling. For two days, as trucks backed in and tipped loads of blue metal at our feet, we helped rebuild the driveway, spreading the gravel with rakes as the rain slanted in from the west. It was as chaotic and frenetic as a military operation, and we were an unlikely outfit – a few genuine labourers, a couple of visitors from London, the kid and me – like a bunch of rogues building a runway for a landing that sounded too fanciful even for Leap. But the word was, Peter Bartlett was flying in from somewhere. He was having a party for his fortieth birthday. Guests were coming from all over and they couldn't be expected to wade through 100 metres of mud and builder's sand in order to reach the threshold.

Peter bought the castle in 1974, as he tells it, 'for the price of a house in Nollamara', a working-class suburb of Perth. His mother was an O'Bannon, a name common in the annals of the Leap, and he said he felt connected to the building the moment he saw it. Once the first stage of restoration is complete in a few months' time, he'll take up residence in the keep. Garrulous and indefatigable, he's a generous and passionate man, the kind of livewire who can hold forth eloquently on any subject until all hours. More than once, having heard him fall suddenly silent in the middle of a sentence, I've looked across the fireside to see him canted back in his wing chair fast asleep, with a mug of tea still balanced on his knee and a half-eaten slice of soda bread clamped in his fist. He speaks of 'bringing positive feelings' to Leap, of 'healing' it by living well here and having others live happily around him. He says he's not bothered about the ghosts, though he's taken the trouble to have a kind of multi-faith exorcism of sorts conducted. He plans to fill the place with books and art, friends and music, and for a week, using a tractor and a hay trailer, Joe and I have been ferrying antiques, Persian rugs, candelabra and crates of books up from a storage shed near Lissanerin.

Peter is a man of antic impulses and infectious energy. He's a maker of friends, a midwife to the friendships of others. 'I want,' he says, 'to make people's dreams a reality.' He's consumed by the notion of continuing Leap's story and changing its course for the better, and it looks as if he's likely to do both. On his birthday the castle keep was full of music for the first time in more than sixty years. Visitors flew in from several time zones. Friends drove down from Dublin, from Birr and Banagher, from Kinnitty and Roscrea, and locals from farms and hamlets all across the valley came walking down the drive, many for the first time. From its front steps to the battlements overhead, the castle was lit up like a paddle-steamer. Many pints were poured and drunk in its freshly swept halls. Poems were recited, telegrams read aloud. It was like a cross between a country wedding and a grand-final shindig. Strangers locked arms and danced and laughed and sang. Guests traded songs in friendly rivalry. Called upon to sing 'Waltzing Matilda' I made a hash of it. The party went on until the early hours and I never heard a ghost joke all night. It was a fine and happy occasion and before dawn it had produced several new Leap stories, some of them louche indeed.

Here where every field and some trees have names, where walls and cottages have names, where a cluster of houses has a collective name to distinguish it from the cluster 500 yards down the valley, place is as serious a proposition as religion. In fact the two are bound together in a way that's both alien and very familiar to me. I count myself lucky to have been here to see and feel all these things, to meet these people, but I feel an ache now, a kind of build-up that is not simply an accumulation of sensations. More than just the constant brooding mass of the castle leaning out at me every hour, it's a weight of story that's almost burdensome. This is not my place; it's bursting with stories but they're not mine to tell. My myths were handed down in suburban streets by the sea, stories of fishermen and jockeys and superhuman women riding in sidecars. I'm a New Worlder, a coastdweller, and this landlocked valley, this world of niches and hedges and low skies, is making me a little claustrophobic.

A few days ago I woke with a light shining in my face. I thought I'd fallen asleep reading and left the bedside light on. But no, it was the sun shining in the window, warm and strong and clean for the first time since we arrived. Spring had come, and it made me think of home.

Up here at Spencer's Cottage, I drag the biro across the page and try to spin the legends and the voices I grew up with into a house of my own. I think of my grandmother sending me up the ladder into the fig tree, hear her voice as she gallops her way through a bit of Browning, a dash of Longfellow. I remember the stories she told as I dropped figs into her bucket. We have our own marvels and ghosts. I have my own stories to tell. A house that sighs and breathes, pushes and pulls, a place of savagery and healing. It's an unlikely idea, but I'm caught in it now. I'll push on and see.

* Not long after these impressions were first set down I was at a dinner in Kinnitty where someone visiting from the coast recounted recently waking at night to see a train of lights on the beach below. As she stood at the window they passed silently, bobbing and dancing until they were obscured by cliffs. It was an unsettling sight. She thought these lights resembled torch flames held aloft by horsemen. In the morning she went down to the strand and saw no sign of their passage. Perhaps it was ball lightning; she didn't know what to make of it. The story stayed with me. It was, I suspect, the germ of what would some years later become a novel. *The Riders* was the book about Ireland I never intended to write.

   The novel I was writing at Leap was *Cloudstreet*.

   Peter Bartlett moved into the castle keep and lived there happily for several months. But he grew ill that same year and returned to Australia for treatment. He died soon after. We were living back in Australia by then. I was on my way to visit him in Safety Bay when I heard the news.

   Leap Castle was bought by the musician Sean Ryan, who has continued the work of restoration.

Chasing Giants

In winter the humpbacks are so close we can hear them breathing. On calm nights my wife and I listen to them crash and leap about as we lie in bed. When a whale slaps its tail against the ocean's surface the noise it makes is peculiarly solid. It's the sound of precision engineering doing its thing with confidence and satisfaction, like the deep, luxuriant noise of an expensive car door closing. Think of a bookie climbing into the Bentley after another day at the track – *thwunk*.

It's hard to stay focused on work during whale season when you hear them all day, see their pillars of vapour from the kitchen window. As a distraction they're worse than the fridge.

Whenever we can, when the wind drops and the gulf glasses off, my wife and I grab the big paddleboards and pick our way through the spinifex to the water's edge. Flat-water paddling is good exercise and generally quite a meditative activity, but most of the time I do it to catch a glimpse of megafauna – I can't help myself – and if we don't encounter whales, manta rays or dugongs, there'll be something smaller to see: turtles, tuskfish, schools of mullet. And there are always surprises: a bobbing knot of sea snakes, a Spanish mackerel that seems to fall from the sky, or a juvenile whale shark pootling along in the shallows long after its fellows have headed north toward Indonesia and the Philippines.

This winter we had our first sighting of sousas. A close cousin of the Chinese white dolphin, *Sousa sahulensis*, or the Australian humpback dolphin, was only described as a species in 2014, and it was exciting to encounter them a few hundred metres from home. To my eye they seemed stumpy, breaching in hurried jerks, and they were hard to keep track of. Unlike the more outgoing bottlenose dolphin, the sousa is shy, even cryptic. A bottlenose will often dart and frolic beneath you to get your attention, to satisfy its curiosity, but as we discovered, a sousa will most likely keep its distance, veering off or diving away when there's a chance of things getting personal. We spent an hour playing cat-and-mouse with the pod and never made eye contact. They didn't want to play.

I've had a passion for cetaceans since I was kid. I'd hardly outgrown my devotion to *Flipper* on TV when I moved to a town where sperm and humpback whales were being hunted to the brink of extinction. Visits to the flensing deck gave me my first intimate look at these immense and majestic mammals. For many years the closest I got to such creatures were the times I shared waves with dolphins in the surf, but in the 1990s, once the whaling stopped and the populations began to recover, I surfed with southern rights in the break and felt the songs of humpbacks ring in my body like the pulses of an MRI. And in the new century, when a 22-metre blue whale – the largest creature on the planet – washed up dead on a remote beach near our place on the midwest coast I was literally all over it, regardless of the cheesy stench. It rotted away foully for years, sloughing vast carpet rolls of blubber, spilling ribs and organs and oozing oil all over the white sand, until all that was left were a few tide-jumbled vertebrae that brought to mind the aftermath of a brawl in a beer garden. Even its dissolution was epic.

So, I confess, I'm a bit of an enthusiast. The sight of humpbacks steaming by on their annual migration is no novelty now, but it thrills me anew every time. When a whale writhes into the air at a distance I get an instant shot of adrenaline. Some days in winter the water erupts with bomb-like percussions. It's like someone's set off a minefield out there with all those welters of spray, all those shining slabs twisting in the air as if blown out of the water.

Binoculars are fine; I give mine a flogging. But when the migration's on I want to be out there amongst it, and as often as I can I paddle out to meet the convoy.

Early in the season, excitement tends to outstrip common sense. It doesn't matter if the pod is already level with our place and hopelessly far out, I'll give chase anyway, telling myself I'll catch up in the end. What this actually requires of course is being able to paddle twice as fast as a 15-metre mammal can swim at idling pace, and keeping it up for the best part of an hour. And believe me, even the lazy cetacean cruising speed of 3 or 4 knots is hard to sustain for long, especially for the middle-aged male tending toward the portly. The first time I tried it I felt like I was re-enacting the final reel of *The Blues Brothers*. This was not strictly a car chase, but it was a hectic and absurd pursuit every bit as overblown and underscripted as the film's. It was a dumb thing to attempt, but like Dan Aykroyd and John Belushi, I'd come to believe I was on a mission from God.

When I finally drew near the pack, blistered and running with sweat, the sun was setting on the ranges and I was kilometres from home. My longsuffering wife, who'd sensibly given up the chase half an hour before, was but a speck on the water behind me. I knew I didn't have much time, but for ten minutes I idled along at a prudent and legal distance as two calves turned to check me out and their mothers rounded up to wait and watch. The youngsters rolled and twisted, making currents with their glistening bodies. They slapped their tails and lifted their heads to take me in and if it hadn't been for the fact that darkness was falling and my house was already lost in the gloom of the desert plain, I'd have stayed for hours.

Later in the season I'm a bit smarter about my whale watching and by then the pods are in so close there's no need for grand chases. In September, on a dropping tide, we paddled out through phalanxes of lagoon rays and squid the colour of molten gold to meet a group little more than a stone's throw from shore. Ahead of them, like an exuberant escort, a posse of sousa dolphins leapt and twirled, chiacking and showing off to their giant cousins. Of course in deducing the sousas had no interest in play I hadn't really considered that they just might not want to play with *me*. They were like kids wired on red cordial. They were enormously entertaining, but they were also handy for gauging the whales' movements. Whenever the big pod dived you could anticipate the point at which they'd surface again because ten or even twenty seconds before they breached, the dolphins would leap in a series of pairs, left and right, curling outward, mugging and spinning like jesters before the court.

That September day the whales slowed; you could feel them easing back on the throttle. As if they'd sensed us and become curious. My wife hung back wisely. Naturally I went in closer. As they let go their breaths, clouding me with gamy vapour, they groaned operatically, and in the muscular depth of that noise you could register the remarkable mass of their bodies. They paused and began to make eye contact, taking me in languorously. It was obvious the adults were considering, making decisions, directing their young. However many times you experience this, it's unsettling. For here is an embodied consciousness on a scale you can't quite assimilate. No matter how familiar you are with the scientific facts and abstract conjectures, it's a shock to encounter this up close. Nothing can prepare you for it.

The youngsters were particularly curious. And when they circled back on me I found myself caught up – caught out, really – because I was no longer keeping a safe or legal distance from the action. I wasn't impinging on their space; if anything, it was the other way round. They rolled and lifted their pecs. They ran leisurely figure-eights around me. The water was shallow and the resultant eddies made it hard to keep my feet.

Now, to have a whale beneath you is a thrill. But to have one slide under you in shallow water is a little nerve-racking. Once I saw what was happening I lifted my paddle and braced myself as best I could. All around me were footprints – churning fields of turbulence – and the dolphins, out skylarking amongst the adult whales at the perimeter, were not going to be any use to me in predicting where the calves were likely to breach. Then, beneath me and slightly ahead, I saw a shadow. For a moment it looked like the profile of a whale swimming across my path along the seabed. But we were in only 5 metres of water and the scale was all wrong. A moment later I realized it wasn't the whole creature I was seeing. This was only its tail. Right beneath me. Getting bigger by the instant, scything up underfoot.

I got ready to jump but at the last moment the calf tilted slightly and its mighty tail broke the surface barely a metre to the left of me. It was slick and black, looking all of a sudden as big as the tailplane of a fighter jet, and as it rose before me, above me, glistening in the sun and shedding water in trickles and droplets, I was in no doubt it could have swatted me dead in an instant. But the tail just hung there, almost perpendicular, while I staggered, flailing like a tightrope artist with only the paddle for a balance pole. After a pause and a moment's inversion, the calf dived, breached just ahead of me and with a throaty bawl coursed away toward the adults.

We paddled homeward, chirping with excitement, swapping observations and laughing at our luck. As we came in across the sandy flats, we startled a few blacktip sharks that had begun their annual aggregation. They were slick and twitchy, each about a metre long, and as they bolted they left festive puffs of silt in their wake. It was like coming home to a fireworks display. It seemed fitting. It was that kind of day.

The Demon Shark

I
Holy and Silent:
On Peter Matthiessen's *Blue Meridian*

If there is a unique cultural inheritance for those who grow up in much of this country it might be nothing more or less complicated than a sense of space, a way of being that Les Murray wryly calls 'the quality of sprawl'. Raised on the beaches of Western Australia I was an heir to this glorious and often unexamined amplitude. There was such an open field before me: the long white beaches, the teeming rockpools and the limestone reefs where I chipped abalone with a screwdriver and a string bag at low tide. The sea itself was too big to be assimilated in a geographical sense; it had more in common with outer space than terrestrial habitat. It was so strange and elusive yet its sensual familiarity made it feel like home. Being in the sea or near it did weird things to my body. All that movement, lush and harsh, all the life, seen and unseen, set my mind a-smoulder. The oceanic scale of things often scrambled my head; the immensity and beauty were too much to process. My thoughts sputtered and fizzed, as hopeless and fragmentary as those of a besotted lover. At day's end, after eight hours in the water, I could only think of more. In its way it *was* love. As a beach kid I knew there were things to be leery of – sucking currents, stings and jagged corals – but I still felt the sea was utterly benign. It was as intimate and mysterious as a mother. I didn't fear it as much as the prospect of being denied access to it. I was an innocent in my Eden.

Well, that was before someone took my cousins and me to the Astor to see Carol Reed's *Oliver!* Traumatic as musicals can be for a boy, I can hardly blame the movie itself, though it did feature the exceptionally unpleasant-looking Oliver Reed who, as Bill Sikes, compounded the early poor impression by beating poor Nancy to death with a club. Apparently family entertainment isn't what it used to be. This was the most violent scene I'd ever encountered in a drama to that point, but I was already pretty stirred up because before the main feature my cousins and I had sat through the trailer for a documentary called *Savage Shadows.*

Savage Shadows was, in large part, a re-enactment of the day in 1964 when Victorian skindiver Henri Bource lost his left leg to a great white shark. The sight of this man being hauled aboard a small boat, threshing and flailing in a slather of blood was, to say the least, galvanizing. At the age of ten I was too young and too shocked to realize that Mr Bource was only acting. The voice-over told us this was real; it had actually happened. And it all looked authentic to me: the hole of his screaming mouth, the whites of his eyes, the outrage of his actual stump. The trailer itself can't have been more than a few minutes in duration but its graphic imagery and sensational presentation left a deep impression, one that many millions of swimmers were to feel a few years later when Spielberg's *Jaws* sent folks lurching from the cinema – and the water – in horror.

The benign sea suddenly had its Satan. Of course this trope was an Australian tradition, but until that afternoon in 1970 I hadn't really internalized it. Afterwards the water was never quite the same.

'The shadow of sharks,' writes Peter Matthiessen, 'is the shadow of death, and they call forth dim ultimate fears. Yet there is something holy in their silence.' As a child in the cinema I understood this first proposition in an instant. It took longer to grasp the wisdom of the second.

In the wake of that cold, sweaty minute in the Astor it wasn't as if I was consciously and constantly afraid of sharks but they were a liminal presence thereafter, something lurking in the water beyond the pleasure of the moment. It hardly ruined my life but it did divide the mind in a way that was new. For along with the creaturely joy of snorkelling in the open water behind the reef there was now a twitch of anxiety. The eye searched for something even when I wasn't looking. Sitting on my foam surfboard, waiting with the pack for the next wave, there was always a little bit of consciousness reserved for the savage shadow.

Beachside aquariums were popular in those days. They weren't the elaborate experience they've since become, with tunnels and moving walkways and thoughtful interpretive information; these were just tanks with thick, distorting windows, a freak show rather than an educational experience. The harried snapper and trevally coursing about in those murky cauldrons were just background. What the punters wanted to see were the sharks: dozy, whiskered wobbegongs, grey nurses with their snaggle teeth and truckers' bellies, bronze whalers so sleek and sinister, and the cruising hammerheads like visitants from hell. Just as Irish country folk tell ghost tales as they hoist a final pint before setting off home down the lonely lanes, local beachgoers liked to contemplate these wraiths on their way to or from a swim. We pressed our noses to the glass and thumped it with our fists. Once you'd seen them you couldn't get enough. This was it, the lurking fear in plain view. They were appalling, these creatures, but seductive, too. Their shapes were inescapable, in the gill-slits of muscle cars, the fins of the latest surfboards. Teenagers wore their triangular teeth on leather thongs around their necks. Along with many schoolmates, I drew the classic whaler outline in countless maths books on sulphurously hot afternoons in class. I was a captive.

I borrowed shark books from the library to stare at the photos of great whites being hauled up grotesquely on docks, their vast girths forced out through their mouths by gravity. People chalked their names upon carcasses and posed po-faced like heroes. I pored over photos of limbs, engine parts and animals cut from the guts of sharks. Shark-hunting was popular in the sixties and there were many images of skindivers Ben and Eva Cropp killing grey nurses with 'bang sticks', or 'smokies', which were spears armed with a shotgun cartridge. There was a famous photo of the elfin Valerie Taylor with her arm in a shark's mouth, the creature wrenching unsuccessfully at the chain mail she'd armoured herself with for the camera. I returned time and again to the grueseome pictures of Rodney Fox who'd been bitten by a great white in 1963. Despite having his lungs and intestines exposed, Fox survived the attack and like Henri Bource had gone back to the sea with the doggedness of a spurned lover.

Newspapers seemed to be full of lurid accounts of shark sightings, maulings, captures. The whole country was obsessed with sharks. It was as if the continent were besieged by armies of them, and of all those species stalking the depths beyond the surf-line none had the pitiless warrior reputation to match the so-called 'white death'. We knew quite little about *Carcharodon carcharias* in the sixties, but some Australians began to go to a lot of trouble to encounter them and to capture images of them close up.

When the groundbreaking documentary *Blue Water, White Death* was released in 1971 I was desperate to see it, but the film passed me by. It boasted the first extended underwater footage of great white sharks ever taken. In the later years of video it seemed perennially unavailable, so the republication of Peter Matthiessen's *Blue Meridian* comes as a consolation of sorts. First published in the same year *Blue Water* was released, it's an account of the making of the documentary, and although written as natural history the passage of time has rendered its social observations as telling as its descriptions of life beneath the waterline.

Matthiessen is acknowledged as one of the world's finest writers of natural history. Best known for *The Snow Leopard* and *The Cloud Forest*, he also has a respectable body of fiction, including my favourite, the arresting *Far Tortuga*. In 1969 the author joined an expedition led by American millionaire Peter Gimbel to find and film *Carcharodon carcharias*, the great white shark. Gimbel had previously earnt fame as the man who took the first pictures of the *Andrea Doria* in 70 metres of water off Nantucket, and his project was financed by the cinema wing of TV giant, CBS. The plan was to find the fearsome predator and to get into the water with it and film it. The first objective was an enormous challenge, the second all but unthinkable at the time. It was the year people went to the moon, an era when discovery and adventure still had some cachet, but even then preparing to swim with great whites was quite an undertaking.

In March 1969 the team of seven Americans and two Australians charter a whale catcher from Durban and set out for the whaling grounds off the eastern coast of South Africa. The Australians are Ron and Valerie Taylor, who are underwater royalty in their home country. According to the expeditioners' intelligence, very big sharks congregate off Durban, especially during the whale hunt. Matthiessen, along as spare hand and observer, is a novice diver and suitably apprehensive at the prospect of climbing into an aluminium cage in the midst of a pack of feeding sharks. His tone of calm curiosity gives his account a sympathy that is grave and illuminating. Witnessing the butchering of whales, he writes: 'Nothing is wasted but the whale itself.' On April 8 when they find their first big aggregation of sharks, Matthiessen describes his descent in the cage: 'When water and body temperatures are so nearly the same, the skin seems to dissolve; I drifted in solution with the sea. In the sensory deprivation of the underwater world – no taste, no smell, no sound – the wild scene had the ring of hallucination. The spectral creatures came and went, cruising toward the cage and scraping past with lightless eyes.'

For hours the crew films the awesome sight of big oceanic whitetips coring the floating carcasses of whales at close proximity. The cages are buffeted, the water swirls with gore, and though the footage is remarkable, no great white appears.

On April 19, to the horror and fury of the Australian divers, Gimbel and fellow cameraman Stan Waterman leave their cage during a similar feeding frenzy. A small shark enters by the open door and the remaining diver is left with it trapped and blundering around with her until it can find the door again. That rattled diver is, of course, Valerie Taylor. The dismay at Gimbel's sudden recklessness begins to open up divisions in the crew, especially between the Americans and the Australians. The author renders the shifts and silences of shipboard life with great tact and subtlety. He becomes fascinated by Ron and Valerie Taylor. Ron in particular interests him almost as much as the elusive white shark itself: 'He is a well-made graceful man with long sideburns and a black monk's cap of unparted hair, a flat gaze – his eyes do not open the way into his mind, but reflect one's own – and a slightly retracted lower jaw; perhaps it is association, but in a strange way that eludes definition, Ron brings to mind a shy and handsome shark.'

Matthiessen learns something of the Taylors' reputations. Spearfishing champions, filmmakers and popular lecturers, they are minor celebrities at home and gurus to those who dive. He the quiet, unassuming genius, she the beautiful, feisty on-camera side-kick – they are professionals in the company of mere adventurers. At the time, Ron is perhaps the best diver alive, capable of amazing feats of courage and endurance, moving in the water as though he were born with gills. Although Taylor seems to know no fear, he takes only calculated risks. He has lost several friends to sharks and every now and then he kills one when it seems to Matthiessen less than necessary.

While the ship steams about the Indian Ocean, all the way to Sri Lanka and back to Africa with no great white in sight and a growing litany of mishaps dogging the company on and off the sea, Matthiessen carefully builds his picture of a strange clash of minds and cultures. The Taylors are prim, conventional Australians of their time and there is real humour in the portrayal of them surrounded by big-talking and foulmouthed Yanks who are cosmopolitan, educated, wealthy and confident. The human drama of this is often more enthralling than the quest itself. Driven to push himself further and further, Gimbel takes more and bigger risks, not only swimming in the midst of slamming, buffeting sharks, but working his way right into the wound of a dead whale so that he is beside the gnashing jaws of the sharks, pressed against their gulping throats. 'A wild fatalism overtook us,' Gimbel tells the author. 'We felt a growing sense of immunity.'

Matthiessen and the Taylors puzzle over this behaviour. Gimbel maintains that he's simply curious: 'he seeks out ways to test what he calls "the limits",' says Matthiessen, 'and of course this search has no real end to it but death'. Gimbel seems driven to challenge the sharks, while to the author Ron Taylor may simply be one.

The expedition moves to South Australia's Spencer Gulf, and another famous local joins the company. Rodney Fox still bears the scars of his 1963 encounter with a great white. It took 360 stitches and a great deal of surgical skill to save him that day but his fascination with sharks has only grown over the years and few have his working knowledge of whites. As they chum for the sharks that seem to perpetually elude them, he and the Taylors are convinced that the wait will soon be over.

When the first specimen finally shows itself the sight is awesome. After the mechanical grotesqueries of the *Jaws* franchise and the intervening years of cage-dive footage to which the contemporary viewer has become accustomed, it's worth contemplating just how dramatic that first sighting must have been. Even Ron Taylor seems to have gotten excited. Immediately, the cages were lowered, wetsuits shrugged on. 'Surging out of the sea to fasten on a horse shank hung from a davit, it stood upright beside the ship, head and gills clear of the water, tail vibrating, the glistening triangles of its teeth red-rimmed with blood. In the effort of shearing, the black eye went white as the eyeball was rolled inward; then the whole horse quarter disappeared in a scarlet billow.'

Underwater, Matthiessen watches the historic filming from his racked and buffeted cage, horrified at the sight of these great otherworldly creatures: 'there was no sense of viciousness or savagery in what they did, but something worse, an implacable need'. As ever, the author is first a natural historian, as dispassionate as he can manage to be, but even he cannot resist the urge to touch – as if he's not immune to the impulse that Gimbel acts upon so extravagantly – the urge to connect momentarily with a greater power. 'Gills rippling, it would swerve enough to miss the cage, and once the smiling head had passed I could reach out and take hold of the rubber pectoral, or trail my fingers down the length of a cold dead flank, as if stroking a corpse: the skin felt as smooth as the skin of a swordfish or tuna.'

Later, the author quotes Peter Gimbel as saying: 'I was filled with a terrible sadness that we had indeed determined precisely the limits we sought, that the mystery was at least partly gone because we knew that we could get away with anything, that the story – and such a story! – had an end.'

I suspect Matthiessen may not have shared this sadness. In this account Gimbel's quest seems to have had more to do with the mysteries in himself than those of the shark he seeks. The author's curiosity never seems to wane, his awe and respect for nature have not dulled with time. Certainly the Taylors have gone on to see sharks very differently, and although more has been learned about the great white since this remarkable jaunt in 1969, no one would dare say the creature is any less a mystery, any less a target of irrational hatred.

The day I began reading *Blue Meridian* an abalone diver known to friends of mine was taken by a great white near Hopetoun, Western Australia. It's impossible to read of an expedition like this without mixed and strong emotions. Appalled, amused, amazed, I still envy Matthiessen his brief touch of the living shadow, an experience from a time when you couldn't have filled a dinghy with those who could claim to have done the same.

---

* Peter Gimbel died of cancer in 1987. Ron Taylor continued to dive until his death in 2012. He too died of cancer. Peter Matthiessen died of leukaemia in 2014, aged eighty-six. At the age of eighty, Val Taylor was still diving with sharks and campaigning for marine sanctuaries.

II
Predator or Prey?

Australians have a peculiar attitude toward sharks. It's pathological and it runs deep. Other cultures have their wolves and bears, their lions and tigers – the carnivorous demon lurking in the shadows. Here there's no growling menace out in the dark. Our demon is silent and it swims.

'Why did God make sharks?' Whenever my kids asked me this I was always tempted to answer: 'To sell newspapers.' Because that's how it feels sometimes. Flip through a Sunday paper this summer. Watch the telly. When it comes to sharks, fear equals money. The more lurid the pics and headlines, the better. Readers and viewers can't help themselves. Advertisers love it almost as much as editors. A bona-fide bad guy. I guess it's what you're left with when you're no longer allowed to burn witches. The shark is our secular substitute for the Devil.

Like most Australians, I grew up with an irrational fear and disgust for the shark. Not that I ever actually saw one. Not alive, not in the wild. Our waters were supposedly teeming with these hideous creatures, but for the millions of hours I spent surfing, spearfishing and boating, I saw none at all.

As a kid I saw a few dead specimens. Divers often killed sharks for sport. When anglers like the legendary Alf Dean 'fought' tiger sharks and great whites they did it for pleasure, for some sense of mastery, then they dragged them ashore and hung them from gantries. I remember enormous, distended carcasses suspended from meat hooks and steel cables on jetties on the south coast. The dead sharks often had their lengths and weights painted on their flanks as if they were machines. Their entrails spilled at our feet through their gaping jaws. And I think of it now: the hundreds and sometimes thousands of kilos of protein, the decades of living and travelling and breeding and ecological job-sharing that are bound up in the body of a single mature shark. All of this reduced to a trophy that lasted a few hours before the creature's body was carted off to the tip. These displays were like public executions, the criminal species strung up for the crowds, as if the only good shark were a dead shark and we needed to see this butchery acted out again and again for our own wellbeing.

No wonder I wasn't seeing live sharks as a kid. Humans had declared war on them. By the time I finally caught sight of a specimen in the wild, some time in my thirties, there were more sharks in our collective minds than there were left in the water.

Picture this. I'm thirteen, standing on a jetty looking down onto a flashing mass of bronze whalers and other sharks. Men are blasting holes in them, shooting them at close range from boats. This is Albany, 1973. The sharks are gathered around the gore-mired flensing deck of Australia's last whaling station. It's a local treat for tourists, having access to such a spectacle. There are half a dozen dead sperm whales floating a few metres away. The water is wild with blood, not just from the writhing sharks, but because someone just beneath me is grinding the head off a whale with a steam-powered saw. Believe me, it's an untidy business to witness. A head the size of a shipping container unseated from the biggest body you've ever seen in your life. It's hard to believe what I'm seeing. It seems a bit wasteful – disgusting, actually – to be butchering such immense creatures for little more than fertilizer and cosmetics. But blokes shooting sharks? That doesn't bother me a bit. I am, after all, a boy of my time and place.

Of course I haven't been that boy for a long while and the culture I grew up in has changed. In my own lifetime Australians have become very conscious of animal welfare and nature conservation. Most people hate to see creatures mistreated. Whether it's a dog being beaten or a bear tortured for its bile, cruelty and thoughtless slaughter offend us. A kangaroo cull or footage from an overseas abattoir will cause outrage bordering on social derangement. But of all creatures subject to routine mistreatment and wanton destruction, the shark remains, for the most part, beyond the range of our tender feelings. We reserve special sympathy, of course, for endangered species. Most of us could not countenance the unnecessary killing of an elephant or a rhino, let alone those scarier creatures, the leopard or the cheetah. After all, these are rare, proud, noble beasts. But the endangered shark? By and large nobody cares.

Yet the shark was here before any of those other 'iconic' beasts. It embodies the deepest experience of prehistory and it still swims in the present. But in the popular mind it's a terrorist, an insidious threat we must arm ourselves against. Bees kill many more Australians than do sharks every year, but there is no war on bees.

The Devil is supposed to get all the good lines, but the shark is mute. It is a creature routinely vilified, and the disgust it produces in us shuts down curiosity and empathy. As a result we tolerate or even participate in acts of cruelty against it that'd be unimaginable were they to involve any other species. In short, the removal of sharks from humane consideration gives humankind licence to do the unspeakable.

The evidence suggests that we'll let ourselves do *anything* to the shark. This is why the barbaric trade in shark fin continues to prosper, why most of the big pelagic sharks have disappeared globally without an outcry, why boys who maim and torture sharks beneath jetties in coastal communities of Australia are unlikely to be reprimanded, let alone convicted of any offence, and it's why right-thinking folks in Sydney and Melbourne are content to buy shark meat under the false and misleading market label of flake, even as the numbers decline. Of all the fishery resources close to worldwide collapse, the shark's is the one least likely to stir our collective conscience. Because essentially, *the shark doesn't matter* – that's the stubborn and perennial subtext. The demonization of sharks has blinded us, not just to our own savagery, but also to our casual hypocrisy.

Sharks are not machines. They are not invincible. They are not cruel – certainly not as cruel as a fourteen-year-old with a Twitter account, or a backroom politician with a grudge. Unlike humans, sharks are not capable of moral evil. In short, they are not at all what we thought they were. For one thing, we need to remind ourselves: there is no monolithic shark. With almost four hundred species, there are as many ways to be a shark as there are to be a human.

You only need to meet a few individual sharks to understand that they're complex and many-faceted, variable in behaviour and form. Some are sociable, even playful. At times they seem to like human interaction. I love dolphins as much as anybody else, but believe it or not I've had more fun with sharks: lemon sharks, tawny nurses, whale sharks, even the ADHD kids of the surf zone, the bronze whalers.

Happily, most of us who spend a lot of time in the water have moved on from the ignorant shark prejudices we grew up with. In the rare instances when a diver or a surfer gets bumped, bitten or even killed, it's now uncommon to hear the survivor or a bereaved relative speak in terms of vengeance or outrage. Anger and hatred are rare. The tone of these harrowed folks is philosophical. The ugliest utterances seem to come from those at a distance, citizens who rarely get their hair wet. They're usually blokes, I'm sorry to say. Men, of course, are far more likely to die on the toilet than from a shark encounter, but when you hear what some politicians and shock jocks have to say on the matter you're led to suspect that before their final straining moment they'd prefer to see every last shark dead.

The year 2011 was the worst for fatal shark attacks in Australia in living memory. Four people lost their lives. These were violent deaths, terrible events. With the help of news media a kind of fever gripped the public imagination, and as a result lots of Australians and foreign tourists were too terrified to swim in the sea. That same year we suffered the lowest road toll since the Second World War, with only 1292 Australians killed. Some of these people died slowly, many were disarticulated. Their blood stained the lawns and streets of many safe neighbourhoods. But there was no media-fanned panic, nobody stayed off the roads – on the contrary, our road usage went up. This most common form of violent death simply doesn't frighten us anymore. The very real likelihood of being mangled in a car is something we've domesticated. That's not simply a contradiction, it's a marvel of human psychology.

The fact is, sharks have so much more to fear from us than we do from them. Worldwide, millions of people are in the water every day of every year – and even with the recent spate of incidents in

Australia, most of them in my home waters, the number of attacks is but a handful. But how many sharks are killed annually? Almost a hundred million. That's 270 000 sharks killed just today. Many of these have their fins amputated while they're alive; they're returned to the water where they drown slowly or die from shock. A third of all open-ocean shark species are threatened. Many of those are keystone species, so when they disappear, the rest of the ecosystem goes haywire. Habitats stripped of sharks begin to produce mono-cultures at best and plagues at worst. The current rate of shark slaughter is savage and is not just unsustainable, but potentially catastrophic for our oceans.

Why are sharks so vulnerable to overfishing? Mostly because they have very modern reproductive habits: they mature late and breed infrequently. When you decimate a population of sharks, the recovery period is perilously long. They simply don't bounce back.

Our nation was at the forefront of the global change in attitudes toward the slaughter of whales and dolphins. This all began in Albany when I was a teenager in the seventies; it unfolded in front of me, and it's had a real impact on my life and work. Cetaceans are charismatic; they have lungs and voices. Sharks, too, are social, but being silent they need others to speak for them. They are now more vulnerable than dolphins and may become more threatened than whales. Their survival is bound up with our own, for a world without sharks will eventually become a world without people. We need to expand our common knowledge and reform our attitude to these beautiful and misunderstood creatures while there's still time.

III
Passing Strangers

At dawn, as the big winter storm looms beyond the horizon, I consult the internet once more and see the readings from the swell buoys spiking. There'll be no work today. I time my run up the coast for low tide. I lock the hubs on the ute and throw the boards in the back. The dog leaps in uninvited.

The track north is narrow and rough. Rain peppers the windscreen. After the best part of an hour I wind my way clear of the capstone and the dunes, through the squatters' huts and out onto the point where a right-hander is reeling down the beach, groomed by the howling nor'wester. I don't hesitate. I get out into the rain squall and suit up. The dog slinks over to the whale carcass like an aunt to a buffet. I know she'll spend the next two hours rolling in it. I have a bottle of detergent to deal with the after-effects. She loves that whale.

I grab my board and step around the mess of bones and blubber. It's only once I'm downwind the stink catches me. Pretty rugged, but better than a few months ago.

At the shore the water's still got an oily sheen to it. I know what that means, but the surf is great and I'll take my chances.

I join the small pack of locals on the peak. We sit about 300 metres out along the edge of an island and take waves in turn, bullshitting and sledging the morning away. The Shaw brothers say the bronzies are back, the same three sharks that have been lurking since the blue whale washed in. It's a heads-up. Good to know. I've seen them once or twice, two smaller specimens and one the size of a fullback. They haven't given us any trouble. But the sight of them twitching and circling out beyond the break certainly gets the adrenaline going.

A set trundles in, makes its slow angling turn toward us, and I paddle out to meet it. I let the first wave go and spin around for the second. It picks me up and I wind down its long, curving wall, mugging at friends as they paddle by. I kick out near the beach where the reek of the whale is worst. My kelpie leaves off blubber-surfing and races down in the mistaken assumption that I'm done. As I paddle out, her high, piercing bark chases after me.

Before I get far, a big set rolls in and I'm caught on the shallow bar in a welter of whitewater. I stand and wait a while, buffeted by every new wall of foam, and when things settle I push back out and start to paddle.

That's when something bumps me. In all this fizzing spume. Something rough. Something as big as I am. It nudges my arm, like a passer-by brushing past in a corridor. It stops, as if confounded, and there's a moment of fraught intimacy, skin to skin. I can't see a thing. Then I feel the sandpapery grind of it as it turns in panic and flees.

The whole encounter lasts maybe two seconds. But in its wake my entire body is lit up with awe and terror. As I pass one of the local deckies I tell him what just happened. He gives me a sideways look and heads to shore without delay. But I stay. I don't know if this close shave has left me feeling lucky or if it's just the rare beauty of the waves rolling in, but I can't call it quits yet.

Bizarrely, the sun comes out. The cold front bores in from the north-west with a sunny escort. And the sea feels friendlier. For one thing, it's easier to see what's moving under the surface, at least in the unbroken water behind the break.

On the beach, the dog barks. She's faint in the distance.

I catch a few more waves and then sit out the back swapping stories with my mate Lifestyle Pete. And then a really hefty set rolls in and we dig hard to reach it before it mows us down. I make it past the first two waves but by the third I'm really scratching. It looms up above me and I feel like a beetle scuttling up the front of a speeding semi. At the peak it's hissing, seething. And somehow I make it before the lip lurches out and heaves me backward onto the sandbar.

I rise to the crest, caught for a moment like a kid on a fence, and I teeter there, grabbing my board, bracing myself for the fall back to the surface below. As I plummet I see the shark, and at the last moment the bronzie sees me. I'm hurtling at him helplessly with only the board as a shield. He's sleek and big-shouldered. In half a second I'm about to land on him. He turns and bolts. I splash down in the tight comma of turbulence he leaves in his wake.

He's chasing mullet, I tell myself. And I'm probably right. Now I'm definitely too buzzed to go in. I surf until my back threatens to go into spasm. I ride a last wave in to the reeking shore and the dog is there to greet me.

---

* The bronze whalers at the point stayed around for a couple of seasons without incident. A few years later, though, about a kilometre south,

a surfer was taken by a great white. Not long afterwards, the West Australian government began a shark cull targeting this endangered species. In its first season the program destroyed 170 tiger sharks, whalers and bullsharks, none of which were implicated in the spate of attacks that provoked it. No great whites were caught, and there was no evidence to suggest the killing program rendered swimmers any safer. In the public outcry that ensued, opponents of the program were vilified as misanthropes. Even so, the cull was discontinued and resources were directed toward non-lethal barriers, aerial surveillance and early-warning systems.

In 2013 two people died as a result of shark attack in this country. The next year the number was unchanged. In 2015 one person died this way. During this same period over three thousand people died violently on our roads. Many thousands more succumbed to heart disease.

Using the C-word

During an interview in 2013, a journalist pulled me up for using the C-word.

'*Class?*' she asked with lifted eyebrow. 'What do you mean?'

I found myself chewing the air a moment. Had I said something foul, something embarrassing to both of us? Discussing two of my fictional characters in terms of the social distinctions that separated them, it seemed I'd broached a topic that wasn't merely awkward, it was provocative. There was a little charge in the atmosphere. I tried not to put it down to the fact that I was talking to an employee of News Corp. The reporter in question is a person of independent mind whose work I admire, but she was, after all, in the employ of Rupert Murdoch, whose editors and columnists maintain a palace watch on what they like to call 'the politics of envy'. A blur of competing thoughts went through my mind. Was she being ironic, or did she really expect me to defend a casual reference to class relations? Was I being paranoid or was this the kind of clarification necessary in the new cultural dispensation? Did the nation's drift to the right mean that we all needed to be a lot more careful about our public language, lest we expose ourselves to charges of insufficient revolutionary zeal?

After a mortifying beat or two, I made a clumsy attempt to explain myself and soon saw that whatever the journalist's own thoughts were on matters of class, the fact she'd challenged me on my use of the word meant she'd somehow done her duty. To whom she'd fulfilled this implicit obligation wasn't immediately clear. Beyond my initial twinge of anxiety I didn't seriously think she had a proprietor or even an editor in mind when she baulked at the offending word. Afterwards I came to the conclusion that a Fairfax journalist or Radio National presenter might well have posed the same question. In itself it was, of course, no big thing; it just caught me unawares. All the same, it was a signal of the way in which something fundamental has changed in our culture. In calling me out over my use of the C-word, the interviewer was merely reflecting the zeitgeist. I should have anticipated it. I've been making assumptions about our common outlook that are plainly outdated.

I don't think it's an exaggeration to say that in contemporary Australia, citizens are now implicitly divided into those who bother and those who don't. It seems poverty and wealth can no longer be attributed – even in part – to social origins; they are manifestations of character. In the space of two decades, during which the gap between rich and poor grew wider than at any time since the Second World War, Australians have been trained to remain uncharacteristically silent about the origins of social disparity. This inequity is regularly measured and often reported.

In October 2013 the OECD's former director for employment, labour and social affairs cited figures that estimated 22 percent of the growth in Australia's household income between 1980 and 2008 went to the richest one percent of the population. The nation's new prosperity was unevenly spread in those years. To borrow former Morgan Stanley global equity analyst Gerard Minack's phrasing about an even worse situation in the United States, 'The rising tide did not lift all the boats; it floated a few yachts.' And yet there is a curious reluctance to examine the systemic causes of this inequity. The Australian political economist Frank Stilwell has puzzled over what he calls contemporary 'beliefs' around social inequality. Australians' views range from outright denial of it to Darwinian acceptance. Many now believe 'people get what they deserve', and to my mind such a response is startling and alien. Structural factors have become too awkward to discuss.

As the nation's former treasurer Wayne Swan learnt in 2012 when he published an essay about the disproportionate influence of the nation's super-rich, anybody reckless enough to declare class a live issue is likely to be met with howls of derision. According to the new mores, any mention of structural social inequality is tantamount to a declaration of class warfare. Concerns about the distribution of wealth and access to education and health are difficult to raise in a public forum without needing to beat off the ghost of Stalin. The only form of political correctness that the right will tolerate is the careful elision of class from public discourse, and this troubling discretion has become mainstream. Which constitutes an ideological triumph for conservatives that even they must marvel at. Having uttered the C-word in polite company I felt, for a moment, as if I'd shat in the municipal pool.

Australia's long tradition of egalitarianism was something people my age learnt about at school. I recall teachers who were dowdy folk of indeterminate politics who spoke of 'the fair go' with the same reverence they had for Bradman or the myth of Anzac. Australia's fairness was a source of pride, an article of faith. Which is not to say the nation of my childhood was classless. Social distinctions were palpable and the subject of constant discussion. In the raw State Housing suburbs of Perth there were definite boundaries and behaviours, many imposed and some internalized. All the people I knew identified as working class. Proud and resentful, we were alert to difference, amazed whenever we came upon it. Difference was both provocative and exotic and one generally cancelled out the negative power of the other. We expressed the casual racism of our time. We played sport with blackfellas but didn't really socialize with them. We laughed at the ten-pound Poms with their *Coronation Street* accents but felt slightly cowed by their stories of great cities and imperial grandeur. The street was full of migrants who'd fled war-ravaged Eastern Europe. Like most of the locals, they worked in factories and on road gangs. They told us kids we were free and lucky and we thought they were telling us something we already knew. As a boy I believed that Jack *was* as good as his master. But I understood that Jacks like me always had masters.

I watched my grandfather work until he was in his seventies. Sometimes I carried his Gladstone bag for him. It seemed to signify his dignified position as an ordinary worker who did a decent day's work for a decent day's union-won pay. He'd started on the wharves in Geraldton and spent decades as a labourer at the Perth Mint, and though the meekest of men he reserved a sly defiance for his 'betters'. He was a union man but his allegiance was more tribal than ideological. The most memorable thing he ever said to me was when I was fourteen or so. Rolling one of his slapdash fags on the verandah of his rented house in sunstruck Belmont, he announced that I should press on with my 'eddication', because 'that's yours for life, and whatever else the bosses can get offa ya, they can't take what's there between yer ears'. This was the same man who'd pulled my mother out of school at fifteen because there seemed no point in her staying on, the bloke whose sons were sent into apprenticeships without a second thought. Twenty years earlier, his world had been narrower, more constrained, and I'm not sure whether he encouraged me out of regret for the curtailment of my mother's dreams or if he was infected by the sense of promise that was in the air with the rise of Whitlam.

The summer of that sage moment, all things seemed possible to working people in Australia. It was as if all those Jacks and Jills with masters began to feel new prospects for their children and grandchildren. As an adolescent in this period of flux, it seemed the frontiers between classes were suddenly more provisional. Some will say class boundaries were always notional, but if they had been as permeable before Whitlam, there was certainly no evidence of it in my family, no sign of it in our street. The lines were fixed. Until the 1970s, young people followed closely in their parents' footsteps. Not just out of solidarity or emulation, but because to a large extent origin was destiny. The children of tradesfolk became tradesfolk and the offspring of doctors tended to find themselves in the professions. The Whitlam government didn't completely bulldoze the walls between classes, but it did knock a few holes in the parapet, and without those liberating gaps my future would have been very different.

Compared to most fields of endeavour, sport and entertainment seem relatively porous in social terms. The arts – which often combine elements of both sport and entertainment – are a little like them in this regard, though historically they have been more class-determined than it's deemed comfortable to admit. Ask any director in a major theatre company in this country how many of their actors were educated in public schools. They'll have to have a good hard think. Traditionally the world of letters has been similarly class-bound, though it has changed in my decades as a practitioner. In Australia, as elsewhere, it was standard procedure for members of the gentry to impoverish themselves for the sake of literature, or to at least fall a few pegs into raffish bohemia along the way. Tom Keneally stood out in Australian letters for a long time as the most visible exception to the class rule. Hailing from Homebush, a son of working people, Keneally wrote himself, by accident or design, into the bourgeoisie. In his early years he laboured in the shadow of Patrick White. The great laureate was invariably presented to the world as an oddball, but in truth White's trajectory embodied the rule. Our purse-lipped jeremiah was a scion of the squattocracy. His was a life of inherited mobility. He began adulthood in spats and ended up scowling contentedly in a cardigan and beret, and to that extent he conformed to a pattern very familiar indeed. He was, whether he knew it or not, the norm.

So as a child of the working class, someone who has prospered to a degree unimaginable by my parents and grandparents, and done so in the arts, of all fields, I am conscious that my own trajectory is atypical. And yet a career like mine is not quite the rarity it would have been a generation ago. Contemporaries like Richard Flanagan, Kim Scott and Christos Tsiolkas will have similar stories to tell. For all our differences as writers and people, we all emerged from what were once termed the lower orders and found ourselves – by reason of income and social recognition – in the middle class. I can't speak for these other writers of my generation, but I am reconciled to my new station. In middle age I am conscious of my good fortune and happy to acknowledge that it's more a manifestation of cultural history than personal talent. It's not that I came into the world empty-handed, I inherited a social tradition. I grew up in a country that codified the dignity of labour, which treasured decency and fairness, where the individual was valued and the collective aspirations of ordinary people were honoured, and I came of age during a social convulsion by which the culture enriched itself in a hectic explosion of hope and innovation. In that sense I consider myself luckier than any lad born to a fortune in a previous generation.

I was the first of my family to finish school, the first to complete a tertiary education. Like my younger siblings, I surfed the pent-up force of my parents' thwarted hopes. For us they wanted a life less subject to the whims of others – the bosses my grandfather spoke of – and they knew that access to education was the key. No one in my family spoke about economics; the future was never about money. What my parents dreamt of was simply a larger, more open existence for their children. Their hopes were rarely expressed in ideological terms. They were not political people and certainly not radicals. They were inspired more by Billy Graham than by the distant and slightly poncy Gough. They urged us to use the gifts we were born with and to refuse to accept the status quo.

We acknowledged class distinctions as a fact of life. In high school and university, class was a constant topic of conversation and study. Even at the utopian apogee of my youth I could never have imagined a time when class might be rendered obsolete by history. I certainly didn't foresee an age when the very word might hang in the air like something forbidden.

In 1995, at a book party in Soho, the literary editor of a newspaper who was decidedly in his cups suggested I was a bit 'chippy'. I was puzzled. Even after the fellow was poured into a cab and my amused London publisher had time to explain the meaning of the term, I remained bewildered. Apparently at the sort of gentlemen's club indispensible to British publishing, it was impolite to mention one's social origins; it made a fellow uncomfortable. Even the most casual, lighthearted reference to class was viewed as 'making a song and dance about it'. I was amongst people who'd either been to Oxbridge or who were pretending they had. Their accents and manners – even those who'd already begun to speak like Jamie Oliver – were rigidly shaped by conceptions of class. As an exotic I'd had something of a free pass that evening – until I mentioned the C-word. Lesson learnt, I filed that evening's faux pas under Foreign Customs. I didn't dream that nearly twenty years later I'd be facing a similar awkwardness at home.

In the past few years some friends have remarked upon my anachronistic class-consciousness. Invariably they're the children of professionals, graduates of elite schools – all of them lovely, decent people. One, the son of an architect, gave me a blue collar for my forty-fifth birthday. It was funny, I enjoyed the joke, but I wonder what he'd have had in store if I'd been a feminist and a bit gender-conscious, or Aboriginal and a tad race-aware.

If I remain preoccupied by class it's not because I'm chippy or resentful. I don't feel embittered or damaged. I have no hard-luck story to tell. But social distinctions continue to fascinate me. Perhaps, if I try to take the most disinterested view, their apparent demise has rendered them more compelling; their political invisibility makes them more vivid. But I find it hard to see class dispassionately because it's still a live issue. I sense it grinding away tectonically in the experiences of relatives and friends, who may not want to talk about class but who are subject to its force every day.

In 2010, when my face appeared on a postage stamp, I had to submit to the good-humoured sledging of relatives at pains to restrain their pride. In my family teasing is a blood sport and a measure of affection, so I copped it with a smile. I enjoyed their refusal to seem impressed. There were lots of jokes about them having to lick the back of my head. But at certain moments it was painful to be reminded that some of them could moisten the stamp and fix it to the envelope but not write the letter it was supposed to carry on its way. These are the family members who only follow my stories in audio format – not because they're too busy to be bothered with books, but because they are functionally illiterate. Their curtailed educations, which have sorely constrained their adult lives, are not a manifestation of character, they are outcomes of class. When I'm with those of my friends who are privately educated, I can't help but be mindful, now and then, of those intimate and often shameful family constraints. Prosperous Australians, even those who've snuck under the wire like myself, forget so easily that others are still living over-determined lives in another economy altogether. Many of them are old neighbours, schoolfriends, relatives, and often they live close by, in the same postcode as you.

When I was young, I didn't know people like me. By which I mean folks who are comfortable, confident, mobile. I never mixed with people from outside my own class. There was no opportunity, and it seemed there was no need. I didn't know anyone who went to a private school. The Catholic kids across the street went to the convent, but that was a step down from state school. It wasn't until I went to university that I came into contact with people my age who'd had private educations. If Whitlam hadn't abolished tertiary education fees in 1974, I doubt I would have made it to university at all. My parents certainly couldn't have afforded full tuition and if there were scholarships available to bright young oiks back then we didn't know about them. Like so many others of my generation who were the first of a family to enter university I was an outrider on a strange and wonderful frontier. All of us were changed as a result. It expanded the curtailed world of my immediate family – exploded it forever.

'The uni', as my parents called it, was a revelation. The campus of the 1970s was a circus. Everywhere you looked there was a performance, an inversion, a spectacle. It was liberating and surreal. Imperious daughters of the gentry experimented with meekness. Roughknuckled boys slowly came out as gay. Confused by all the costume and panto, some of us began shyly to ask each other about our backgrounds. For many, the schools we'd come from had given us a certain restricted confidence that only pertained within tribal boundaries. Even the posh kids were wrong-footed by the new rules. We were all at sea, only revealing ourselves to one another in cautious increments. We looked wistfully to our new teachers as they strolled the corridors with remarkable aplomb. The tenured Marxists in liberal arts courses were not the first bourgeois citizens I ever encountered but they were the first I spent significant time with. Their self-assurance was epic, marvellous, dizzying. Some of them took modish intellectual positions and had delusional self-hating politics but what was most intriguing about them was not the choices they made, but the fact that they'd had so many choices to make. Range of choice, I discovered, was a key indicator of class. Some choices are conferred by birth while others have to be won by hard work. A few can only be achieved by legislation.

I didn't miss the determined certainties of being working class. Nor did I miss its self-limiting tribalism. But I probably wasn't prepared for the growing self-interest of the class I gradually rose to. For if there's solidarity at work anywhere in our society these days it's among the very rich, and the middle class has watched and learnt. Middle Australia is increasingly class-conscious and it looks to bolster its interests at every turn.

Once the old class-based educational barriers had been down for a decade, Australia seemed to have broadened somewhat. By the

1980s the working class was harder to identify. Manufacturing was on the wane, but tradespeople began to earn incomes that were once the preserve of the middle class. It was confusing, even upsetting, for some Australians to learn that a plumber might earn more than a teacher. This was well before the minerals boom that enabled a bus driver in the Pilbara to pull down the salary of a doctor in Hobart.

But despite all these changes, class never disappeared from cultural consciousness. Surprisingly, it wasn't the poor and over-looked resorting to class discourse. The union movement that had once given voice and language to class struggle had either been smashed or imploded. Margaret Thatcher declared there was no such thing as society and Australian governments gradually inter-nalized that view and appropriated policies that sprang from it. Governments of both major parties oversaw a transition from col-lective citizenship to consumer individualism that remade our con-ception of education, health and taxation. Federal ministers – Labor and Liberal – who'd been educated in the era of Whitlam promptly pulled the ladder up after them. It was pay-as-you-go for my kids. Or graduate in debt. Workers were encouraged to see themselves as contractors, employers as entrepreneurs. Looking back it seems to have been something of a counter-reformation, an ugly regression. But it wasn't the vanquished workers pressing the language of class warfare into service, it was the growing middle class.

The success of Middle Australia didn't bring the confidence you'd expect. By the turn of the century these prospering folk, now called 'working families', seemed defensive, even a little besieged, and the class basis of much of their social discourse was either unacknowledged or completely unconscious. The boho-bourgeois inner city has long been plagued with smugness, something the suburban middle class might aspire to if only it weren't so anxious. It takes a deep level of entitlement to be smug. Middle Australia settled for just being fractious and snooty. Only after the turn of the millennium did we begin to hear successful tradespeople being called 'cashed-up bogans'. What else could that signify but class anxiety? Very quickly a large cohort of middle-class people found a means of codifying contempt for those rough-handed interlopers who'd been elevated by the minerals boom into Middle Australia without the benefit of the social conventions and tastes the old middle class was born to. What was the source of all this anxiety? That Jack might leapfrog all his masters and give them the finger in passing? That they, Menzies' apparently Forgotten People, might be overtaken by the lower orders?

When I was a kid, most people in the suburbs were likely to describe themselves as battlers – code for unpretentious, working-class toilers. Nowadays, largely as a result of the nation's remarkable prosperity, the social centre has broadened to the degree that Middle Australia is normative. People are still just as likely to describe themselves as battlers, but their historically large incomes bely the nature of their struggle, which often has more to do with material ambition than any real hardship. In many instances the 'battles' of Middle Australia are self-imposed. But in recent years they have been valorized and enlarged. Nowhere was this more obvious than during the Howard years when the term 'Howard's battlers' was deployed as a deliberate attempt to appropriate the power of class language while simultaneously declaring class a dead issue. Once it was rebadged, the middle-class cohort the conservatives had first courted and then ennobled felt increasingly emboldened to expect greater patronage, extra tax cuts, more concessions, a larger slicer of the welfare pie. As a result all subsequent governments were forced to contend with a middle class with an increasing sense of entitle-ment to welfare. And these funds were duly disbursed – largely at the expense of the poor, the sick and the unemployed.

This, of course, was the real politics of envy at work. Howard exploited middle-class resentment of the so-called welfare class and pandered to a sense of victimhood in Middle Australia that Rudd and Gillard either couldn't or wouldn't see. Battlers morphed into 'working families' as prospering Australians were taught to minimize their good fortune and expect more state aid. From the subsidization of private schools to the tax rules favouring the superannuation prospects of the already comfortable, this is the new welfare paradigm. Evidence of it was everywhere before the 2013 federal election as single mothers were stripped of income and middle-class parents who earnt up to $150 000 a year were promised a full wage for six months to stay home and look after their own children.

As the *Sydney Morning Herald*'s economics editor Ross Gittins wrote in a column in the lead-up to the poll, 'If you think the class war is over, you're not paying enough attention.' He said: 'The reason the well-off come down so hard on those who use class rhetoric is that they don't want anyone drawing attention to how the war is going.' To suggest that ours is a classless society, or that matters of class are resolved because of national prosperity and the ideological victory of the right, is either tin-eared or dishonest. At least the Americans are brutally frank about it. Gittins went on to quote Warren Buffett who declared: 'There's class warfare alright, but it's my class, the rich class, that's making war, and we're winning.'

Australia may be dazzlingly prosperous, and keen to project a classless image to itself and others, but it is still socially stratified, even if there are fewer obvious indicators of class distinction than there were forty years ago. Accent surely isn't one of them. Postcodes can be telling but not conclusive. Even a person's occupation can be unreliable, and the world of surfaces has never been trickier to read. In an era of lax credit regimes, what people wear or drive is misleading, as is the size of the homes they live in. Australians have begun to live ostentatiously, projecting social aspirations that owe more to the entertainment industry than to political ideology.

The soundest measure of a person's social status is mobility, and the chief source of mobility is income. Whether you're born to it or accumulate it, wealth determines a citizen's choice of education, housing, healthcare and employment. It's also an indicator of health and longevity. Money still talks loudest, even if it often speaks from the corner of its mouth. Even if it covers its mouth entirely. And governments no longer have a taste for the redistribution of wealth. Neither are they keen on intervening to open enclaves and break down barriers to social mobility. Apparently these tasks are the responsibility of the individual.

Where once Australia looked like a pyramid in terms of its social strata, with the working class as its broad base and ballast and the rich at the top, it's come to resemble something of a misshapen diamond – wide in the middle – and that's no bad thing in and of itself. I say that, of course, as a member of the emblematically widening middle. The problem is those Australians the middle has left behind without a glance.

In recent years the incomes of the top fifth have outgrown those at the bottom by more than four times. At the other end there are the poor, who make up almost 13 percent of the population. The most visible of them will always be the welfare class: the sick, the addicted, the impaired and the unemployed, who only exist in the public mind as fodder for tabloid TV and the flagellants of brute radio. But if ever there was a truly Forgotten People in our time it must be the working poor. These folk, the cleaners and carers and hospitality workers, excite no media outrage. They labour in the shadows in increasingly contingent working situations. Categorized as 'casuals', the only casual element of their existence is the attitude of the entities that employ them. Often on perpetual call or split shifts, their working lives are unstable. Many of them women, a significant proportion of them migrants, they have little bargaining power and low rates of union representation. As Helen Masterman-

Smith and Barbara Pocock vividly documented in their 2008 study *Living Low Paid*, these are the figures ghosting down the corridors of hospitals and five-star hotels. They stock the shelves of supermarkets in the wee hours. They mind the children of prosperous professional couples and wash their incontinent parents in care for an hourly rate most middle-class teenaged babysitters can afford to turn their noses up at. It is upon these citizens that the prosperity of safer families is often built.

For these vulnerable Australians there is little mobility. And precious little of what mobility affords – namely, confidence. The cockiness that irritates the old middle class when they encounter FIFO workers with their Holden SS utes and tatts and jet skis is rare amongst the labouring poor. For years I worked in a residential highrise where the looks on people's faces in the lifts and on the walkways ranged from wry resignation to unspeakable entrapment. Single mothers on shrinking benefits, injured workers on disability allowances, middle-aged people staggering back from a night at Woolworths. Even the most functional and optimistic of them seemed tired. They were not exhausted from partying, from keeping up with all their dizzying choices; they were worn out from simply hanging on and making do. As an accidental tourist in their lives, I was struck by this weariness. And I felt awkward in their presence. Their faces and voices were completely familiar. They smelt like the people of my boyhood – fags, sugar and the beefy whiff of free-range armpit – but despite the cheerful, noncommittal conversations we had on our slow ascents in the lift, I felt a distance that took many months to come to terms with. Like the expatriate whose view of home is largely antique, I was a class traveller who'd become a stranger to his own. For all my connection to family, for all the decades I'd spent in fishing towns amongst tradespeople and labourers, the working class I knew was no more. My new neighbours were living another life altogether.

The sociologist Zygmunt Bauman writes about the contrast between the 'light, sprightly and volatile' working lives of mobile citizens at the top of society who are underpinned by those largely without choice and prospects. Comfortable, confident people, heirs of the new individualism, often view strangers in cohorts below them in astoundingly superficial terms, as if they have adopted a look, chosen an identity – as they frequently do themselves – as if life were a largely sartorial affair. Faced with your own surfeit of choices, it's easy to assume everyone has so many. The 'liquid' elite understands exotic poverty – it rallies to it tearfully – but it often fails to recognize domestic hardship: poverty of choice, poverty born of constraint, the poverty that is working servitude or the bonded shame of unemployment. Despite the angelic appeal of market thinking, there is no gainsaying the correlation between success and certain family backgrounds, geographical locations, ethnicities and schools. Pretending otherwise isn't simply dishonest, it's morally corrosive.

The culture that formed me was poorer, flatter and probably fairer than the one I live in today. Class was more visible, less confusing, more honestly defined and clearly understood. And it was something you could discuss without feeling like a heretic. The decency of our society used to be the measure of its success. Such decency rescued many of us from over-determined lives. It was the moral force that eroded barriers between people, opened up pathways previously unimagined. Not only did it enlarge our personal imaginations, it enhanced our collective experience. The new cultural confidence this reform produced prefigured the material prosperity we currently enjoy. It is government intervention as much as the so-called genius of the market that has underpinned our national wealth and it amazes me how quickly we've let ourselves be persuaded otherwise.

I have no illusions about overcoming class distinctions completely. Nor am I discounting the role that character plays in an individual's fortunes. But it disturbs me to see governments abandoning those at the bottom while pandering to the appetites of the comfortable. Under such conditions what chance is there for the working poor to fight their way free to share in the spoils of our common wealth? No one's talking ideology. There is no insurrection brewing. For many Australian families a gap in the fence is all the revolution they require. But while business prospers from the increased casualization of its workforce, and government continues to reward the insatiable middle, the prospects of help for the weakest and decency for all seem dim indeed.

Lighting Out

The news came in April but it took weeks to sink in. The book was finished, my publishers were happy. Some days I felt drunk with relief. The rest of the time I had my doubts and suspicions, and I was beset by a strange and mounting urge to get in the car and head for the border. To go where and do what? I had no idea. I just wanted to get out and go. So one day in May I hit the road. My hands were shaking. As I wound up the parched escarpment above Perth, through horse paddocks and orchards and into the jarrah forests, the first cold front of the year rumbled in my wake.

Lighting out for the border is problematic in a country as stupendously large as ours. For a West Australian it's no small thing to get to the state line. Driving from Perth to the Northern Territory takes the best part of a week. The shortest route out of Western Australia is to traverse the Nullarbor Plain into South Australia, a trip of only a couple of days. The last time I'd made that crossing was in the summer of 1969. In those days the Eyre Highway was a vicious limestone track and the journey was the first real travel adventure of my life, after which I set my mind on being a writer. I was nine and a half. Thirty years later I was having second thoughts.

On that previous trip I made the trek with the family in a Hillman Hunter station wagon towing a box trailer converted into a rudimentary camper. Out on the great plain where the blacktop petered out to a limestone track we pulled over to prepare ourselves for the ordeal. Until that point we'd endured only heat and boredom, but when we saw the towering plumes of white dust barrelling our way we knew things were about to get lively. Every oncoming vehicle laboured under a roofload of shredded tyres and mangled rims. Some cars were without windscreens, others looked partially disassembled, and as they hit the civilized bitumen beside us, drivers and passengers alike looked demented. The old man got out and sealed the doors and windows with masking tape. Then we said a travelling prayer and pounded out across the treeless space, teeth rattling in our heads. It was mad fun. For the first hour. In our little English car we were higher than anything else in the juddering landscape, but the chalky dust was infernal and the vibration like nothing I'd ever experienced.

Decades later I swept across the smooth, quartzy bitumen in airconditioned comfort with Marcus Clarke's *For the Term of His Natural Life* playing on the stereo. Late that first day, having made a modest 600 kilometres, I camped on the wooded outer edge of the goldfields where the earth was the colour of chilli powder and the sky a chemical blue. The bark of salmon gums hung in strips like unravelling bandages and as I gathered firewood in a road-daze

I thought of poor Rufus Dawes, the convict character I'd puzzled over as a boy. My mother had given me Clarke's novel the year we crossed the continent. It was the first grown-up novel I read. I hadn't realized the connection when setting out this time, I'd just snatched the audio tape off a rack in haste, something to pass the time and ward off thoughts of my own book.

I cooked dal over the fire and watched the stars. The night looked clear enough to throw a swag down on the dirt but I expected the cold front to overtake me before dawn so I sacked out in the back of the LandCruiser and slept so deeply I didn't hear the roadtrains lumbering by in the distance or even the rig that was pulled up nearby when I woke at first light.

That morning I drove past saltpans and vast eucalypt woodlands into monochrome treelessness. The overcast sky spilled to earth, its blotchy greys hard to distinguish from the cloudy puffs of knee-high scrub stretching windblown and insubstantial to the horizon. The gunmetal two-lane ribboned out changeless until the afternoon surprise of Madura Pass when there was a sudden decline as the Hampton Tableland gave way to the hypnotic Roe Plains. Down on the flats it was all sky. It was like travelling across the seabed, which is more or less what that land is. Everything looked scoured, as if one giant swell had just receded and another was about to come surging in. The only thing separating me from Elsewhere, it felt, was this low, dun-coloured shelf I was pelting across. I drove until I ran out of daylight and when I climbed down onto the dirt I felt stoned. Collecting firewood, boiling a billy – such things seemed to require immense concentration. A gale gathered force from the south-west – the front I'd been outrunning. It came ripping in across the saltbush. There was nothing out there taller than a dog to offer resistance to the elements, nothing between me and the horizon, me and the sky. Even the earth's crust was thin. Beneath me was a limestone karst system stretching inland from the Southern Ocean.

It was hard not to feel vulnerable. This place felt more remote and exposed than the wilderness of the far north Kimberley.

Crouched in the back of the rain-lashed vehicle, eating leftover dal, I recalled how in 1969 we camped in enormous gravel scrapes like moon craters. Nothing lived there; they were desolate, claustrophobic pits whose pink ramparts shielded the wider landscape from view. Puzzled at being deprived of the horizon my brother and I climbed the gravel bund and walked barefoot into the country beyond. You could hear tiny creatures rattle and flutter in the low scrub. From here the world went on forever, like a dream. Apart from the road scar, there was nothing to see that looked like anything much to us: no fences, nor buildings, nor lights, nor people. We didn't know it but that week our father slept with a hefty stick beside him in the trailer because he'd heard on the coppers' grapevine a madman was preying on travellers out there on the plain.

As the storm rocked the LandCruiser on its springs somewhere short of Mundrabilla I locked the doors and went to sleep alone.

Ceduna, the first actual town across the border, was the logical end point for this less than logical road trip. Unless I wanted to press on to Adelaide – and then why not crack on to Melbourne and Sydney, to finish by staring out upon the Pacific? Maybe. For the moment Ceduna was enough; if I got up early and went like hell I'd make it by dark. All I remembered of it from childhood was a wind-ravaged caravan park and a late-night shower in thongs in a reeking ablution block.

At first light I hit the road. Taj Mahal on the stereo. I was relaxed now. I could do this for days. The road was wide and flat and all but empty. The driving was effortless. I ploughed on, foot on the floor, mind mercifully blank.

Suddenly I was in South Australia, blowing along the brink of the Bunda cliffs. I caught glimpses of the wild sea, streaks of spume, spray in the air. I'd been through Eucla and Border Village and crossed the state line without even registering them. It's a wonder I wasn't stopped; I was driving like a fugitive.

Then, quite suddenly, the trance lifted. I don't know why. I eased off the throttle and pulled over. I clambered down into the buffeting salt wind and felt all the momentum leach away from me. I watched a rain squall hammer in across the heath and knew I was done; I'd lost the urge to go any further. I wanted to climb back up, pull a U-turn and head home. But I was only a few kilometres out from the White Well ranger station and the head of the Great Australian Bight. At least that was a landmark. And there might be whales, something memorable to seize upon as punctuation. I made myself get back in and drive those extra few minutes.

At the lookout I stared down into the storm-torn sea. Spray misted my face as waves hurled themselves against the crags. If there were whales out there I couldn't see them. I gave it three minutes. Then I got back in the car and drove west. Ceduna could wait for another occasion. And so could all the other places I remembered from my childhood adventure. I filled up and headed for home, and thanks to the long-range tanks I wouldn't need to stop for anything but sleep. I was locked in, hurtling, pausing for nothing: not the dune-covered telegraph station at Eucla nor the Cocklebiddy caves and the blowhole at Caiguna. And though I've always wanted to make the trek out to the Eyre Bird Observatory I blew on past the turn-off.

But the road back looked different. I saw things I hadn't noticed on the outward leg. Like the roadkill, for instance: so many roos and emus and reptiles twisted and split at the shoulder of the highway. Every few minutes there'd be something sprawled directly in my path, a dark hump of flesh under a poultice of birds. How had I not noticed this carnage before? What had I actually been taking in these past days? Had I seen anything except the horizon?

Once I'd registered the highway gore it was pretty much all I saw. I fixed on the crows in particular, the way they feasted at the gravel shoulder in querulous brigades. The road was so flat and straight and empty that these congregations were visible for kilometres. Massed in the shimmering distance they were legion. They didn't even look like birds, they could have been people out there gathered for ceremonial purposes: mourners, dancers, singers, all leaping and crooning and feeding behind an aqueous veil. With such a distance to cross between sighting each new aggregation and reaching it, I had a long time in which to anticipate, to puzzle and wonder. And I must have seemed so far off and inconsequential to the birds themselves because once I finally reached them they seemed startled, even affronted. Most stirred and cranked themselves aloft. Some merely stepped back at the last possible moment and shrugged like bored labourers in the slipstream.

Now and then, in the sky above these roadside gatherings, I caught the profiles of kestrels and hawks. Late in the day I saw a wedgetail eagle, a magnificent specimen the colour of mahogany. Its great wings were spread. Wind rifled through its plumage as it lay there, knocked flat on its back at the roadside. The spectacle shook me. I couldn't help but take it personally because it brought back the summer I'd tried so hard to put behind me.

I pressed on miserably until dusk when I came upon a solitary grove of eucalypts clumped together conspicuously on the plain. I'd begun to make camp in the lee of these emaciated gums when a car with a caravan pulled up almost on top of me. In a funk I packed my gear and drove another kilometre into the low scrub beyond. I grilled a T-bone on two sticks over some hard-won coals and when it was ready I fumbled and spilled it into the fire. I ate it disgustedly, ash and all. I was tired but too unsettled to climb straight into the sack.

The previous November, after nearly seven years of mostly pleasurable work, I'd boxed up the manuscript of my latest novel so it could be sent to the publishers before the deadline. At twelve hundred pages, weighing 6.5 kilos, it was a hefty parcel. My daughter, ten years of age, could never recall a time when I was not working on this story; it had been the backdrop to her life and its completion was something of a puzzle to her. In the rest of the family there was cautious relief. No one, including me, could quite believe it was finally over. It wasn't.

At the end of that momentous day my wife came home from work to find me exactly as she'd left me six hours earlier – standing white-faced at the desk, straightening pages, leafing through, reading passages and restacking them. For months I'd harboured a gnawing doubt and during the day it had become uncontrollable. I was paralyzed by the hardening realization that the entire thing had taken a wrong turn in the final draft. It didn't work. It was a turkey, a terrible mistake. I should be burning it, not sending it. After twenty years as a novelist I was about to blow a deadline for the first time. Worse, I'd have to can the book completely. But it had already been advertised. Not my idea, but there it was. There was a production schedule, a publication date, a title in the public realm. For me this was a disaster. Never before, at the approach of a deadline, had I had a manuscript so far away from being a book.

I told my wife the novel was a wash. I'd have to cancel it or begin rewriting immediately. She advised me to do nothing until I'd cooled off; I should get some rest and seek counsel, there was time yet. It didn't feel to me as if there were time for anything but despair, but I held off burning the manuscript and sent it to a couple of luckless friends before limping off for the summer holiday.

Summer was a disaster. The wind never let up. I lay awake every night in a slimy sweat and spent the daylight hours brooding. I was doing nothing at all but beneath the weight of those wasted years I could not rest.

Eventually my friends called. They were kind; their verdicts confirmed my suspicions. They thought there was a novel buried in the manuscript and they had many suggestions about unearthing it, but by this time I'd lost faith in the story and didn't believe I could salvage it. Worse, I'd lost all confidence in my abilities as a writer. I'd certainly had bad days before, but not weeks and weeks like this. I couldn't control the panicky conviction that my gifts had deserted me. Every book I read only confirmed what was beyond my reach. The great pleasure of reading became a misery. I'd begun the summer trying to be philosophical. There'd be other novels, I told myself; nothing is ever really wasted. I could learn from this. I just needed to accept it. But then I wondered if there would be other novels. It began to feel there might be nothing left, no stories, no craft, no sustaining impulse. I was sick, ashamed, bitter, afraid.

The holiday petered out unhappily; we went home early and I met the new year in the grip of an unfocused rage. Depressed, unreachable, sleepless for days on end, I was a malignant presence in the house.

One Saturday night, having thrashed about into the small hours, I got out of bed, walked down to the office and confronted the manuscript on the desk with its many boxes of drafts and notes. I hated the sight of that pile – hated even touching it – but I was furious enough to rip the brown paper wrapping off and stare again at the title page. After a couple of moments I sat down and sharpened a box of pencils. Then in a weird, vengeful spirit I cracked a ream of green paper and began the whole thing once more from the beginning.

It was as if a fever had come upon me. I was angry at the story, at the wasted time, at myself. I squirmed in my seat, hardly able to credit the fact that I was embarking on this journey again. It was a crazy thing to do but it felt no worse than rolling around in bed and just thinking about it. The tedium was immeasurable. I felt as though I were bashing back up a long, stupid detour in order to find the old track and the only thing propelling me was fury. That anger scoured every page, every word. The tip of the pencil felt hot, as if it channelled rage, and my mind was no wider than the pencil itself. I didn't know it but in my madness I was testing the boundaries of an ancient puzzle, namely how to get a camel through the eye of a needle. And as I was to discover, it mightn't be a pretty business but it's certainly possible.

First kill your camel. Next, light a big fire. After that get a cauldron big enough to hold your hapless dromedary. If it becomes necessary, hack the beast of burden to pieces and keep the pot at the boil for days on end. Then take a straw and a suture needle and begin spitting your rendered camel through the tiny aperture. Just don't expect to enjoy yourself. And for pity's sake, do it in private; this is a spectacle no one else should ever have to witness.

I'm only half joking about this, because that's what the process felt like. I didn't regret the murder of my camel. I was grinding up years of work, masticating it and spitting words back onto the page in a stream as thin and hot as an oxy-flame.

By two-thirty next afternoon, when I staggered up from the chair, I had twenty fair sheets. I went home, slept a few hours and returned. Mostly I came and went in the dark, seething, disassociated and slightly deranged. Fifty-five days later I had a novel. It was six hundred pages shorter than what I'd set out with, a different book, but at least it was a book. And there was still time in which to have it edited, set and bound. I sent it off. My publishers seemed happy. But I didn't know what or how I felt. So I bunked off.

I sat up late that last night on the Nullarbor. When I ran out of firewood I sat in the dark with the stars lording it over me. It was clear and cold out there; I could feel my thoughts sliding back to the book. In the end I took a pill to make me sleep but it was a restless night. At dawn I drove back to the blacktop and put the rising sun behind me. I was agitated again. The relative calm of the previous couple of days was gone.

In the middle of the morning I overtook two cars, one of which seemed to be towing the other on a perilously short rope. When I blew by I saw there was no towrope at all; the two drivers were simply entertaining themselves, all but touching bumpers in an effort to relieve boredom. At noon the road finally veered a little. I pulled in for fuel at Balladonia. Coming out of the roadhouse dunny I saw the tailgaters introducing themselves to the tailgatees. Both parties were in high spirits.

That afternoon I lost count of the wedgetail eagles patrolling the highway. Hunkered on shaggy legs over the burst remains of mammals, they were an impressive sight. As I approached them, barrelling along at full tilt, they collected themselves in ponderous articulations of bone and feather and sinew to get themselves aloft. In flight they were majestic, every one of them a glory to behold. But they bothered the hell out of me. Each new eagle brought to mind the fifty-five monstrous days and nights of summer. I thought of the six hundred pages I'd slashed from my novel without a second thought. Not all those lost pages were gone because they were poorly written. Whole scenes, chapters, characters and subplots were discarded for being suddenly surplus to requirements. They were the good country I'd back-burnt to save the homestead. Cutting a manuscript is usually a pleasure, relatively easy to do for being so obviously beneficial to the project. But I'd never slashed and pruned on this scale before, nor had I done it at such heinous speed. I suspected I'd made errors of judgement, expunged sections I could have retained. It took me half a day out there on the treeless plain to understand my agitation: I was grieving for lost material.

And the eagles? Well, from year to year and draft to draft there was a scene I could never bring myself to part with, a sequence in my little landscape romance when a man and a woman, driving down a coast road in hostile silence, hit a wedgetail that blunders against the windscreen. The shock causes the driver to veer off the road and almost roll the vehicle. For a few moments they sit dumb as the bird recovers, gathers its great wings, and in a scramble of talons and feathers takes to the sky. It had always been a pivotal point in the story, a fraught moment of change between the two characters. And then one night in summer, like a man bulldozing his home paddock to keep the fire front at bay, I bladed the scene off without hesitation. Too melodramatic, implausible; nobody's going to hit a wedgetail eagle with their car. So, in an instant, at the slash of a pencil, it was gone, another couple of pages out – on to the next thing. And in my besieged state, having found the ruthlessness required to save the book, I thought the scene was gone for good.

But now, as the hours passed and the sun overtook me, I began to see that it was only gone from the novel. I hadn't been able to expunge it from memory. Because I had it all there again, pressing against me: the room I was in when I first wrote it, the rank smell of the carpet, the bobbing heads of pigeons at the crud-smeared window, the rusty rooftops below. I could still see the clean white page and feel the excitement of knowing I had something good to fill it with. Not that the scene was easy to get right. The pains I went to in trying to describe the way the bird struggled for purchase on the duco, its tawny feathers blurred against the glass. I laboured over the moment of collapsing resistance between the man and the woman, the way the natural world corrals and inflames and inspires them. I'd *been* there; I'd inhabited that moment. By sheer force of work I'd made it so real to myself it resonated as an experience. And now, having consigned it to the rubbish bin, I was overcome with regret. All these wedgies, they had me going now; I was thinking of all the other good pages I'd chucked in the bin, the years of labour

I couldn't just shrug off with a purgative road trip.

I'd never had qualms like these before. A feeling of bereavement over a turning point in a book – it was ridiculous. Look, I told myself, you got lucky: you found the novel in the manuscript. You clawed back out of a pit and spared yourself a lot of embarrassment. And, okay, you're a little shaky, talking to yourself out here on the open plain, but at least you've got some sort of book coming out at Christmas; you get to keep the advance – think of the breathing space. Besides, the eagle business probably was a bit florid; you're better off without it. So buck up!

And I did what I could to talk myself down, but the raptors didn't let up.

In the middle of the afternoon, before the Nullarbor began to give way to the first woodlands of the gold country, I saw in the distance a pair of eagles fighting over the remains of something at the roadside. They had the unhurried authority and the sloping shoulders of bankers. As I rushed onward something dark fluttered up between them. The land beyond was piled green with trees like treasures these birds stood guard before. Hell, I was sick of them now. As I bore down upon them I saw the two wedgetails had the body of a third eagle between them. A little unlikely, but there it was. Probably mown down by a truck. They were struggling over the carcass, each bird with a wingtip in its beak so that in the midst of this tug of war the dead raptor rose from the gravel to its full span, dancing upright, feathers bristling in the wind. I was tired and slightly loopy, it's true, but it looked to me as if that eagle were taunting me, capering at the roadside as if to say, *Here I am, not gone yet!*

I flew by. I drove on long after I should have pulled over and I thundered through the salmon gums into the wheatbelt and out toward the coast. I did 1300 kilometres that day. In the final hours I felt every bump in the road. I wondered what it was, this mixture of sadness and exhilaration I was coming home with.

Stones for Bread

Then cherish pity, lest you drive an angel from your door.
WILLIAM BLAKE

'If a child asks you for bread,' Jesus of Nazareth said, 'will you give him a stone?' He seems to have been a man of many awkward questions. On the face of it, this one is a no-brainer. Yet it continues to trouble us. In contemporary Australia, the so-called Lucky Country, when children arrive on our shores pleading for bread – what do we give them?

To those inspired by Jesus' teachings, Palm Sunday is profoundly important. It's a reminder that we walk in his footsteps. We try to carry his liberating impulse with us, to honour it and keep it alive. In communities all over the globe, people walk together for peace and reconciliation. And not just Christians, people of every faith and of no faith at all unite to express shared values and yearnings, a common humanity, the things that bind us rather than those that separate us.

Some of us remember this day particularly as one on which an itinerant prophet spoke truth to power. The Nazarene arrived at the gates of Jerusalem in a calculated parody of imperial pomp: instead of a stallion he rode a borrowed donkey, in place of an army he'd brought along a bunch of holy fools who threw cloaks and palm leaves in his path as if he were some kind of big shot. This was a peaceful act of dissent, a passive provocation, and it was the beginning of a sequence of events that got him executed a week later. Christ's ideas, the teaching his followers came to call The Way, were an affront to the common sense of the time. They were so offensive they could not be tolerated.

And many of us who mark Palm Sunday are the same sort of lily-livered specimens who made up the rabbi's hapless entourage two thousand years ago; we are their echoes. Our purpose is not to praise the conventions of the day, but to dissent from them. We're here to call a spade a spade, to declare that what has become political common sense in Australia over the past fifteen years is actually nonsense, and not just harmless nonsense – it's vicious, despicable nonsense. Something is festering in the heart of our community, something shameful and rotten. It's born of a secret, one we don't like to acknowledge, which we hide at a terrible cost.

You see, we're afraid of strangers. We're even scared of their traumatized children. Yes, this big brash rich nation trembles. When people arrive with nothing but the sweat on their backs and a crying need for safe refuge, we're terrified. Especially if they arrive by boat. It seems the boat makes all the difference. So great and so wild is our fear of maritime arrivals, we can no longer see victims of war and persecution as fellow humans. This fear has deranged us. It overturns all our civic standards, our pity, our tradition of decency, to the extent that we do everything in our power to deny these people their legal right to seek asylum. They're vilified as 'illegals' and their suffering is scoffed at or obscured. Our moral and legal obligations to help them are minimized, contested, or traduced entirely.

Our leaders have taught us we need to harden our hearts against these folk. The political slogans have done their work, the mantras of fear have been internalized. We can sleep at night because these *creatures*, these *objects* are gone. We didn't just turn them away, we put stones in their empty pockets and made them disappear.

But will we sleep easy? I wonder.

We weren't always this scared. I was a young man when we opened our arms and hearts to tens of thousands of fleeing Vietnamese in the 1970s. We looked into their traumatized faces and took pity. We didn't resort to cages or gulags. We took these strangers into our homes and halls and community centres. They became our neighbours, our schoolmates, our colleagues at work, and their calm, humane reception reflected the decency of this country. Malcolm Fraser asked the best of us, and despite our misgivings we rose to the challenge.

Fifteen years ago the nation's leaders began to pander to our fears, and now they are at the mercy of them. Fear has turned us. In our own time we have seen what is plainly wrong, what is demonstrably immoral, celebrated as not simply pragmatic but right and fair. Both mainstream political parties pursue asylum-seeker policies based on cruelty and secrecy. A hard-hearted response to the anguish of others is popular; it's the common sense of our day.

In the time of Charles Dickens child labour was common sense, too. So was the routine degradation of impoverished women. Charity was punitive and the suffering of children inconsequential. The poor of Victorian England were human garbage. Common sense saw them exported, offshored in chains to a gulag out of sight. For many of us, these despised objects are our forebears.

My convict ancestor was a little boy when he was transported, what is now known as an unaccompanied minor. I've been thinking of him lately, this child consigned to oblivion; public events make it unavoidable. And after reading of the sexual abuse of defenceless women on Nauru and Manus Island, the instances of assault by guards, the epidemic of self-harm, I've been wondering how it could be that these things have happened in our time, on our watch, with our taxes, in our name.

From a grisly past, from brutish conventions, Australia emerged to build something better than Victorian England. We distinguished ourselves with a tradition of equality, humanity, solidarity. Until recently we thought it low and cowardly to avert our gaze from someone in need, to turn our face from them as though they didn't exist. That's where our tradition of mateship comes from. Not from closing ranks against the outsider, but from lifting someone up, helping them out, resisting the craven urge to walk by.

Nowadays we don't see refugees' faces at all, and that's no accident. The government hides them from us, in case we feel natural human sympathy. Pity is no longer a virtue but a form of weakness. Asylum seekers have been turned into cargo, contraband, criminals. Quite deliberately, human decency has been supplanted by a consensus built on hidden suffering, maintained by secrecy, cordoned at every turn by institutional deception. This, my friends, is the new common sense.

According to this new dispensation Australia does not belong to the wider world. We're nobody's fool. We have no obligations to our fellow humans, unless it suits us. Why? Because we are exceptional and therefore beyond reproach. What makes us so special is not clear but we are determined, it seems, to distinguish ourselves in the world by our callousness, by our unwavering hardness of heart. We will not be lectured to by outsiders – or, come to think of it, by insiders either – about human rights, torture, or the incarceration of children. We'll bluster at critics and bully whistleblowers into silence. We'll smear their reputations. In the diplomatic language of Tony Abbott, we'll shirtfront them.

But to live as hostages to our lowest fears we must surrender things that are sacred: our human decency, our morality, our self-respect, our inner peace. To passively assent to this new convention is to set out together on a road that leads to horrors. To exile and cage children 'for their own good', to prolong misery 'in order to save life', to declare that the means will justify the end is to echo the lies of tyrants.

If this is common sense I refuse to accept it. I dissent. I have no special moral powers. And I say these things in sorrow. But I know when something's wrong, and what my country is doing is wrong.

Prime Minister, turn us back from this path to brutality. Restore us to our best selves. Turn back from piling trauma upon the traumatized. It grinds innocent people to despair and self-harm and suicide. It ruins the lives of children. It shames us and it poisons the future. Give these people back their faces, their humanity. Do not avert your gaze and do not hide them from us.

In another time, perhaps soon, our common sense will be seen as nonsense. And we'll have to ask ourselves, Was it worth it? This false piece of mind – was it worth the price paid in human suffering? How will we account for ourselves?

Jesus said: 'What shall it profit a man to gain the whole world only to lose his soul?' And I wonder: What does it profit a people to do likewise, to shun the weak and punish the oppressed, to cage children, and make criminals of refugees?

Children have asked us for bread and we have given them stones. We filled their pockets with rocks and pushed them back upon the deep.

So turn back, my country. While there's still time. Truly, we are better than this.

Remembering
Elizabeth Jolley

I was eighteen when I met the novelist and short story writer Elizabeth Jolley. Fresh out of high school I enrolled at Curtin University, then known as the Western Australian Institute of Technology, and found myself in one of her writing classes. I'd never heard of her or her work, but she was the first published writer I ever encountered. She was fifty-five years old and after years of rejection she was in the process of becoming famous.

God knows what I expected, but I hadn't anticipated this genteel old lady in the hippie dress and sandals. She had a lovely soft, hesitant voice, a posh English accent that brought the hairs up on the back of my defensive working-class neck, and she seemed to think that the best way to win over a roomful of kids in op-shop suits and lime-green hair (or in my case, flannel shirt and Adidas Rome joggers) was to begin the class with a few *Lieder*, courtesy of the trusty cassette player she set up on the sill of the non-opening window. I was fascinated by her windswept English teeth. And those granny glasses she wore might have given even Janis Joplin second thoughts.

To be honest, my initial impression of Elizabeth was in keeping with my general disenchantment as a writing student. At that time WAIT was the only Australian university offering a degree in creative writing and I had hopelessly unrealistic expectations of it. I must have confused this fledgling enterprise with the sorts of graduate programs available at Iowa or Stanford, courses I couldn't hope to afford or even qualify for academically. Those famed departments were staffed by major poets and novelists, writers even an eighteen-year-old from Karrinyup might have heard of. But after some early excitement I found myself enrolled in a bog-ordinary BA course with a trendy seventies media bent. Sure, there was writerly stuff on offer, but up close it looked a bit naff. The staff heavyweights taught the real units – the academic end of the deal – but creative writing was mostly left to writers of very modest reputation and experience who wielded no power in the department. As I saw it, WAIT made a big noise about creative writing but never hired accordingly. I imagine things have changed considerably with the years, but back then this institutional imbalance really rankled. In retrospect it would appear the English department preferred to make heavyweights of their own rather than recruiting them from outside.

Of course it was hardly fair of me to expect a Wallace Stegner or Malcolm Bradbury to be teaching in a provincial undergraduate course such as this. I was a kid who knew nothing. But I stayed in the course until I got a degree, and even did a postgrad year. I'm grateful for those four years, but there were times when I felt I'd been sold a pup. During that first class with Elizabeth, as Germans warbled away in glorious monaural from the windowsill, mine wasn't the only face that fell just a little.

When you're a kid you assume you're the only work in progress, that everyone above you, those you look to, have evolved to a level of angelic achievement. But the WAIT writing course, like the department and the literary culture beyond it, was still finding its way, making itself up as it went along. In her publishing career, Elizabeth was likewise still finding her way. She'd published a book of stories with a local press and had some radio plays broadcast. Having written for years, she was struggling to break through all kinds of cultural, gender, geographical and generational barriers. This was several years before Penguin published *Mr Scobie's Riddle* and *Woman in a Lampshade*, almost simultaneously in 1983, when Elizabeth became an unlikely Perth hero in a national literary scene run from Sydney and Melbourne.

At the time it was a significant achievement for a West Australian. It wasn't just that the odds were against you, it took quite a bit of steel to leave the western fold. Writers from Perth felt a burden of loyalty to the Fremantle Arts Centre Press, which did so much to nurture local work, and many were nervous about forsaking its hospitality in the hope of a wider audience and the chance to actually earn royalties. But finding a bigger publisher made a massive difference to Elizabeth's career, and probably her life, and the timing of the move was fortunate; those two books, the strongest of her early period, found their way into the homes and consciousness of many new readers, and other books soon followed to cement her reputation.

Those of us who knew Elizabeth a little could only marvel and cheer as her career blossomed. In the small world of Australian letters it looked as if the eighties belonged to her; she was everywhere. Impossible as it seemed, she was fashionable. And although she appeared baffled by the perennial affirmation, she rose to meet it graciously, and to some certain extent knowingly. She became, in the words of *The Guardian*, 'the laureate of the dotty'. And the work came so quickly, ten books in as many years. I was still a student when it struck me that she was drawing upon a stock of unpublished material going back years, perhaps decades, and it was true – when she arrived in Australia from Glasgow in 1959 she brought with her a trunk full of letters and manuscripts. Some of that material may have been too painful to bring to light then, and some seemed to have been reworked in and for the moment.

At the peak of her fame she published the novels *Foxybaby* (1985) and *The Well* (1986). They were lesser works but they were greeted with near universal acclaim from the critical establishment. By this time she'd been groomed as an eminence and a character by the university, and become nearly indispensable to its reputation. She was, despite her public persona, a worldlier person by then, and perhaps more calculated. But she eventually returned to work that was less performative, and considerably more personal. To my mind *My Father's Moon* (1989) and *Cabin Fever* (1990) are her greatest works, freighted with loneliness, bereavement and desire. Here she seems to have broken free of the grotesqueries and masking humour that sometimes looked like a sly form of crowd-pleasing. These novels leave an afterglow. I can remember where I was when I read them. After years of being contemptuously dismissed by editors and publishers, it must have been no small thing for her to risk the adulation she'd come to enjoy, but in her late novels and novellas there is little of the antic daffiness that brought her work to attention. Instead something more austere and raw emerges.

Even Elizabeth's jacket photographs began to change, reflecting a new confidence. She was captured gazing levelly at the camera, specs off, no smile, nary a twinkle. In a tribute to her published in the now defunct journal *Indigo* the poet Philip Salom suggests that this new direction might have cost Elizabeth critical support, which would be sad if true, but hardly surprising. Either way I can only concur with his assessment of these late works as her best. They seem to me the work of someone in deadly earnest, at full stretch, beyond any need of approval.

But in the late 1970s, when I spent most time with her, Elizabeth probably had more determination than confidence. She was yet to be liberated and quickened by the affirmation of readers and critics. In those early years at WAIT, I think many of us who were Elizabeth's students learnt to write alongside her, or perhaps it's more accurate to say in her wake. We were there to witness the way she learnt to teach, and to publish. And her publishing career was every bit as instructive as her classes. Long after that single year I was in her class she was still teaching me how to be a writer.

Writing, the act itself, remains a personal mystery – Elizabeth taught me that early. Its processes and origins are hard to articulate and are sometimes best left to explain or conceal themselves. Whether writing can be taught with any rigour or by any system or with any realistic expectations is an open question. But publishing the stuff is something closer to a political science. This can be learnt. The public and procedural aspect of the writing life involves negotiations and accommodations bewildering to the innocent arts apprentice but hardly unfamiliar to, say, the employee with hopes of advancement. A peculiar suite of skills, which have nothing to do with art, needs to be acquired in order to survive honourably. When it came to such things as discretion, charm and oblique professionalism, Elizabeth had no peer. She had a passive-aggressive genius, a gentle way of patronizing while appearing to be patronized, indulging while seeming to be indulged, and I have no doubt that her years in the academy, about which she could be scathing in private, armed her well in this regard. She might have looked the fey old lady in sandals but her survival instincts were keen. For someone with such an unbusinesslike mien, she was rather good at taking care of business – and then covering her tracks. In one form or another she saw the value in deft representation. In life and in work, she'd been forced to take the long view.

I'm often asked what it was like to be taught by Elizabeth Jolley and I'm hesitant to answer, because many who ask have already formed a settled impression and they don't like you mucking it up. In terms of the mechanics of craft, I learnt much more at the feet of people I never met. I also learnt plenty from teachers at WAIT who didn't write fiction or poetry at all. I certainly didn't learn to write dialogue at Elizabeth's feet, especially not in the vernacular. For someone so musical she had a tin ear for talk, unless characters spoke Edwardian or Mittel-European. To her, anyone less cultured must have simply sounded cockney. She was good on atmosphere, with interiors, and the natural world; good at alerting you to what you could do with them on the page. Some Australian and American writers have been better teachers than practitioners of their craft: Elizabeth wasn't one of them. In my experience, particularly of those early years, her writing far outstripped her skills as a teacher.

Yet the student of writing often learns despite what they're being taught, either by defiance or by watching the teacher rather than engaging with the lesson, and I think the latter probably applies to much of my time with Elizabeth. She had no enthralling program, no killer technique, no charismatic presentation. She did have an eccentric persona, but for a young student this was as much an obstacle as a delight. Several of my classmates, some of whom became considerable writers, might now be glad to have been in Elizabeth's classes, but I know that at the time they felt they'd learnt nothing useful from her. I am likewise glad to have been in her strange orbit, for though I was often bewildered by her in class I did learn things from her that are still important to me.

In the teaching of writing she focused on the thing itself, the story or the poem before us. She didn't entertain much talk of theory; at that time her sensibility owed more to the English and German Romantics than to anything modern, let alone postmodern. Her awe for the mystery of language was tempered by the practical realities of the artisan, and this combination had an enduring effect on me. She was cautious with words and stories but not ideologically suspicious of them. She politely resisted the pseudoscientific discourse sweeping through the department. These were the early days of semiotics, the Cuisenaire rods that preceded the murkier calculus of cultural studies. When it came to music, however, she was a believer, almost a mystic. She held to it as a life force, and again this was instructive and sometimes also sweetly stubborn. For her it seemed to literally inspire story and language, and she often tried to 'work us up' with it. To many of us the *Lieder* were a bit of a stretch, but Neil Diamond was a bridge too far.

She took her work as a teacher seriously. That meant, God bless her, she took our work seriously too, and that decency must have cost her something. When she commended you faintly on an image or a line of prose you had the sense that she'd dipped briefly into the same reservoir of respect – for nature, for human experience, for language – she reserved for Goethe or Rilke. But she was thrifty in all things, and praise was no exception; she offered it carefully, with a sense of proportion. Despite her daily encounters with the gormless, the mulish, the self-deluded, the shiftless and the hopelessly untalented, she maintained a kindness and consideration that strike me now as heroic. I'm not just referring to her courtesy – she was courteous whether courtesy had been earned or not – but to the way she gave credit for the work and intentions and efforts of others. While most of us were surely wasting her precious time she nevertheless gave us her full attention, she sought and fixed upon whatever flicker of promise she could detect in our generally dreadful offerings, and she offered her comments with a delicacy and tact that seemed to belong to another time and place. I know from my own brief and undistinguished months of trying to teach that a similar generosity was beyond me.

Elizabeth said that when she sensed something promising or exceptional in a piece of student writing she would read it to her husband Leonard for his comment. She told me she did this with several of my stories, and I have no doubt she meant it as a compliment because she was still reminding me of it decades later. She read to him once she'd settled him in bed, hours before she turned in herself. As a youth, and even as a man in middle age, I could barely picture such a scene because the Jolleys were not ordinary folk. To a boy from rough-and-ready Karrinyup they were larger than life, like characters from Thomas Mann: physically unprepossessing, crippled in Leonard's case, but cultured and sensitive people for whom art was vital business.

Elizabeth appeared to defer to Leonard in all things. He was an imperious little man with good taste and a notoriously sharp tongue, and as the librarian at the University of Western Australia he'd enjoyed considerable status within their social circle, but these were the years in which Elizabeth's reputation began to match and then eclipse his, and her apparent deferrals were not nearly as straightforward as they seemed. So it wasn't the idea of these grand figures bothering to waste time on my raw divots of prose that impressed me so much as the prospect of my lumpen fictional world intersecting with the complex dance of their domestic life, for theirs was a peculiar milieu indeed. And as we were later to discover, partly fictional in itself. When a bit of work got the nod from both of them you took it seriously – well, I did. I don't know whether, in those early years, Elizabeth ever really deferred to Leonard's judgement or if she just liked to mask her own praise in his, but their combined verdict of approval felt like approbation from the board of governors.

In those writing classes, once I'd reconciled myself to Elizabeth's cultural and generational strangeness and learnt to negotiate her scything wit and the shielding genius of her persona, I wrote my first real stories. Some were published in magazines and one I later included in my first collection. Under Elizabeth's surveillance my first novel began life as a radio play, a form I've always hated and in which she excelled. The genre was her idea but the script was all my own miserable doing. After the book's publication in 1982 she was gracious enough never to mention its squalid origins. She understood, as few others can, the art of literary salvage.

As a teacher she had the kind of humility that allowed her to stand aside. She didn't feel the need, or perhaps the entitlement, to wade into your work or your fictional world with her gumboots on. She looked for what you were *trying* to do, not just what you'd failed to do. She did not require you to write like her or to address her special fictional concerns. But she expected you to take your work at least as seriously as she did.

Elizabeth wrote to be published. As a result of her own long and often thwarted apprenticeship she had more practical advice about the business of submitting work for publication than anyone else I ever encountered. Like Tom Keneally on the other side of the continent, she was a pro trying to lift herself from the swamp of amateurism that still prevailed in Australian letters. Her ideas were pragmatic, her outlook seasoned by disappointment, by the cycles of fashion, and by politics and personality. She had plenty to say about endurance and self-belief, about editorial pettiness, geographical hubris, and deep prejudices surrounding age and gender. She let you know which editors to avoid, which magazines to try repeatedly, who was asleep at the wheel, who 'forgot' to pay, who was an out-and-out liar, and how fickle the entire enterprise was. In sending manuscripts to editors you had to be systematic, even cold-blooded, keeping distance between yourself and the work. You had to understand the virtues of order; you did your homework about who it was you were submitting to. And there was plenty of solemn chat about clean envelopes and good staples.

She was a mine of information, and in a publishing sense a class warrior along with it. She took the business of publishing as seriously as she did the art of writing. She was not an amateur, was not content to be viewed as one, and she refused to be coy about being a pro. Elizabeth believed in craft – absolutely, passionately – but she also relied on tradecraft. It's so hard to make a living as a writer, and much harder if you're too precious to find out how publishing works. To Elizabeth this was simply good housekeeping, and any interest you showed in this kind of professional development – the grubby, industrial side of being a writer – was eagerly rewarded. Within her teaching environment and the writerly ecosystem of the period, this made her exceptional, and was a brisk antidote to the evasive boho insincerity about publishing that still wafts around writers' gatherings. Elizabeth was a romantic with discreet but steely ambition. She couldn't abide dabblers or pretenders. She'd never call you a wanker to your face, but she had a certain distant look, a pursy set to the mouth at times that did the work for her.

I don't mean to imply anything mercenary here, only that Elizabeth had good strategic impulses. Even while publishing from the wrong side of the country, she managed to negotiate the strange undertow that prevails closer to home. She had an unholy knack for wrong-footing the locally embittered or envious, and she always did it with a smile. A writer from an anxious provincial city like Perth could hardly have sought better counsel.

Elizabeth pioneered the servicing of reading groups. Before these became mainstream they were a pretty daggy, if badly understood, part of civilian reading culture, and in the west most of them were in the bush. In the early 1980s Elizabeth drove gamely all over rural Western Australia to meet isolated book clubs, to drink their tea, dazzle them, answer their questions. There was a generosity about this as well as a lack of preciousness, and these readers became her first constituency. Without publicity or publisher support she developed a broad and loyal readership, one that became rusted on for life. The people who met her in those farmhouses and tiny country halls quite rightly adored her, and she slyly flogged them books from the boot of the car while she was at it. She was a one-woman literary festival, a roadshow, returning with stories to tell, a few bob extra, and an acute understanding of her audience.

Although she was modest and self-deprecating, Elizabeth did have a very strong sense of her own dignity, and of the value of her work as both teacher and writer. You failed to see this at your own peril, for when she was offended or angry her disappointment was, despite its quiet expression, quite chilling. I can testify to this from the day I owned up to withholding my best work from class. I'd been sending stories to magazine editors without showing her. In their stead, to satisfy course requirements, I'd begun handing in things I knew were second-rate but good enough to pass. I was disillusioned with the broader course and keen to make some kind of headway in what I thought of then as the wider world. The long view was beyond me.

She'd noticed the inferior work and puzzled over it, and I was quick to explain and very slow to see how she felt about it. How could it matter? I thought. Why waste good stories to pass some crap unit in some mickey mouse course? What was her problem? Callow and self-absorbed as I was, I couldn't see how disrespectful and unnecessary this substitution was, how lacking in mutuality. Elizabeth had given of her comradely best, and she expected mine in return. She offered respect and had a right to have it reciprocated, regardless of how I felt about the degree. She'd never once made an obstacle of herself. She always kept the faith, served the work. And here I was, treating her like some tenured time-server. She was hurt, and told me so in language so genteel it flew by like birdsong. I was halfway home before I began to understand what a bollocking she'd given me. In the decades afterwards it pleased her to remind me of this episode, with an affectionate and vicious twinkle of the eye, preferably with an audience. I had to take every wild embellishment, every fictional flourish – and, believe me, there were plenty of them – as my just deserts.

The launch of Elizabeth's second collection, *The Travelling Entertainer and Other Stories*, in November of 1979 was my first experience of a book launch. The Fremantle Arts Centre hosted a gathering of citizens from the requisite three postcodes of the day and there was the kind of riesling on offer that has happily since gone the way of the flagon. There were fine speeches by Ian Templeman and the author herself, and piles of the handsome book, which cost $4.50. To me everyone seemed very old and venerable and alien. My girlfriend and I were excited and wildly uncomfortable. I'd written a novel myself by then and had begun another. I wondered if this was what lay in store. In truth it didn't look all that promising. We stood in line to have a book signed and Elizabeth was ebullient and tipsy and terribly funny. In that spidery hand, which I would recognize anywhere, she wrote the inscription:

> *For an intimate friend*
> *Tim Winton*
> *I look forward to your book*
> *Elizabeth Jolley 14.11.79*

Even at nineteen I got the joke. We were friendly, Elizabeth and I. In time she would dandle my children on her knee. We had friends in common, shared the same agent, and corresponded fitfully over the years. We phoned one another to confer on professional matters because in this we spoke the same language and trusted each other's judgement and discretion. Yet warm and comradely as our acquaintance was, we were never intimate friends. Her inscription is the sort of thing you scrawl at book launches after a couple of glasses of plonk in a roomful of luvvies, with a nod and a wink and a gentle dig. This, dear boy, she may as well have said, is what lies ahead. Gird yourself. Keep your game face on. Intimate friends, won't this give them a laugh in a few years' time!

Beyond her circle of intimates – and she made good and loyal friends – Elizabeth was too guarded, too performative in her way, to be easily knowable. To the rest of us her battiness was an essential part of the persona. She was always kind, ever funny, but later in life the routine became harder to read. She'd pretend not to remember you for a moment then drill you with some cringeworthy detail from decades previous. With Elizabeth confusion was expected, a wily comeback only moments away. You sensed a quip in the wings, even when in later years it often failed to arrive. In this, I think it's fair to say, she gave of herself what she could, as she could. Right up to the end and after it, in person and on the page, Elizabeth Jolley kept us guessing.

Sea Change

In the early light of morning I back the dinghy into the water, jerk it free of the trailer and leave my father holding the painter while I park the vehicle at the foot of the dune. As I walk to the water's edge I see the bait truck rolling onto the jetty a few metres away beneath a haze of gulls. Out at the edge of the lagoon, a crayboat steams in through the passage in the reef.

The old man has the outboard running, but he's still standing in the shallows. He's over eighty now and climbing aboard isn't the simple matter it once was. We get him in, one stiff leg at a time, and before I can leap in after him there's a swirl and a huff behind me as one of the local dolphins surfaces an arm's length away. It sidles in, cocks an eye at me, and familiarity being what it is, I haul myself aboard without a backward glance. The dolphin drifts along-side, rises on its tail, and lets off a few shameless squeaks, but I'm immune to all entreaties. Still, before I can put the motor into gear it leans its scarred head into the boat and tries one last time to charm its way into a free feed.

'Go on, you lazy bugger,' I say. 'Get your own.'

As we get under way, the dolphin shadows us, jumps, flashes ahead to ride the bow wave. But none of the old moves pay off and eventually it peels away to join the others rounding up herring in a pack along the bay. We skate across the lagoon with its mottled seagrass pastures and anchor in a sandy channel to fish for whiting.

'How many are we allowed these days?' asks the old man.

'Thirty,' I say.

'Only thirty?'

'Dad, thirty's still a good feed.'

He shrugs. I guess things seemed better, freer in the old days. As kids in the thirties and forties, he and his siblings caught crays and herring and silver trevally from the shore. They collected their own maggots for bait and humped their catch home in hessian sacks. Sometimes, as the stories have it, they caught more than they could carry. Back when there was so much more coast than there were people living on it, the sea was mad with fish.

'I spose thirty'll do,' he says.

I cut bait and look out over the water, the hulking white dunes, and the low roofs of the hamlet in the narrow margin between them. The good old days may be long gone, yet here we are, as ever, launching a boat from the beach in a quiet bay under cloudless skies, bobbing on clean water. In an hour we'll have enough sweet-tasting fish to feed two households. Not so long ago we'd have fished until we ran out of room in the esky. Now, thank God, thirty whiting will do.

Since I was a teenager, when I first began to write stories for a living, I've mostly stayed close to the wilder shores of Western Australia. The places most precious to me are those where the desert meets the sea. The littoral – that peculiar zone of overlap and influx – continues to sustain my spirit and fuel my work.

In the early 1990s I wrote a little memoir called *Land's Edge* to describe the beach culture I grew up in and the natural world that inspired me. Back then I was the father of young children. I loved introducing my kids to the lifestyle I knew as a boy and which my parents and grandparents had enjoyed before me. We lived in a fishing community of six hundred people. The school was over the road, the beach was only a block away and dunes loomed over everything, strange and changeable as the sea itself.

In many ways the conditions of our life together as a family were very modest. We certainly didn't have much money, but to my mind we lived very well. After a couple of years in Europe I'd come to observe just how constrained a prosperous modern life could be. So I was conscious of how privileged our coastal existence was, and grateful for it. Every day as a matter of course we did what other folks did on their holidays, we pulled craypots before breakfast, snorkelled with sea lions on our lunchbreak, and bombed off the jetty at sunset. Some weeks we ate only what we'd grown in the garden or caught in the bay. Squid, abalone and crayfish were standard fare. Whenever the swell and wind were gentle enough I took a small boat out through the reef pass to deeper waters offshore to supplement our diet with dhufish, snapper and black-arsed cod.

Having inherited all this bounty we had to count ourselves as some of the luckiest people alive. We'd done nothing to earn it – the living ocean was simply passed down to us – and for that gift I will always be grateful.

This summer just gone I took my granddaughter into the sea for the first time. She wasn't walking then, so she clung like a barnacle as I waded in with her. It was lovely to feel her shudder with the strangeness of all those competing stimuli – the surges of current and light and noise, the spill of waves across her delicate skin. What a thrill it is for a sun-damaged old beachcomber to initiate another generation, to feel that I'm passing on a kind of saltwater birthright – a healthy sea. Yet only a fool could suggest that little girl's coastal inheritance is secure.

It's hardly controversial to say the world's oceans are in peril – that's been the consensus view amongst marine scientists for years. Many great fisheries have collapsed. Ninety percent of the biggest pelagic fishes are gone. Coral reefs are in strife. Land clearing and rapid coastal development have put insupportable pressures on many marine ecosystems, and as terrestrial sources of mineral wealth are exhausted, the oceans become the new frontier. The world's population has exploded and all the fishing, drilling, building and dumping is catching up with us. Even before we consider the prospect of acidification from global warming, we're headed toward a situation where the oceans can no longer tolerate what humans dish out.

Hunting and gathering are in my blood. Fishing is an integral part of my family culture. I have lived most of my life in communities where people either fish for a living or fish to simply feel alive. But I've also lived long enough to witness a diminution in the seas, and to notice a fragility where once I saw – or assumed – an endless bounty. I was slow to comprehend all this; the image of the slowly boiling frog fits me perfectly.

In the nineties I got used to diving longer and deeper to find abalone where not long before getting my quota had been easy work. Prize species like dhufish and snapper became locally scarce, and all around me boats got bigger as recreational fishers had to venture further and further out to catch a feed. You didn't need to be any sort of boffin to know something was wrong; fishing, even for hobbyists, had become hard work. Eventually I understood that I wasn't merely a witness, I was a part of the equation. As was every person I knew.

Of course the worst of what was happening at sea was not taking place in my backyard. By world standards what I was seeing was relatively mild. Europe and Asia had dead zones already. Closer to home in the Pacific, plastic gyres the size of cities were beginning to appear. Catastrophic oil spills like the *Exxon Valdez* disaster of 1989 seemed safely distant. But twenty years later, the illusion of immunity was shattered when, for seventy-four days, the Montara platform spilled oil into the Timor Sea off Western Australia. Suddenly problems facing our marine environment were no longer over the horizon. I began to read some of the emerging science and got a clearer picture of what my senses were already telling me, and it was this slow realization of a global threat and trouble at home that stirred me to become an activist. It was obvious that all of us, even Australians, needed to change our behaviour. The science suggested we should reduce our consumption and set aside areas of marine habitat as sanctuaries for regeneration.

In 1997, a few years after I became the honorary vice-president of the local branch of the Australian Marine Conservation Society, I published a little book called *Blueback* in which a woman and her son fight off a development juggernaut that threatens to destroy the lonely, pristine bay they live on. It was only a fable but in it I was wondering what it took to save a precious place. Some years later I'd have cause to wonder if perhaps I hadn't unconsciously been rehearsing for a new phase of my life, because it was shortly after publication that I found myself in a battle for just such a place. During the years of the Save Ningaloo campaign it often felt as if I'd gotten myself snagged in a far less wishful version of my own novel. And it felt as if the story was not only uncontrollable but inescapable.

Once Ningaloo Reef was properly protected in 2003 it was

evident that the stewardship of our oceans had become a main-stream concern in Australia. People expected their national heritage to be defended, and nothing seemed more precious than the sea around them.

After Ningaloo I tried to return to the reclusive life I'd enjoyed before, but one contest quickly segued into another and now I find myself more or less permanently enmeshed, as if I never will climb out of that little book after all.

All these years later I continue to go to the water every day to surf, wet a line, set my craypots. I'm not the gung-ho fisher I once was, yet whether it's a few squid, a quick snorkel or a sunstruck idea at the jetty, I'm still feeding off the ocean in every possible sense and I owe it a debt. So the rabble-rousing goes on.

It's exhausting, but I'm glad to have played a small part in this cultural sea change. In a few weeks the Australian government is expected to declare a chain of marine parks running from the Southern Ocean to the Coral Sea. Just as our forebears set aside terrestrial reserves for respite and study, for non-extractive recreation and as a form of prudent planning for future generations, marine parks are a means of preserving representative and vulnerable habitats. Work on this process began in 1999 when Liberal prime minister John Howard established the National Oceans Office. Until Tony Abbott rose to the Liberal leadership the initiative was bipartisan. It's also broadly popular. Polling suggests an overwhelming majority of Australians support the establishment of these parks, so the plan should not polarize citizens. Again, the scientific consensus is substantial. It's not a matter of fisheries management, it's about the preservation of ecosystems. The Gillard government has a massive opportunity to create an enduring legacy. It also has a chance to distinguish itself politically, to define itself in a polity obsessed with reactive, short-term twitches and fixes. This is a moment for the future, so you can expect to hear the voices of the past rail awhile. You'll still meet the odd geezer whining that he can't shoot roos in a national park. Sixty years ago blokes like that had plenty of company but now they're a fringe element, maddies. And sixty years hence you'll doubtless find anglers who cannot accept that some bits of the ocean are for fish and not fishing, but again there probably won't be many. Most rec-fishers are philosophical about marine parks, they have a sense of justice and proportion. When they get past the backward bluster and realize that most coastal waters will remain open to fishing, they can't see what the fuss is about.

There will, however, be commercial casualties in this process and it's vital that affected fishing operators are bought out on just terms with dignity. Government must ensure it finds the will and funds to achieve this. And it has to show a bit of courage in taking on some of the bigger vested interests at sea, not just industrial fishing, but the big players of oil, gas and coal whose activities have a serious impact on the marine environment. Few Australians have any idea how much territory is locked up in oil and gas tenements. In Western Australia alone they encircle every important coral reef from Ningaloo to the Montebello Islands, from the Pilbara to the precious Rowley Shoals. The public is only just beginning to see the threat the Queensland coal industry poses to the future of the Great Barrier Reef as more and more coal ports are mooted.

Federal environment minister Tony Burke has hard decisions to make about how much habitat he reserves inshore on the continental shelf – where fishing pressures are most extreme and where most Australians interact with their marine environment – and how much territory he's brave enough to deny industrial interests. There's already an emerging emphasis on reserving abyssal waters at the expense of the contested grounds closer to shore, as if the low-hanging fruit of large offshore zones might make up for how little protection our inshore waters will be afforded – a case of never mind the quality, feel the width. My instinct is that Tony Burke genuinely cares about the outcome. My hope is that he'll resist the urge to fudge. At such a prosperous moment in our history, with so much more at stake for the Australian people than the next political cycle, the boundaries Burke sets may speak not simply to his character and that of the Gillard government, but to the kind of legacy my granddaughter and her kids will have after he and the government and I are gone.

Now and then, when things get bleak and it feels as if nothing really changes, I think of a hole I once swam in at the Montebello Islands, north of Ningaloo. It's a crater a kilometre across, left by a British nuclear bomb in 1952. A strange place to go for a snorkel, I know. There wasn't much to see down there besides glassy sand and weird, white worms. Only a few years before I was born this wanton destruction – the blowing of islands from the sea and the irradiation of entire ecosystems – seemed necessary to secure world peace. Today the Montebellos are nature reserves, their coral reefs teeming with dugongs, whales and spangled emperors, and parcels of the islands are sanctuary zones that should be extended. The shift of mindset, the cultural sea change required to get from bombing them to preserving them – all in the span of a single lifetime – is immense.

People develop. They change. As individuals, yes, but also as families, communities and nations, and the nuclear crater at the Montebellos is a handy reminder of just how much and how quickly. It seems odd to say that a swim in a radioactive hole can be restorative, that it can engender hope, but that's how it felt afterwards as I stood on the boat and thought about how far we've come. In the years since, that hope hasn't faded.

* In 2012 Tony Burke declared the world's largest system of marine parks. When he came to power in September 2013, the new prime minister Tony Abbott announced a moratorium on all new marine parks and

a review of those recently declared. He was removed from office less than two years into his term, but both the freeze and the review have continued under Malcolm Turnbull and his various environment ministers. All indications suggest the government is likely to reduce protection.

Barefoot in the Temple of Art

As you approach the National Gallery of Victoria, along a boulevard jangling with trams in downtown Melbourne, it's easy to see why former director Patrick McCaughey called it 'the Kremlin of St Kilda Road'. It's a massive rectangular block whose blue stone walls have something of the penitentiary about them, and in a quarter teeming with tourists and commuters it manages to retain a perpetual and sinister remoteness. There are no windows. The only break in the mass is a portal arch so tiny it could be a mouse-hole from a *Tom and Jerry* cartoon. Only when you step through that arch do you see the building's inner skin. There's no portcullis here. All that stands between you and Australia's greatest art collection is a falling sheet of water.

The water wall has been disarming pedestrians and delighting children since the museum's unveiling in 1968. Today, on a hot morning in the summer holidays, kids linger to feel the current sluice through their fingers. It's a treat to watch them. It takes me back.

You could say the NGV and I got off to an awkward start. When I first visited, nearly half a century ago, the new building on St Kilda Road had been open less than a year; it was Melbourne's fresh civic triumph, a trophy the city's burghers and bohemians could share and dispute over. But I was of neither tribe. I arrived at her door sweaty and barefoot, a scruffy nine-year-old interloper from the western frontier.

I grew up in a hardy, utilitarian environment, where nobody you knew had ever finished school, where practical skills were valued and beauty, art and language were mere frippery. It seemed there was a cultural moat between me and the speculative dreamworld I later learnt to call art. But there were larger barriers to contend with – distance chief among them. Perth was popularly considered the most isolated city in the world. The 'real' Australia, the one we saw on TV and in magazines, lay elsewhere, somewhere beyond the heat haze of the treeless plain. It was hard not to feel that everything you knew was inconsequential.

Feeling overlooked, even spurned by the eastern states, which make up two-thirds of the landmass, westerners like us suffered the prickly anxiety felt by provincials the world over. We dreamt of making the great crossing to the Other Side, if only to confirm it wasn't all it was cracked up to be. The trip across the Nullarbor was a rite of passage. When my family made the trek in the summer of 1969, a drive longer than that from London to Moscow, there wasn't even a sealed road linking Us to Them.

The privations of that journey, the juddering corrugations and choking dust, were a test of character, but we were sure our ordeals would not be in vain. Keen for us to experience the great world beyond, my parents had taken us out of school early. There was, they said, so much to see and do and learn, and Melbourne was a town where *things happened*. We'd visit the hallowed stands of the Melbourne Cricket Ground, walk the streets where cop shows like *Homicide* and *Division 4* were recorded in glorious black-and-white, and finally, most importantly, we'd tarry in the shadow of the Sidney Myer Music Bowl, where only a year or two earlier the legendary Seekers had played a homecoming concert to two hundred thousand fans, the largest audience in Australia's history.

It took more than a week to reach Melbourne. We knocked the dust from our clothes and worked our way through the sites of pilgrimage and, though no one would admit it, our hearts were sinking. The place looked ordinary. The trams were jaunty in their anachronistic way, but nothing about Melbourne appeared any more potent or Australian than the places we knew. The MCG was just an empty hulk. The scene of The Seekers' triumph, without our white-bread troubadours to enliven it, didn't have much to excite a nine-year-old either. Even Mum and Dad seemed a tad underwhelmed, but they lingered dutifully at the foot of the stage as we kids chased up the freshly mown amphitheatre toward the final stop on the itinerary.

Mum had shown me pictures of the brand-new museum whose massive stained-glass ceiling and groovy water wall had featured in magazines and newspapers. By all accounts the place was terribly modern. But that hot day, footsore as we were, its chief promise was water. We bolted through the parkland from the Music Bowl to the fortress on St Kilda Road, and there, for a moment, we stood awed before the gallery's moat-like fountain pools. Then, like the heathens we were, we dunked our feet and splashed about and were happier than we'd been all day. To me the water was special relief. I'd stubbed both big toes and the flapping scabs were a nuisance. Even before our parents arrived, adults were sooling us out of the water.

Dunking, they said, was disrespectful. Didn't we know this was art?

Once we'd dried off on the hot pavement, we knew better than to touch the tantalizing sheets of the water wall that lay like a shimmering curtain between the portal arch and the mysteries within. We fell into line and followed our parents through the arch. We were on our best behaviour. Mum gobbed on her thumb and cleaned our faces, but when we presented ourselves at the ticket office, we learned that we would not be admitted. Barefoot supplicants were not welcome in the temple of art.

Mum was shamed. We kids were mortified. But there was worse to come, because Dad was irritated and determined to press the point. Fine for him, safely shod in his rubber thongs, but for the rest of us, shrunk back into a knot of ignominy, it was awful. After trying several dud approaches – including the point that, thanks to our recent wading, at least our feet were clean – he made a breakthrough. He told the attendant we were from Queensland and suddenly all resistance ceased. It seemed that for yokels from the tropic north they'd make allowances. We were in!

It was a victory nearly wasted: I was so embarrassed I could barely absorb what lay before me. And this is how I came to be acquainted with Henry Moore. For many minutes I lurked behind his *Draped Seated Woman*, hiding my grievous feet, trying to regain some composure. The sculpture could have been a parked car for all I cared. Still, I had time to take it in after a fashion, and there was something consoling in its mass. Its curves were confusingly voluptuous. It was, as Mum had promised, *terribly modern*, but there was a quality to it I later recognized as humane. I didn't just take shelter from it, I took heart. And from there I set off to see what else I could find. I roamed free.

In the great hall I craned to take in Leonard French's much discussed stained-glass ceiling. It would have been great to lie on the floor to see it better, but given recent events I didn't dare.

From there I wandered the courts and galleries, seeking out local legends like Tom Roberts and Frederick McCubbin whose colonial images were familiar from school. I lingered at Russell Drysdale's *The Rabbiters*, the title of which sounded traditional and whose colour range looked old-timey, but it struck me as weird, almost haunted. Was this modern? I didn't know. But I couldn't stop looking at it. In the halls of the European masters I was all at sea. I stopped only to take in works that were monumental or whose artists were famous enough to ring a bell. Like Rembrandt, whose *Two Old Men Disputing* brought to mind a pair of cricket fanatics in an aged-care facility, still going on with their infernal statistics in their PJs. It was a picture you fell into. You could look at it for the rest of your life and forever wonder what the story was.

There were many things I didn't understand, stuff that made me uneasy, stripes and splashes and globs on pedestals that had me scratching my head. There seemed to be no limit to what people could think of, and that was a giddy feeling. On and on the galleries went. And on and on I trekked, until finally I yielded in dismay, backtracked like a sunburnt Hansel and found my clan hunkered by the entrance, spent and waiting.

Passing back by the water wall to the familiar world, I had a dim sense I'd seen something special. I knew I was no genius but I didn't want to be ordinary and if I'd learnt anything from the excursion it was what people could do when they saw past the everyday. There was no single experience that made me want to live by my imagination, but I don't doubt the pivotal effect this visit had. Within a year I was telling anyone who'd listen that I was going to be a writer.

So it was a treat, this summer, to return to the NGV, no longer a new sensation, now an institution. There have been changes. The palazzo-style building on St Kilda Road has been rebadged as the NGV International and the handsome Australian collection has been rehoused in the Ian Potter Centre at Federation Square, across the Yarra. Recent renovations have afforded the old building more exhibition space, and on the day I arrived I found the halls teeming with visitors.

From the exterior it's still quite a daunting building, but happily the museum-going public is not as easily intimidated as it once was. That sullen philistine reverence has fallen away. Children and their parents run their hands delightedly up the cascading sheets of the water wall and even if, in the years since my first visit, the aesthetic effect of the piece has become hard to distinguish from the display windows of Chinese restaurants, it's a pleasure to see ordinary folks reaching out, making contact, claiming the place as they enter.

Inside, the democratic spirit continues. Not only is admission to the permanent collection free, children are welcomed without reservation. The morning of my visit, kids were lined up to ride the glittering brass carousel ensconced in the building's central court. In the great hall, where Leonard French's monumental stained-glass ceiling remains, they lay on the floor, pointing and writhing. It was a joy to see a grandmother shuck her shoes and chase her charges from one end of the hall to the other in her horny bare feet.

Sadly, the ceiling itself hasn't fared well with the years. Its scale remains impressive, and like the water wall it's earned a public fondness, but caught at the wrong moment it looks like the world's largest crochet rug ready to be spread across the knees of a giant philanthropist.

Henry Moore's once controversial *Draped Seated Woman* is still there, too, handy as ever, though smaller than I remember, and there's something about her pin head and blank face that now seems disrespectful. Close by in the new sculpture garden is Pino Conte's *Tree of Life*, which features an infant clinging stubbornly to its mother's breast. This babe could be any age. The mother's arboreal trunk is sensually rendered but her mass is implacable. It's a lovely, muscular celebration of the life urge and if I were to bring one of my grandkids to the NGV, this would be our first stop.

In the labyrinth of the European galleries, noticing for the first time what a solid collection of religious art the museum has amassed, I came upon Titian's *Monk with a Book* and saw what a worldly fellow he is. Where a pious man might prefer to be seen looking heavenward, our friar has been caught seeking some action closer to home. Do I sense a woman in the wings, a visit from the bookies? Rembrandt's *Two Old Men Disputing* is still there, luminous as ever, and further along, in the gallery dedicated to seventeenth- and eighteenth-century works, I met a new acquisition – Jean François Sablet's gorgeous portrait *Daniel Kervégan, Mayor of Nantes*. The revolution-era burgher is rendered with rare sympathy. His is the face of a plain, trustworthy man with tired, soulful eyes. Here is the sort of citizen-leader the communards must have dreamt of. But in this world-weary visage there's no hint of the Terror to come.

With the familiar past behind me, I rested over a pot of Darjeeling and reflected on the changes that have come to the museum. Apart from the structural additions, about which I have mixed feelings, the most telling improvements are social. The courts of the David Shrigley show were thick with kids drawing responses to the work. The spillover from the Jean Paul Gaultier carnival was evident upstairs as the young and curious coursed through galleries, snapping and texting as they went. The temple of art no longer spurns the young and uninitiated.

Within the collection, the most telling change is the growing prominence of Asian art. When I was a kid, Australia had barely begun to emerge from the moral murk of the White Australia Policy, and the NGV's holdings remained trenchantly Europhile. At the entrance to the Asian collection is a smouldering piece by an Indonesian artist, Haris Purnomo. *Orang Hilang*, a work of remembrance for the disappeared activists of the Suharto years, has the happy effect of inoculating the occidental viewer against narrowly ethnographic expectations. Yes, the galleries feature works of tradition and antiquity – like the Jin Dynasty Guanyin and many precious ceramics from Japan and China – but there's a keen appetite for contemporary exemplars and Purnomo's piece helps set the tone. Here, an old man with a limpid stare and a telling scar at the base of his neck wears the names of the missing like wounds. Words are too dangerous to utter. His mouth is covered. His eyes and the patchwork of plasters speak for him.

Despite its naked political intent, it's a beautiful object, and of all the paintings in the building it's the one I saw people linger over longest.

I stayed the entire day and saw but a fraction of what was on offer. Following the spent kids and their guardians out past the water wall, I thought again of that boyhood visit. I first entered the NGV barefoot and cowering, but I was so taken with what I saw that I forgot to be embarrassed. I strode out of the place like a man in boots.

ACKNOWLEDGEMENTS

Some of these pieces have appeared previously, often in earlier forms: 'Havoc' in *The Monthly*; 'A Walk at Low Tide' in *Edgelands,* the catalogue for an exhibition by Idris Murphy and Paul Martin, Warburton Gallery, Glasgow; 'Repatriation' in *The Monthly, Prospect* and *Ecotone*; 'Betsy' in *The Good Weekend*; 'The Wait and the Flow', adapted from an interview with Tim Baker, which appeared in his 2007 book *High Surf*; 'In the Shadow of the Hospital' in *Granta*; 'The Battle for Ningaloo Reef' in *The Bulletin*; 'Letter from a Strong Place' in *Overland*; 'Holy and Silent' in *The Independent Monthly*; 'Predator or Prey' in *The Good Weekend* and *Turning the Tide*; 'Using the C-word' in *The Monthly*; 'Lighting Out' in *The Bulletin*; 'Stones for Bread', first given as a speech at the 2015 Palm Sunday Walk for Justice in Perth, later published in *The Age* and the *Sydney Morning Herald*; 'Remembering Elizabeth Jolley' in *Indigo*; 'Sea Change' in *The Good Weekend, New Statesman* and on BBC radio; 'Barefoot in the Temple of Art' in *The Economist/Intelligent Life*.

Les Murray's 'Poetry and Religion' is quoted with the kind permission of the author (published in *Collected Works*, Black Inc., Melbourne 2006). The publisher acknowledges the dual copyright licensors for 'Trouble You Can't Fool Me': written & composed by Frederick Knight & Aaron Varnell, published by Sony/ATV Music Publishing Australia; 'Trouble You Can't Fool Me' (words and music by Frederick Knight/Aaron Varnell) © Irving Music, Inc./Universal Music Publishing Group, all rights reserved, international copyright secured. Reprinted with permission. Peter Matthiessen's *Blue Meridian* is published by Harvill Press, London, 1995.

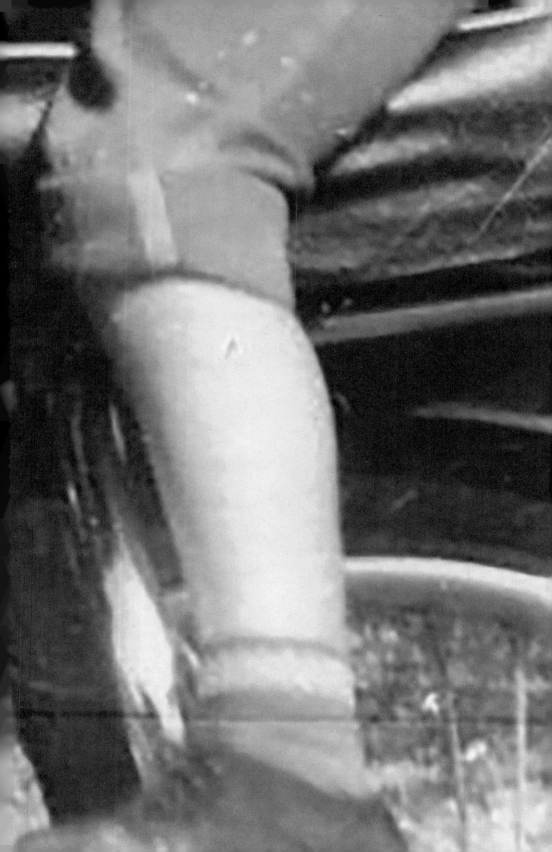